THE OPERATING ENVIRONMENT

**Peter Campkin,
William Duncan and
David Morgan**

FINANCIAL TIMES
PITMAN PUBLISHING

FINANCIAL TIMES

MANAGEMENT

LONDON • SAN FRANCISCO
KUALA LUMPUR • JOHANNESBURG

*Financial Times Management delivers the knowledge,
skills and understanding that enable students,
managers and organisations to achieve their ambitions,
whatever their needs, wherever they are.*

London Office:
128 Long Acre, London WC2E 9AN
Tel: +44 (0)171 447 2000
Fax: +44 (0)171 240 5771
Website: www.ftmanagement.com

A Division of Financial Times Professional Limited

First published in Great Britain in 1999

ISBN 0 273 62876 3

British Library Cataloguing in Publication Data
A CIP catalogue record for this book can be obtained from the British Library

10 9 8 7 6 5 4 3 2 1

Typeset by M Rules
Printed and bound in Great Britain by Clays Ltd, St Ives plc

The Publishers' policy is to use paper manufactured from sustainable forests.

THE
OPERATING
ENVIRONMENT

◆ Contents

Contents

Contents

Preface

Although the book is primarily aimed at Core Module 3 – The Operating Environment – for the BTEC Higher National Diploma in Business, the work may also be beneficial to students taking GNVQ Advanced Level Business and other business-related NVQs. Further, the work may also appeal to students taking the introductory stages of professional courses, such as those of the Chartered Institute of Marketing (CIM) and the Institute of Personnel Development (IPD).

Each chapter starts with a statement of Chapter objectives. As you work through each chapter it is worth remembering the objectives stated. To further assist your learning they are referred to again in the Chapter summaries.

Another feature of the text is the inclusion of *Financial Times* articles which will serve to illustrate some important aspects of the business environment.

Most chapters contain one or more sections entitled Further resources, which give you further information on the topics covered in the chapter. These sections include Internet addresses, as they are becoming a very important source of up-to-date information on the changing business environment. Such an example is shown below.

Further resources

The business environment

General

Quality daily and Sunday newspapers. Current affairs programmes on TV and radio.

Further reading

Worthington, I. and Britton, C. (1997) *The Business Environment*. London: Financial Times Pitman Publishing.

Palmer, A. and Hartley, R. (1996) *The Business and Marketing Environment*. Maidenhead: McGraw-Hill.

At the end of each chapter you will find Assignments to test your understanding of key aspects of the text.

Acknowledgements

We would like to acknowledge the kind assistance of Denise Thompson, Jeanette Campkin and Kaori Tsujimato.

Introduction to the business environment

Chapter objectives

By the time you have read this introduction you should understand:

◆ **what is meant by the term 'the business environment';**

◆ **how to classify factors that are present in the business environment.**

Introduction

It is important that students of business understand the nature of the business environment and how the various factors present in that environment impinge upon organisations. The word environment is not being used in its ecological sense, to mean the natural environment, but to mean those politico-legal, economic, socio-cultural and technological factors external to the organisation which have a bearing on the way in which the organisation responds and behaves. This does not mean that organisations cannot influence the environment in which they operate in order to reduce uncertainty. For example Airbus Industries is a consortia of UK, French, German and Italian aircraft manufacturers. They collaborate, in order to compete with the large US and other world plane makers, thereby seeking to maintain a relatively stable environment.

In using the word organisation, we are mainly concerned with business organisations, ranging from the one-person-owned sole trader right through to the huge transnational corporations which may have sites in several countries around the world. There are, however, other organisations which are controlled by the State, such as government departments, like the Department of Health, and the Courts of Law, like the High Court.

It is important to understand the nature of the environment and to distinguish between static and dynamic environments, and simple and complex environmental conditions. A static environment is one that is not undergoing significant change, whereas, in a dynamic environment, conditions are changing rapidly.

'Simple environment' means that the environment is not difficult to understand. In complex environmental conditions, however, the environment is difficult to comprehend. For example, the former public services in monopoly positions such as gas, electricity and water operated in a relatively static and simple environment. However, a large multinational computer manufacturer operates in a dynamic and complex environment.

There are various ways of classifying the environment. In this book, environmental factors will be addressed by using the acronym PEST. This stands for Political, Economic, Social and Technological. Such factors are present in what is termed the far, general or contextual environment. The near, operational or immediate environment, on the other hand, includes individuals and organisations which have an interest or potential interest, and directly or indirectly influence the activities of the organisation. These are known as stakeholders. It is useful to distinguish between internal and external stakeholders. Internal stakeholders include individuals and groups of employees and managers, whereas external stakeholders include customers and suppliers.

The main consideration of this book is, however, to focus on the PEST factors, to be more elaborate, the politico-legal, economic, sociocultural and technological factors, which are the interdependent and uncontrollable factors that influence business organisations. Therefore, the book is structured in the following way.

Part 1 – The politico-legal environment

The politico-legal environment includes the role of government in business and in the economy in the United Kingdom. In Chapter 1 we examine important statutes (Acts of Parliament) that affect business, for example, those statutes which protect the consumer and the employee. After reading this chapter you should also be able to understand what is meant by the terms nationalisation and privatisation.

In Chapter 2, we explain the political process in the UK, enabling you to distinguish between the various functions of government, namely, the legislature, the executive and the judiciary. The legislature is Parliament, which consists of the House of Commons and the House of Lords. The executive comprises the Cabinet and various government departments such as the Department for Education and Employment. We provide an outline of the judiciary and the courts of law, as well as the structure of local government.

Chapter 3 on the European Union (EU) explains the major institutions of the EU – the Commission, the European Parliament, the Council of Ministers and the European Court of Justice (ECJ). Primary pieces of EU legislation are known as the Treaties, such as the Treaty of Rome (1957) (the EC Treaty). Secondary EU legislation is in the form of regulations, directives and decisions. The making of such legislation is outlined in the final part of this chapter.

Chapter 4, which deals with the law relating to business, distinguishes between civil law and criminal law. It also introduces the law of contract and the law of tort (a tort is a civil wrong such as trespass and negligence). Finally, it describes and explains the sources of law, principally judicial precedent and legislation, the legal system (the courts) and the role of legal personnel such as judges, barristers and solicitors.

Part 2 – The economic environment

Part 2 includes a consideration of both the micro and macroeconomic environment of the UK and the international economic environment. Chapter 5 on the microeconomic environment looks at the functioning of individual parts of the economy such as the price mechanism and various forms of market structure. Chapter 6, which examines the macroeconomic environment considers the workings of the UK economy as a whole. It also describes the circular flow of income, as well as the various macroeconomic objectives and policies of the government. This chapter also briefly outlines the workings of the UK financial system.

Chapter 7 examines the international economic environment. It discusses the benefits of free trade and outlines restrictions to free trade that have developed. In recent years, regional economic groupings such as the EU have grown in importance. Further, recent developments in central and eastern Europe have changed the nature of the international economic environment. Finally, this chapter considers the economic role of various international organisations such as the World Trade Organisation (WTO) and the International Monetary Fund (IMF) will be considered.

Part 3 – The sociocultural environment

Part 3 explains the relationship between demography and business. Chapter 8 defines key demographic terms such as birth rate, mortality and migration. Further, it explains the importance of demographics and demographic statistics to business and government.

Chapter 9 identifies key social trends such as lifestyles, households, transport and education. It also outlines the implication of some of these trends for business and government.

Chapter 10 on the social responsibility of business provides you with an introductory understanding of business ethics and further develop the stakeholder concept.

Part 4 – The technological environment

Chapter 11 defines what is meant by the word technology and assesses the impact of technology on business, for example in factories, offices and shops and the impact on individuals. Finally, it provides you with an appreciation of the impact of the Internet on individuals and on business.

Part 1

THE POLITICO-LEGAL ENVIRONMENT

Introduction

'Can't live with it, can't live without it.' This phrase could sum up the relationship between business and the state. Rules are made and amended by Parliament, government departments, local councils and the European Union (EU). Certain actions require approval from the relevant authority. This can impose a heavy burden on business, but the advantages of a regulated state are great too. Unfair competition can be dealt with, criminal law can impose sanctions for illegal actions and civil law can protect the interests of business.

The first four chapters of this book describe the structure of the political and legal systems that affect business within the United Kingdom.

The role that government plays, at its various levels, is outlined in Chapter 1. That chapter also considers the different approaches to government involvement that can be taken. Nationalisation and privatisation are discussed. A brief outline is given of the principles of major areas of importance to business: consumer protection, competition law, employment law and planning law.

The political process in the United Kingdom is described in Chapter 2. Two key questions are answered: Who makes the decisions? and How are they made? Parliament, the Prime Minister, the Cabinet, government departments, the civil service and local government are all considered.

Since the United Kingdom joined the European Economic Community (EEC) (as it was then known), Europe has played an important role in British life. The European Communities Act 1972 provided that 'All such rights, powers, liabilities, obligations and restrictions from time to time created or arising by or under the Treaties, and all such remedies and procedures from time to time provided for by or under the Treaties, as in accordance with the

Treaties are without further enactment to be given legal effect or used in the United Kingdom shall be recognised and available in law, and be enforced . . .'. This means that law created within the framework of the European Union shall be as much a part of English law as that made by the Westminster Parliament and the British courts. Chapter 3 describes the institutions of the European Union and outlines EU law.

Chapter 4 deals with the law relating to business. It summarises the main divisions of law and gives an introduction to legal language. This chapter describes the court structure and sets out the different sources of law.

Major reforms are currently being discussed which may greatly change our system of government. These issues are dealt with in Part 1 of this book. The Treaty of Amsterdam will, if ratifed, alter European law, reducing the number of legislative procedures to three: assent, co-decision and consultation. The assent procedure is not described in this book as it is of little relevance to business. Some minor changes will be made to the co-decision and consultation procedures. Perhaps the greatest visible impact will be on the renumbering of EC Treaty Articles. The Articles of particular relevance to this book are set out in the following table.

Old Article(s)	New Article(s)	Description
85	81	Competition law
86	82	Competition law
137–144	189–201	European Parliament
145–154	202–210	Council of Ministers
155–163	211–219	Commission
164–188	220–245	European Court of Justice
169	226	Action against a Member State
177	234	Preliminary Rulings
189	249–252	Types of legislation and legislative procedures

1

The role of government

Chapter objectives

By the time you have read this chapter you should be able to:

♦ outline the various roles played by the state;

♦ understand the impact that government decisions have on business;

♦ understand the key principles of regional policy; consumer protection law; competition law; employment law; regulation and privatisation.

Introduction

For the last century political debate has been dominated by the question of the role of the state in business. At one extreme is the view that the state should organise all aspects of the economy and business behaviour. The government should set economic objectives and the government, through its ownership of the means of production and using the power to plan and intervene, would be able to ensure that these objectives were met. The classic statement of this view is to be found in *The Communist Manifesto* (*see* Exhibit 1.1).

At the other end of the political spectrum is the view that any state involvement will be a corrupting influence. Adam Smith argued that the most efficient allocation of resources would be achieved by the unfettered operation of the free market. He claimed that the effect of individuals pursuing their own self-interest would be to produce a market in which wants were met at minimum cost. He refers to the operation of 'an invisible hand', matching supply to demand at the optimal price (*see* Exhibit 1.2).

Exhibit 1.1 The means of revolutionising the mode of production

1   Abolition of property in land and application of all rents of land to public purposes.

2   A heavy progressive or graduated income tax.

3   Abolition of all right of inheritance.

4   Confiscation of the property of all emigrants and rebels.

5   Centralisation of credit in the hands of the State, by means of a national bank with State capital and an exclusive monopoly.

6   Centralisation of the means of communication and transport in the hands of the State.

7   Extension of factories and instruments of production owned by the State; the bringing into cultivation of wastelands, and the improvement of the soil generally in accordance with a common plan.

8   Equal liability of all to labour. Establishment of industrial armies, especially for agriculture.

9   Combination of agriculture with manufacturing industries; gradual abolition of the distinction between town and country, by a more equitable distribution of the population over the country.

10 Free education for all children in public schools. Abolition of children's factory labour in its [then] present form. Combination of education with industrial production.

Source: Marx, K. and Engels, F. (1848) *The Communist Manifesto*.

State intervention undermines the proper operation of the free market, leading ultimately to insufficient supply or costly overproduction and waste. Supporters of this view would point to the inefficiency which led to shortages and the ultimate collapse of communism in central and eastern Europe, and the spiralling costs and food mountains associated with the Common Agricultural Policy (CAP) of the European Union.

Most countries have followed a path between these two extremes. On the one hand, the free market has failed in important respects (*see* below), whereas the economic system created by the Communists in central and eastern Europe has collapsed. All states have a mixed economy, although the degree of state involvement varies. Even the most free-market of economies (such as the United States) involve the government in economic management, regulation and preparation of the basic legal framework for business. This chapter looks at the role of government in Britain's business environment.

The failures of the free market are as follows:

1   Failure adequately to meet demand for goods and services, because they are 'unprofitable' – defence, social services, education, mass transport.

Exhibit 1.2 The free market view

The quantity of every commodity brought to market naturally suits itself to the effectual demand. It is the interest of all those who employ their land, labour, or stock, in bringing any commodity to market, that the quantity never should exceed the effectual demand; and it is in the interest of all other people that it never should fall short of that demand.

If at any time it exceeds the effectual demand, some of the component parts of its price must be paid below their natural rate. If it is rent, the interest of the landlords will immediately prompt them to withdraw a part of their land; and if it is wages or profit, the interest of the labourers in the one case, and of their employees in the other, will prompt them to withdraw a part of their labour or stock from this employment. The quantity brought to market will soon be no more than sufficient to supply the effectual demand . . . if, on the contrary, the quantity brought to market should at any time fall short of the effectual demand, some of the component parts of its price must rise above their natural rate. If it is rent, the interest of all other landlords will naturally prompt them to prepare more land for the raising of this commodity; if it is wages or profit, the interest of all other labourers and dealers will soon prompt them to employ more labour and stock in preparing and bringing it to market. The quantity brought thither will soon be sufficient to supply the effectual demand.

Source: Adam Smith (1776) *The Wealth of Nations*, Book One, Chapter 7.

2 Merits of certain goods and services cannot be properly measured by price – for example libraries, cultural matters.

3 Failure of the price mechanism to take into account externalities – pollution, congestion etc.

4 Resources allocated on ability to pay rather than need.

5 Tendency to alternate between periods of under-utilisation of economic resources (recessions with high unemployment) and periods of insufficient supply (with rapidly increasing prices) – the so-called 'boom and bust cycle'.

Economic management

Further resources

Government involvement in the economy

General

Government involvement in the economy is covered by academic material which deals with the fields of economics and government. It is also a fact of everyday life, so you should find frequent reference to the topic in daily newspapers and magazines such as *The Economist*.

Further reading

Bain, K. (1987) *Government and the Economy*. Harlow: Longman.

Barnett, J. (1982) *Inside the Treasury*. London: Deutsch.

Begg, D., Fischer, S. and Dornbusch, R. (1991) *Economics*. Maidenhead: McGraw-Hill.

Cullis, J. and Jones, P. (1992) *Public Finance and Public Choice*. Maidenhead: McGraw-Hill.

Hutton, W. (1996) *The State We're In*. London: Jonathan Cape.

Lawson, N. (1993) *The View from No. 11*. London: Corgi.

UK Government. Department of the Treasury. Annual. *Financial Statement and Budget Report* ('The Red Book'). London: HMSO.

Internet addresses

Office of Fair Trading: http://www.open.gov.uk/oft/ofthome.htm

Oftel (Telecommunications): http://www.oftel.gov.uk

The Treasury: http://www.hm-treasury.gov.uk

Every year the Chancellor of the Exchequer presents his budget. In his speech to the House of Commons he outlines the state of the economy, and the policy objectives he intends to follow. Specific measures are announced to achieve those objectives. Gordon Brown began his Budget speech in July 1997 by stating, 'The Budget that I lay before the House today represents more than an allocation of resources and an accounting of revenues . . . behind the numbers and statistics the central purpose of this Budget is to ensure that Britain is equipped to rise to the challenge of the new and fast-changing global economy.' He used the Budget to introduce measures which he hoped would give stability to the economy and so encourage investment. Other means used to encourage investment included tax changes – for example, reducing corporation tax and increasing capital allowances. Through fiscal measures (taxation and public expenditure) and monetary policy a government seeks to shape the business environment.

One of the most powerful tools for managing an economy is control over interest rates. High rates should reduce the demand for borrowing, thereby slowing the economy. When inflation threatens to rise, as it did in the summer of 1997, interest rates will be raised to reduce inflationary pressures. When the economy is in recession rates will be cut to encourage the economy to start moving again.

The bank rate or, as it was later known, the minimum lending rate, was once decided upon by the Chancellor of the Exchequer in consultation with other ministers. Since the 1970s direct political control over the day-to-day running of interest rate policy has been deliberately decreased. In May 1997 the Chancellor of the Exchequer announced that he would no longer set rates, but the Bank of England was to be given operational responsibility for setting short-term interest rates to achieve the government's inflation target.

Legislator for the general framework

Business operates within the legal framework of the country. Company law determines the nature of business enterprises, and sets down detailed regulations which govern the formation, management and dissolution of business organisations. Every day business organisations are involved in a multitude of relationships which are governed by law. We will consider the principles of law relating to business in Chapter 4. It is the government, acting through Parliament, which lays down this general framework.

Important statutes for business are as follows:

◆ Business Names Act 1985
◆ Companies Acts 1985 and 1989
◆ Company Directors Disqualification Act 1986
◆ Criminal Justice Act 1993 (Part V)
◆ Employment Rights Act 1996
◆ Health & Safety at Work, etc. Act 1974
◆ Insolvency Acts 1986 and 1994
◆ Town and Country Planning Act 1990
◆ Trade Union and Labour Relations (Consolidation) Act 1992

Consumer protection

English law has traditionally steered clear of intervening in contracts between two parties. This approach was based on the view that the State should not interfere in bargains made privately. The principle was *caveat emptor* ('let the buyer beware'). This might have been appropriate for bargains between equals, but has proved unfair in a time when most contracts are between large corporations and individual consumers. Instead of being able to negotiate as an equal partner the consumer is forced to accept the terms laid down. With the help of lawyers some companies prepared standard contracts which attempted to exclude all liability, even when the company was to blame. An extreme example of this was seen in the case of *L'Estrange* v *Graucob* (1934). Graucob Ltd supplied a vending machine to L'Estrange, and the 'small print' of the contract excluded all liability even in the event that any failing was completely the fault of Graucob Ltd. Despite the fact that the machine supplied did not work, L'Estrange was liable to pay for the machine but Graucob successfully avoided all liability for the failure to work. The court held that L'Estrange had accepted all the terms in the contract.

Increasingly Parliament has restricted the right of companies to exclude liability. The current rules are to be found in the Unfair Terms in Consumer Contracts Regulations 1994. Parliament has also laid down terms which, though not written in a contract, are to be implied. This means that ordinary consumers have a legal right to expect that any goods they buy are of satisfactory quality. The Sale of Goods Act 1979 s 14(2) said that goods must be of 'merchantable quality'. In considering what that meant for cars the judge in *Bernstein* v *Pamsons Motors (Golders Green) Ltd* (1987) held that factors such as the safety of the car, the ease of repair, the effectiveness of any repair, the cumulative effect of minor defects and possibly cosmetic factors are relevant. In order to avoid a narrow, legalistic interpretation of consumers rights, Parliament has amended this to require goods to be 'of satisfactory quality' and fit for the purpose, including any particular purpose mentioned by the purchaser to the seller (14(3), Sale of Goods Act 1979). If the purchaser tells the seller that he wants the goods for a particular purpose, then the seller is bound unless he explains that the goods will not be suitable for that purpose. In the case of *Kendall* v *Lillico* (1969), Brazilian groundnut extraction was sold to a company which the sellers knew would use it in the production of food for cattle and poultry. The goods contained a substance which was toxic for poultry. It was held that it was therefore unfit for the purpose as described. Section 13 of the Sale of Goods Act 1979 says that where goods are sold by description there is an implied condition that they will match the description.

Important consumer protection legislation is as follows:

◆ Consumer Credit Act 1974

◆ Consumer Protection Act 1987

◆ Sale and Supply of Goods Act 1994

◆ Sale of Goods Act 1979

◆ Sale of Goods (Amendment) Act 1994

◆ Trade Descriptions Act 1968

◆ Unfair Terms in Consumer Contracts Regulations 1994

Further resources

Consumer protection

General

There is a wealth of material to be found, some of it in academic textbooks. The Office of Fair Trading (OFT) publishes a series of useful leaflets which are available directly from the OFT or your local Trading Standards Office.

Codes of Practice for particular industries are available. These include the British Code of Advertising Practice, published by the Advertising Standards Authority (ASA) and 'Good Banking' from the British Bankers' Association (BBA) and the Building Societies' Association (BSA).

Further reading

Harvey, B.W. and Parry, D.L. (1996) *The Law of Consumer Protection and Fair Trading*. London: Butterworths.

Howells, G. (1995) *Consumer Contract Legislation*. London: Blackstone Press.

Jackson, D. and Smith, A. (1994) *Consumer Protection*. Jordans.

Internet address

Office of Fair Trading: http://www.open.gov.uk/oft/ofthome.htm

Competition law

Rationale

Competition brings benefits to the economy, in that efficient producers are allowed to outperform inefficient ones, and consumers have the advantages of lower prices and choice. There are constant threats to competition, as monopolies and oligopolies form. Strong producers or suppliers can use their strength to block competitors. In order to protect the market, governments have sought to pursue policies to ensure that competition is not threatened.

United Kingdom competition policy

The institutions and policies of UK competition policy are described in Chapter 5. In 1997 the Monopolies and Mergers Commission (MMC) was asked to consider the proposed merger between Bass plc and Carlsberg-Tetley plc. Its report (*Bass PLC, Carlsberg A/S and Carlsberg-Tetley PLC – A Report on the merger situation*, Cmnd. 3662) shows the approach taken by the MMC. Although the MMC found that 'The proposed merger would lead to some net efficiency gains' it held that 'these benefits would not be sufficient to outweigh the adverse effects'. The MMC took the view that 'the proposed merger would lead to a reduction in the number of major brewers and would give Bass a significant increase in market power, as a result of which we expect wholesale and on-trade retail prices of beer to be higher in the longer term than would otherwise be the case. On-trade retailers and the consumer would suffer. In the short term, regional brewers and independent wholesalers could also be adversely affected because Bass Carlsberg-Tetley might choose to lower its prices to target their markets selectively.'

European Union competition policy

Competition policy plays an important role in the work of the European Union. The Union began, and remains, as a common market – with the objective of promoting free trade within that market. Lack of competition would threaten this objective. In particular anti-competitive behaviour can:

◆ bar entry of new firms into the common market; this could ultimately lead to stagnation, not only restricting the free movement of goods, persons, services and capital but threatening the economic well-being of the Union and its citizens;

◆ inhibit intra-community trade, by allowing companies to restrict the supply of goods and services;

◆ make community goods uncompetitive in world markets;

◆ limit consumer choice; the European Union is not just for business, but has sought to improve the standard of living and quality of life for all citizens.

The Treaty establishing the European Community has a special section specifically dealing with competition (Title V, 'Common Rules on Competition, Taxation and Approximation' – Chapter 1, 'Rules on Competition'). The two major provisions are found in, and known as, Article 85 and Article 86. The rules do not apply only to

Exhibit 1.3

The blocking of the Bass/Carlsberg-Tetley deal

Whether enjoying a quiet pint after work, or downing shorts on a Friday night bender, few Britons will have spared a thought yesterday for what the government has done to improve their evening out over the past decade. Squalid pubs have been refurbished, new bars opened, and a far wider range of beer is now readily available. The vertical tie between brewer and pub that shut out both investment and choice is collapsing fast.

Yesterday Mrs Margaret Beckett, the trade and industry secretary, slammed the shutters firmly on an effort by two of Britain's biggest brewers to regain the kind of market power they used to enjoy in the old days. By blocking the proposed takeover by Bass Brewers of Carlsberg-Tetley, she has sent a clear signal to the brewing industry that any attempt by a handful of leading companies to dominate UK beer production will be thwarted.

Bass's attempt to become Britain's biggest brewer, with 37 per cent of the UK market, has its roots in the government beer orders published eight years ago.

Introduced after a lengthy competition inquiry, these set out to reduce progressively the arrangement, known as the tie, whereby brewers owned large estates of public houses which were obliged to sell their beers, and no others.

The beer orders obliged the biggest brewers to divest part of their pub estates. Some of these pubs were detached into arms-length companies; others were bought by regional brewers or by opportunist entrepreneurs who created a new kind of independent pub retail company, responsive to consumer taste rather than brewery production targets.

The industry overhaul is incomplete. As the Monopolies and Mergers Commission report published by Mrs Beckett yesterday puts it 'The beer industry in the UK is in transition.'

Since 1989, the number of national brewers has fallen from six to four, as Courage merged first with Grand Metropolitan's brewing arm and then Scottish & Newcastle.

Scottish Courage, the beer division of Scottish & Newcastle, has emerged as the UK's biggest brewer, accounting for 28 of every 100 pints sold. Under a complex deal signed last August, Bass – number two in the industry with 23 per cent of the market – planned to merge operations with Carlsberg-Tetley, ranked third with 14 per cent. C-T had already rejected a merger with Whitbread, which is fourth with 13 per cent.

Bass and Carlsberg reckoned that by combining UK brewing and distribution they could have saved Pounds 90m a year, a key step in rebuilding profitability.

Consumption of beer in the UK has been declining gently for years. But since 1985, the proportion of production sold by off-licences and supermarkets has grown from 17 per cent to 28 per cent.

Brewers now own only one pub in three, compared with more than half in 1985. New, independent pub chains account for a third of the total. As the amount of beer sold through their pubs has slumped, brewers have been forced by the independent retailers to compete on price.

There has been a massive shift in market power. According to the MMC, the wholesale price of beer has fallen by 8 per cent in real terms over the past four years. During the same period, prices paid by drinkers have risen by 10 per cent.

The MMC concluded that merging C-T with Bass Brewers would give Bass a 'significant' increase in market power. If it were allowed to proceed, the four-man inquiry said, 'we expect wholesale and on-trade retail prices of beer to be higher in the longer term than would otherwise be the case. On-trade retailers and the consumer would suffer.'

The MMC said regional brewers and independent wholesalers would also be disadvantaged, because Bass Carlsberg-Tetley might choose to cut prices in target markets.

With the deal blocked, both Bass and Carslberg, the Danish parent of C-T, are expected to introduce sharp cost-reduction measures in an effort to improve the cash flow and returns on capital of their brewing businesses. The Transport & General Workers' Union estimated that the merger would have cost 2,000 jobs. Blocking it might cost more. Sir Ian Prosser, Bass chairman, said last night that Bass Brewers, which operates eight breweries in the UK would respond to the block with a two-fold strategy. On the one hand, it would continue to build high-margin brands such as Caffreys and Carling Premier. On the other: 'We will continue to look to reduce our cost base.'

Carlsberg told the MMC that it feared C-T, which has five breweries but no tied estate of its own, 'might be unable to survive in current market conditions' if the deal was blocked.

Mr Ebbe Dinesen, chief executive, will brief employees on cost reductions on Monday. But both C-T and its parent say they are now confident that C-T, with five breweries and two strong brands – Tetley bitter and Carlsberg lager – can survive. If that is so, the block will keep the industry under pressure, but consumers will not be disadvantaged.

Source: Ross Tieman, *Financial Times*, 28 June 1997.

companies which have their place of 'residence' in the European Union. Article 85 applies to all arrangements between undertakings 'which may affect trade between Member States and which have as their object or effect the prevention, restriction or distortion of competition within the common market'. Article 86 applies to any abuse of a dominant position 'within the common market or in a substantial part of it . . . in so far as it may affect trade between Member States'. Companies based outside the EU can therefore be subject to EU competition rules, and many of the leading cases involve American firms or their subsidiaries.

Article 85 bans 'agreements between undertakings, decisions by associations of undertakings and concerted practices which may affect trade between Member States and which have as their object or effect the prevention, restriction or distortion of competition within the common market'. There are three essential elements to the definition:

a collusion between undertakings;

b which must affect trade between Member States;

c which has as its object or effect the distortion of competition within the common market.

We look at each of these in turn, examining first what is meant by collusion, and then at what the term 'undertakings' encompasses. Article 85 recognises three forms of collusion:

a agreements;

b decisions of associations of undertakings;

c concerted practices.

Agreements – this concept is wider than a legally binding contract, and can include 'gentlemen's' agreements, or an unsigned agreement. In *AEG-Telefunken* v *Commission* (1983) the company prohibited the resale of its goods, except to dealers who had been 'approved'. The European Court of Justice (ECJ) held that, although the refusal appeared to be the unilateral act of one party (AEG-Telefunken) 'refusals of approval are acts performed in the context of the contractual relations with authorised dealers' and therefore came within the definition of agreement. The fact that the prohibition was honoured by dealers showed their tacit agreement.

Decisions of associations of undertakings are decisions taken by trade associations. The actual legal nature of the assocation is not relevant. The rule affects only binding decisions not mere recommendations.

Concerted practices have been defined as 'A form of co-ordination between undertakings which, without having reached the stage where an agreement properly so called has been concluded, knowingly substitutes practical co-operation between them for the risks of competition' (*ICI* v *Commission* (1972)). It can be difficult to know whether certain behaviour, (such as a price change by the major companies in an industry at about the same time), is a concerted practice or the effect of true competition. To prove that there is a concerted practice it is necessary to show some evidence of contact between undertakings. This could be a meeting (Polypropylene cases (1991)) or advance notice of price rises (*Ahlström* v *Commission* (Woodpulp cases) (1988 and 1993)).

The term 'undertakings' can include company, partnership, sole trader or association. It includes public undertakings (*see*, for example, the case of the pre-privatised British Telecom in *Italy* v *Commission* (1985)), inventors (*Reuter/BASF*) and even an opera singer (*Re Unitel* (1978)). It is important to note that the behaviour of a subsidiary will be imputed to its parent.

The second requirement is that the collusion must affect trade between Member States. Part of the purpose of this rule is to set the appropriate jurisdiction. Collusion which doesn't affect trade within the Community will be dealt with by national bodies unless there is no impact within the territory of any part of the European Union. The key principle was described in *Sociéte Technique Minière* v *Maschinenbau Ulm* (1966): 'it must be possible to foresee with a sufficient degree of probability on the basis of objective factors of law or of fact that the agreement in question may have an influence, direct or indirect, actual or potential, on the pattern of trade between Member States'. Agreements which affect the whole of a country are of especial concern, since they tend to compartmentalise the market on national basis. In *Consten & Grundig* v *Commission* (1966) it was made clear that even if the deflection in trade has the effect of increasing trade, it will still fall foul of Article 85.

Finally the collusion must have as its object or effect the distortion of competition. Either will suffice. In *Sociéte Technique Minière* v *Maschinenbau Ulm* (1966) it was said that a market analysis might be necessary to consider the effect. Such an analysis should take into account:

◆ the nature and quantity of the goods or services involved;

◆ the market share and turnover of the parties;

◆ the effect on parallel importers;

◆ whether the market is dominated by an oligopoly;

◆ the barriers a new company would have to overcome in order to enter the market.

If the aim of an agreement is not to restrict competition the offending clauses are examined to see if they are necessary to achieve the aim of the agreement. This is sometimes known as the rule of reason.

The ECJ has allowed agreements in the following circumstances:

◆ where protection is an 'indispensable inducement' to finding a business partner if the product is new or is the first export into new territory;

◆ where the restrictive provisions are necessary to allow a distribution franchising system to work properly;

◆ where a selective distribution network has been established on the basis of objective qualitative criteria.

The Commission can grant exemptions to agreements that breach Article 85. Two types of exemption exist.

First, an individual exemption can be applied for. In response the Commission may give 'negative clearance', which is a formal decision that Article 85(1) does not apply, or an 'exemption', which is a formal decision stating that Article 85(1) does apply but exemption is granted. However, because of the complexity of competition law, the practice is that exemptions are normally only given in 'priority' cases, and all other applications are given a 'comfort letter'. Article 85(3) requires that four conditions are met, two negative and two positive. Any agreement must (a) contribute to improving the production or distribution of goods or to promoting technical or economic progress, (b) while allowing consumers a fair share of the resulting benefit, and which does not (c) impose on the undertakings concerned restrictions which are not indispensable to the attainment of these objectives and (d) afford such undertakings the possibility of eliminating competition in respect of a substantial part of the products in question.

It has proved more useful for the Commission to grant 'block exemptions'. The Commission sets down in legislation the circumstances in which agreements will be exempted from Article 85, without the need to apply for an individual exemption. Examples can be found in the Exclusive Distribution Regulation 1983/83; the Exclusive Purchasing Regulation 1984/83 and the Patent Licensing Regulation 2349/84. The following terminology is often used:

1 **White clauses**: clauses which are restrictive of competition but are eligible for block exemption.

2 **Black clauses**: clauses which if included will make the agreement ineligible for exemption.

3 **Grey clauses**: clauses which do not usually breach Article 85(1) but which are listed for certainty.

Article 86 covers the other major area of EU competition law. This article prohibits the abuse of a dominant position (*see* Exhibit 1.4).

Dominance has been defined in *United Brands Co* v *Commission* (1978) as 'A position of economic strength enjoyed by an undertaking which enables it to prevent competition being maintained on the relevant market by giving it the power to behave to an appreciable extent independently of its competitors, customers, and ultimately of its consumers'. In the case of *AKZO* v *Commission* (1986) the Court added a further element: 'The power to exclude competition . . . may also involve the ability to eliminate or seriously weaken competition or to prevent potential competitors from entering the market'. In order to establish whether there is a dominant position it is necessary to consider the following issues:

Exhibit 1.4 EC Treaty, Article 86

Any abuse by one or more undertakings of a dominant position within the common market or in a substantial part of it shall be prohibited as incompatible with the Common Market in so far as it may affect trade between Member States.

Such abuse may, in particular, consist in:

(a) directly or indirectly imposing unfair purchase or selling prices or other unfair trading conditions;

(b) limiting production, markets or technical development to the prejudice of consumers;

(c) applying dissimilar conditions to equivalent transactions with other trading parties, thereby placing them at a competitive disadvantage;

(d) making the conclusion of contracts subject to acceptance by the other parties of supplementary obligations which, by their nature or according to commercial usage, have no connection with the subject of such contracts.

Source: EC Treaty (1957), Article 86.

1 **Relevant product market**. In *United Brands Co* v *Commission* (1978) the issue was whether the relevant product market was bananas, in which case United Brands clearly had a dominant position, or whether it was fruits generally. The Court considered whether there was cross-elasticity of demand. It found that consumers were unlikely to swap between bananas and other fruits. Another relevant determinant of the relevant product market is cross-elasticity of supply. In the *Continental Can* case (1973) the Court found that other potential competitors might be able to enter the market by simple adaptation.

2 **Relevant geographical market**. In addition to considering the current geographical market, it is relevant to assess how easy it would be to transport the products in question.

3 **Market share**. Although it has proved difficult to lay down a percentage of market share which would give rise to a dominant position, this is a key determinant of dominance.

4 **Market structure**. A detailed consideration of the structure of the relevant market is important in assessing whether a particular company has dominance.

5 **Barriers to entry**. Consideration will be given to the practical barriers which could deter new competitors from entering the market. These can include the cost of entering the market; the existence of established distribution and the strength of brand loyalty. If a company behaves as if it has a monopoly, it will be treated as if it had one.

Dominance alone will not be enough to found an Article 86 action. There must also be an abuse of that position. No definition of abuse is found in the Treaty, but listed below is some of the behaviour that has been found to constitute an abuse. The ECJ has ruled that an intention to harm need not be proved, harmful effect is sufficient.

The following practices have been found to be abuses:

◆ **predatory pricing**: selling at very low rates in order to keep competitors out of the market – *AKZO* (1986);

◆ **refusal to supply** – *Boosey & Hawkes* (1987);

◆ **rebates** to 'loyal customers' are caught by Article 86 but quantity discounts are allowed;

◆ **tying**: adding supplementary obligations to part of a contract;

◆ **excessive prices** which bear 'no reasonable relation to the economic value of the product supplied';

◆ **acquisition of a company which had an exclusive licence for competing technology** – *Tetra Pak* (1988).

Enforcement proceedings are brought by the Commission, which can act on its own initiative, respond to a complaint or react to an application for an exemption. The Commission's Notice on Co-operation (1993) stressed that complainants should look to protect their effective rights directly before national courts and not by laying complaints.

In the first stage of an investigation the Commission can request from the governments or the competent authorities of Member States, undertakings or associations of undertakings, 'all necessary information'. The Commission asks for specific information by a stated date but there is no obligation to comply. However supplying misleading information can lead to a fine. Once this stage has been completed the Commission can adopt a decision ordering that the information be supplied. Failure to comply at this stage can result in fines or penalty payments.

Regulation 17/62 outlines the powers and procedures for the use of the Commission's enforcement powers. Article 14 gives to the officials authorised by the Commission the power:

a   to examine the books and other business records;

b   to take copies of or extracts from the books and other business records;

c   to ask for oral explanations on the spot;

d   to enter any premises, land and means of transport of undertakings.

Safeguards to protect the rights of undertakings are set out in Articles 17 and 19.

The Merger Control Regulation (1989) allows the Commission to approve or ban mergers which would have an impact across the European Union. In 1997 a merger was proposed between Boeing and McDonnell Douglas. Although both companies were American the merger would have had a major effect on the choices available to airlines based in the European Union. A number of matters of concern were raised by the European Commission, which could have ruled against the merger. While this would have had no legal effect on a merger in America, it would allow the Commission to fine the merged company if it continued to operate in the European Union. The Commission eventually dropped its objections.

Employment law

We shall see in Chapter 4 that agreements in business are regulated by the general law of contract. One form of relationship has however attracted the special interest of government. This is the law which relates to employment. Individual employees have certain rights which are defined and protected by law. Provision is also made to regulate the activities of trade unions.

Any individual applying for a job has a right not to be discriminated against on the grounds of sex or race. Sex discrimination law can be found in the Equal Pay Act 1970 and the Sex Discrimination Acts of 1975 and 1986. The right to equal pay has been interpreted to include not just salary, but sick pay, holiday pay and working hours. The Equal Pay Act 1970 (as amended) applies this right to 'like work', 'work rated as equivalent' and 'work of equal value'.

Any difference of treatment between employees must be due to genuine material factors other than sex. It is therefore perfectly legal to have different rates of pay based on different skills requried, greater length of service or the geographic location of work.

Discrimination on the grounds of sex in the recruitment, promotion, training, benefits or dismissal of employees is outlawed by the Sex Discrimination Acts of 1975 and 1986. Two forms of discrimination are recognised by the courts. Direct discrimination is defined as treating someone less favourably on the grounds of their sex, race or disability. Indirect discrimination is more subtle. It involves setting a condition which a member of a specific group is less likely to be able to satisfy. To demand that all lecturers be at least six feet tall would in practice mean that women are less likely to be appointed.

The Equal Opportunities Commission (EOC) is responsible for ensuring that sex discrimination is discouraged. It can promote test cases in the courts, but it is the issuing of codes of practice and the investigation of complaints which are most effective.

Racial discrimination is covered by the Race Relations Act 1976. This legislation takes a similar approach to the Sex Discrimination Act. Discrimination is prohibited in the advertising for, engaging or dismissal of employees and in their conditions of employment. The Commission for Racial Equality (CRE) plays a similar role to the EOC. It too produces influential codes of practice.

The Disability Discrimination Act 1995 establishes a statutory right of non-discrimination for disabled people in employment. Section Four states that:

(1) It is unlawful for an employer to discriminate against a disabled person –

    (a) in the arrangements which he makes for the purpose of determining to whom he should offer employment;

    (b) in terms on which he offers that person employment; or

    (c) by refusing to offer, or deliberately not offering, him employment.

(2) It is unlawful for an employer to discriminate against a disabled person whom he employs –

    (a) in the terms of employment which he affords him;

    (b) in the opportunities which he affords him for promotion, a transfer, training or receiving any other benefit;

    (c) by refusing to afford him, or deliberately not affording him, any such opportunity; or

    (d) by dismissing him, or subjecting him to any other detriment.

Any employee who works for over eight hours a week is entitled to receive a written statement of particulars of the employment contract. This should be supplied within two months of starting work and should contain:

◆ the names of the employer and employee;

◆ the date on which employment began;

◆ whether any service with a previous employer (in the event of a takeover or other transfer of an undertaking) forms part of the continuous period of employment;

◆ pay rate or scale and the frequency of payment;

◆ hours of work;

◆ any holiday or holiday pay entitlement;

◆ provisions for sick leave and any sick pay entitlement;

◆ pensions and pension schemes;

◆ length of notice be given by either party for termination of the employment, or the expiry date if it is a fixed term employment;

◆ the job title;

◆ details of disciplinary and grievance procedures, or a reference to where they may be found.

If there is no express agreement on the amount of pay, the employee is entitled to 'reasonable pay'. This amount would be established by the courts on the particular facts of the case. In the past wages councils set minimum pay for particular industries and most countries have a legally set minimum wage. The UK introduced a statutory minimum wage in 1998.

The importance of government involvement in the workplace can be seen in the area of health and safety at work. European Union regulations deal with specific industries as well as providing for general rules. The Health and Safety at Work etc. Act 1974 is the major piece of British legislation in this area. Its approach is to set down the general duties of employers and employees. The Health and Safety Executive (HSE) provides advice, codes of practice and detailed rules to help employers and employees to fulfil these duties.

Dismissal from employment is also highly regulated by law. Employees are given legal rights which apply in the event of redundancy or dismissal. Infringement of these rights can be challenged before an industrial tribunal.

Trade unions were set up by their members to press for improvements in the terms and conditions of their employment, and to protect themselves from the power of the employers. The rights of trade unions as bodies, and of individual workers, have frequently been the subject of legislation. In *Taff Vale Railway Co. v ASRS* (1901) it was held that a trade union could be sued for damages resulting from industrial action. This decision was followed by the Trade Disputes Act 1906, which gave a certain level of immunity. The main matters of controversy since have been the right to join a union; the right of a union to be recognised by an employer; and the right of an individual not to join a union.

The Conservative governments of 1979–97 passed a series of laws to restrict trade unions. Their view was that trade unions were a threat to the operation of market forces and were responsible for high wage costs and low labour productivity. Employers were given new rights to sue trade unions, extra procedures were required before industrial action could be taken and the internal conduct of union affairs became more tightly regulated.

Further resources

Employment law

General

A number of useful reports have been produced by the Employment Select Committee of the House of Commons (now the Education and Employment Committee).

Further reading

Carr, C.J. and Kay, P.J. (1997) *Employment Law*. London: Financial Times Pitman Publishing.

Deakin, S. and Morris, G.S. (1998) *Labour Law*. London: Butterworths.

Internet address

http://www.compulink.co.uk/~llkbw/employment_law/Emplaw.htm

Regulation

Whereas in a command economy the government intervenes in business decision making, in a market economy the government does not seek to be so directly involved. However government may still wish to ensure that high standards are maintained. The Department of Trade and Industry (DTI), in a memorandum to the House of Commons Select Committee on Trade and Industry, explained that 'the system of arm's length economic regulation by Directors General independent of the government was intended to leave the management of the privatised companies free, without Government interference, 'to promote "a competitive market and to protect the interests of consumers in those areas where competition had not yet developed, or where natural monopoly is likely to remain"'.

Two recent reports from the House of Commons Select Committee on Trade and Industry give a detailed background and assessment of the regulators. They are the reports into Energy Regulation (First Report, 1996–97) and Telecommunications Regulation (Third Report, 1996–97).

The principal regulators are as follows:

- Electricity   OFFER
- Gas   OFGAS
- Telecommunications   OFTEL
- Water   OFWAT

The banking and financial service industries are regulated by a series of statutes including the Banking Act 1987 and the Financial Services Act 1986. Both statutes have been greatly amended over recent years. Exhibit 1.5 considers current problems and future reform in this area.

Planning law

There are many different planning authorities. For most of England the county and district (sometimes known as borough) councils share the responsibilities for planning (*see* below). However some areas have unitary authorities (*see* Chapter 2), which carry out the tasks of both county and district councils. Certain areas have special planning authorities.

Roles of planning authorities

County councils

The roles of county councils in relation to planning covers the following:

- the winning and working of minerals, the erection of buildings or the use of land in this connection;

Exhibit 1.5

Financial complaints system faces reform

Three ombudsmen have joined forces to explore ways of ensuring that consumer complaints are handled more efficiently under the planned reforms of financial services regulation.

It could lead to all financial services complaints initially being handled at a single point of call. Under current arrangements, complainants contact whichever of six ombudsmen they think most suitable to handle their grievance.

The banking, building society and insurance ombudsmen have jointly commissioned a study to look at the feasibility of setting up a common point of access – an idea the government is believed to favour. Last year the three ombudsmen received more than 100 000 complaints or inquiries from the public.

The study will also examine the needs of the other financial services ombudsmen in investment, pensions and personal investments. Critics say consumers often do not know which ombudsman to contact with a complaint, meaning they either take no action or get passed from pillar to post.

Mr Walter Merricks, the insurance ombudsman, said: 'It should be advantageous for someone who has a complaint involving a number of different institutions to be able to contact a single point. This is particularly the case where it is not obvious which ombudsman is involved – such as where a bank is selling an insurance policy or an insurer is selling a mortgage. However, we need to know the costs and practical implications which is why we have commissioned the study.'

The arrangements for ombudsmen under the planned unified regulatory system – dubbed Super – SIB because it will greatly enhance the role of the Securities and Investments Board – have still to be clarified.

Broadly, there appear to be two options. One would leave the existing system broadly unchanged, with different ombudsmen but closer collaboration between them, possibly within the same building.

The alternative would see all retail financial services business subject to a single ombudsmen set up by statute.

In a speech earlier this week, Mr Mark Boleat, director general of the Association of British Insurers, said the logic of a single point of call was 'absolutely right'.

But he warned that changes to ombudsmen arrangements under the new regulatory system could be complex, costly and disruptive.

One cause of complexity is that several of the ombudsmen schemes are voluntary, others are by contract (under the Financial Services Act) and one is statutory (under the Building Societies Act).

SIB chief attacks 'serious defects' in City regulation

Sir Andrew Large, the outgoing chairman of the Securities and Investments Board, has criticised the system of two-tier City regulation for causing delays in resolving financial scandals such as the mis-selling of personal pensions, John Gapper writes.

Sir Andew, writing in SIB's annual report, argues that the two-tier system, which the government is to reform, has 'serious defects' and is 'inherently less efficient and effective than it could be'.

Sir Andrew says the case for reforming the structure of regulation under which self-regulatory organisations such as the Securities and Futures Authority are monitored by SIB, became 'overwhelming' because of its flaws. There has been 'not just independence but hostility' among the regulatory organisations, which has made it more difficult to clear up the pensions mis-selling, and co-ordinate responses to financial failures such as that of Barings.

'Even the regulatory response to the conduct of certain UK firms in world copper markets, which is generally seen as a considerable success, could have been more robust under a more cohesive structure', Sir Andrew writes.

Sir Andrew says he cannot conceal his disappointment at the lack of progress over the pension mis-selling scandal. 'Despite our efforts to remove the remaining roadblocks it is only now that I sense a greater willingness on the part of the major players to deal with this candal and put it behind us,' he says.

The report shows that Sir Andrew's remuneration rose to Pounds 203 609, against Pounds 181 086 the previous year.

Source: Christopher Brown-Humes, *Financial Times*, 27 June 1997.

◆ searches and tests for mineral deposits;

◆ the disposal of mineral waste, and the use of land or the erection of buildings in connection with the extraction or transfer of sand, gravel, crushed rock, cement etc.;

◆ any development affecting a National Park;

◆ any development or class of developments prescribed by the Secretary of State for the Environment as being a county matter.

District councils

District councils deal with all planning applications other than those reserved for county councils. (In certain areas joint planning boards or committees bring together representatives from a number of councils in an area.)

Enterprise zones

Enterprise zones have certain limited planning powers related to an area managed by an 'enterprise zone authority'.

Urban development areas

In urban development areas there are limited planning powers related to an area managed by an 'urban development corporation'.

Housing action areas

In housing action areas there are limited planning powers related to an area managed by a 'housing action trust'.

Ownership

Nationalisation

Is it better, in the interests of the whole economy, for certain industries to be in private hands or to be run by the state? This question is at the heart of the debate over nationalisation or privatisation. Nationalisation involves taking companies and their assets – often all the companies in a particular industry – into state ownership. Privatisation is the reverse process.

In British political history the Labour Party has supported nationalisation whereas the Conservatives have generally preferred private ownership. However in certain circumstances the Conservatives have nationalised – for example they brought Rolls Royce into public ownership to save it from going out of business.

Nationalisation was seen as a solution to particular problems. When the Labour Government of 1945–51 took key infrastructure industries into public control it was to overcome years of underinvestment and neglect, sometimes exacerbated by the controls imposed during the war. The second wave of nationalisations in the 1970s was to deal with important manufacturing industries which were associated with low levels of innovation and poor management (*see* Table 1.1).

Table 1.1 Major nationalisations

Institution or industry	Date of nationalisation
Bank of England	1946
Coal	1947
Electricity	1948
Transport (inc Railways)	1948
Gas	1949
Iron and steel	1951 (and 1967)
British Leyland	1975
Aircraft building	1977
Shipbuilding	1977

Privatisation

The Conservative governments of 1979–97 pursued a policy of selling off state assets. The period 1983 to 1988 saw the high-water mark of this policy, when a major part of the assets of the public sector was sold into private hands. As well as raising large amounts of revenue for the government, the policy sought to 'roll back the frontiers of the state'. It was claimed that privatisation would improve the efficiency and performance of companies which were no longer under political or bureaucratic control.

Further resources

Privatisation

Further reading

Butler, E. (1988) *The Mechanics of Privatization*. London: Adam Smith Institute.

Pirie, M. (1988) *Privatization. Theory, Practice and Choice*. Aldershot: Wildwood House.

Table 1.2 sets out the major privatisations of the 1980s and 1990s.

Table 1.2 Major privatisations

Company	Date of privatisation
Amersham International	1982
Associated British Ports	1983/4
British Aerospace	1981/5
Jaguar Cars	1984
British Gas	1986
Rover Group	1986
British Airports Authority	1987
British Airways	1987
British Petroleum	1981/7
National Bus Company	1980/8
British Steel	1984/8
Water	1989/90
Electricity	1990
British Coal	1995/6
British Rail	1996

Exhibit 1.6

Bumpy but beneficial disposals

Privatisation, forever associated with the name of Margaret Thatcher, is a huge and continuing success story. It is by no means over. There is more to come in continental Europe, east and west, and in the developing countries. It is difficult to name a government that proposes to extend state ownership of manufacturing or service industries, easy to list countries in which sell-offs are under way.

No, I have not suddenly turned from pink to blue, being ever green. Yet we consumers should be grateful for privatisation. I find it easier to catch a bus in London than at any time in my life. It is a pleasure to fly British Airways, though not cheap. British Telecom never stops ringing up offering family rates. You may think I am getting carried away by my own rhetoric, but let me assure you that even the subsidiary of British Gas that installed a new boiler a few wintry weeks ago did it well.

This may explain why John Major has written to everyone on the share registers of the denationalised utilities, a mailshot in the dark. The prime minister warns against the windfall tax proposed by the Labour party. It might influence a few single-share holders to vote Tory. It is a risk, though.

Putting publicly owned companies on the market is still unpopular. After water was unloaded the 'favour more privatisation' line in the polls fell sharply, to be overtaken by the graph of support for more nationalisation. So says Peter Hutton, director of the polling firm MORI, who has tracked attitudes to denationalisation over 20 years. Sales of individual companies have always been strongly opposed in advance, water most of all. The Tories have usually proceeded anyway. They are now distinctly nervous about privatising the Post Office or declaring an intention to sell London Transport.

Exhibit 1.6 continued

Perhaps we shall hear more about these at a lecture on privatisation due to be given by Kenneth Clarke on Tuesday. The chancellor will launch the last of four reports on privatisation prepared by Nera, a consultancy, for the Centre of Policy Studies, a Tory think-tank. The first told us that safety standards have not deteriorated under private management, the second that the taxpayer benefited from denationalisation, the third, published this week, that labour productivity has risen. Of course it has. Thousands of unskilled workers have been fired. I wonder how much that cost in dole payments.

Nera III warns us that an open market is as important a determinant of efficiency as private ownership. When faced with strong competition, even publicly owned enterprises shed labour and sharpen their management. Nera IV, due out next week, reviews airports, electricity supply, telecoms, gas and water. Prices have fallen in real terms for four of them. Water is the exception. Its bills have shot up. Service quality improved in all except gas, where it fell.

The ifs and buts that pepper these Nera papers constitute a broad recognition that the process has been imperfect. I agree. BA ruthlessly exploits its market dominance. Water monopolies are slow to repair their pipes, the work supposed to be covered by their increased charges. Many industries were sold too cheaply, partly as a result of the ability of the nationalised-industry managers, looking to future gold, to befuddle officials.

Robber barons have replaced public servants in the boardrooms of most of the new plcs. Sometimes the same individual changes personality as soon as the stock certificates are printed. More than a few shameless brigands have stuffed their pockets. We can all add to this picture of opportunism, using only a little imagination. All of it needs redress. Yet the central point remains. A world in which governments ran businesses has been transformed. Today private managements do the job better.

Thus despite the flaws in its execution, denationalisation is a remarkable achievement, one that Britain's Conservatives can justifiably proclaim as their bequest. They may be about to be ejected from office, but while in residence they have made a difference. This was not planned. It just sort of happened. No single genius, not even Lady Thatcher, drew up a blueprint for the disposals. Britain's Treasury nudged a willing government from sale to sale. The ideology followed the fiscal urge.

The conventional wisdom is that there will be no more privatisations once Labour comes to power. There are not many large conventional businesses left to sell, apart from the postal service and London's underground trains. The many companies spawned by the broken-up British Rail need tidying up. Connections between them and to buses should be enforced by regulation. But the ambition of the leader of what was formerly the people's party is to establish Labour as pro-business. It should sell companies on the list of remaining tiddlers.

I would add one more whale. The trunk roads and motorways constitute a service that is best paid for at the point of use. We greens would like the cost of using the roads to account for disturbance of the environment, in fair competition with the privatised rail services. That would change our lives. Let the roads be privatised. Any takers?

Source: Joe Rogaly, *Financial Times*, 8 February 1997.

Chapter summary

Government decisions have an important impact on the performance of the United Kingdom economy. In addition legislation may affect many aspects of the running of a particular business. This chapter has highlighted the particular influence of regional policy, consumer protection law, competition law, employment law, regulation and privatisation.

Assignment

Prepare a report on the measures, described in Exhibit 1.7, that the Chancellor was using to influence the workings of the economy.

Exhibit 1.7

Budget 1998: Brown plans tax overhaul to boost jobs

FT

Gordon Brown yesterday announced an overhaul of Britain's tax and benefits system to encourage work and enterprise, but the City believes he has left it to the Bank of England to slow the economy and fight inflation. In a wide-ranging radical Budget, the chancellor confirmed that he will replace family credit with a more generous tax credit paid through the wage packet. This will allow low earners to keep more of every extra pound they earn and will provide a family where someone works full time with a guaranteed income of at least Pounds 180 a week.

Mr Brown also announced that the government was undershooting the public spending target it inherited from the Conservatives for this year by Pounds 1.5bn. The savings will be spent next year on health, education, public transport and boosting the Treasury's contingency reserve.

In a shake-up of the national insurance system, Mr Brown announced a Pounds 1.2bn cut in employees' contributions worth Pounds 1.28 a week to everyone in work from April 1999. The burden of employers' national insurance contributions will be shifted from lower-paid jobs to higher-paid ones. 'For too long we have done too little to help those who work hard to advance up the ladder of opportu-

nity,' Mr Brown declared. 'The cap on aspirations must now be lifted.'

Bringing forward real increases in road fuel duty will yield Pounds 1.1bn for the chancellor next year, contributing to a negligible net fiscal tightening of Pounds 165m. The tightening will rise to Pounds 915m in 1999–2000, but this is more than accounted for by the short-term impact of corporation tax reforms flagged last year. In essence, the Budget is broadly neutral.

Economists doubt this will be enough to prevent the Bank of England raising interest rates again, but the chancellor's aides believe the City has not yet recognised the fiscal tightening this year. The pound reached its highest trade-weighted level in nine years.

The chancellor acknowledged that sterling's strength hurt manufacturers, but warned their pay settlements were rising. 'It would be the worst of short-termism to pay ourselves more today at the cost of higher interest rates, fewer jobs and slower growth tomorrow,' he said.

Mr Brown predicted the economy would grow by 2.5 per cent this year if employees showed restraint. 'If wage bargaining proceeds in the same short-termist way as in the past, growth could slow to 2 per cent.'

These forecasts are slightly lower than last November's. Mr Brown also predicted inflation would peak at 3 per cent this year and presented an optimistic Pounds 6.5bn forecast for the current account deficit.

The chancellor cut his forecast for public sector borrowing this year (excluding the windfall tax) from July's Pounds 13.3bn to Pounds 5bn. This reflects spending restraint and unexpectedly buoyant revenues from income tax and value-added tax. The downward revision from Pounds 5.9bn to Pounds 3.9bn for the next year is deliberately smaller, in case revenues slow again. The chancellor also used the Budget to focus financial support on children rather than marriage. Mr Brown announced that the married couple's allowance would be cut by a third from 1999, financing a Pounds 2.50 a week increase in child benefit.

In a controversial move, Mr Brown also suggested that child benefit might be subject to the higher 40p rate of income tax, to pay for further increases. Treasury officials believe this could raise Pounds 700m.

For business, Mr Brown announced he would go ahead with November's proposal to scrap Advance Corporation tax, cut the mainstream rate from 31 per cent

▶

Exhibit 1.7 continued

to 30 per cent and introduce payment by quarterly instalments. The chancellor promised not to raise mainstream corporation tax for the rest of the parliment.

Small and medium-sized businesses will be exempt from the requirement to pay quarterly. Their capital allowances will be set at 40 per cent, to encourage investment.

The chancellor also announced a Pounds 50m venture capital fund for universities. The Enterprise Investment Scheme and capital gains tax reinvestment relief will be merged and tax relief raised by half to Pounds 150 000.

Mr Brown also announced controversial reforms to capital gains tax, arguing that the existing system 'rewards the short-term speculator as much as the committed long-term investor'. Long-term investors will face lower rates, but the institute for Fiscal Studies has described this idea as 'deeply flawed'.

As expected, the chancellor back-tracked on his planned tax-free Individual Savings Accounts (Isas). The savings industry had accused him of retrospective taxation by limiting to Pounds 50 000 the amount transferable from existing Tessas and Peps into the new savings account. All capital accumulated in existing schemes will continue to enjoy relief.

Stamp duty will also rise for house sales above Pounds 250 000. Establishing his green credentials, the chancellor raised the landfill levy and announced lower licence fees for vehicles with clean engines. Scale charges for fuel provided by employers will also rise. The chancellor also announced a review of industrial energy use.

Source: Robert Chote, *Financial Times*, 18 March 1998.

2

The political process in the United Kingdom

Chapter objectives

By the time you have read this chapter you should understand:

◆ **the structure of the Executive;**

◆ **the structure of Parliament;**

◆ **the structure of other government institutions;**

◆ **the procedure for making laws in the United Kingdom.**

Introduction

Political events are a major influence on the stock market. Government policies can encourage business, or create major difficulties. Laws govern almost all aspects of business behaviour. Planning permission must be sought from the local authority; grants from government departments and the European Union may be applied for and the taxman must be paid.

Government has become all-pervasive. To survive in business it is necessary to know how law is made, and who the decision makers are.

It is traditional to distinguish between three functions of government. Governments carry out their tasks through the use of law. Laws are (a) made by the legislative power, (b) administered by the Executive, and (c) interpreted by the judiciary.

In the United Kingdom the legislative power is held by 'The Queen in Parliament'. The role played by the monarch is purely formal – opening each session and giving the Royal Assent to bills which have been passed by the two Houses of Parliament. These are the elected House of Commons and the currently un-elected House of Lords.

Exhibit 2.1 The future of the House of Lords

The present Labour government has promised to reform the House of Lords. In its 1997 Manifesto the Labour Party said:

As an initial, self-contained reform, not dependent on further reform in the future, the right of hereditary peers to sit and vote in the House of Lords will be ended by statute. This will be the first stage in a process of reform to make the House of Lords more democratic and representative. The legislative powers of the House of Lords will remain unaltered.

The system of appointment of life peers to the House of Lords will be reviewed. Our objective will be to ensure that over time party appointees as life peers more accurately reflect the proportion of votes cast at the previous general election. We are committed to maintaining an independent cross-bench presence of life peers. No one political party should seek a majority in the House of Lords.

A committee of both Houses of Parliament will be appointed to undertake a wide-ranging review of possible further change and then to bring forward proposals for reform.

The government chose not to begin this process of reform in the 1997–8 session, in order to concentrate upon its other major constitutional reforms.

Executive functions are carried out at a national level by government departments headed by ministers. At the head of the Executive is the Cabinet, presided over by the Prime Minister. The person most likely to be able to gain support in the House of Commons, normally the leader of the majority party, is appointed as Prime Minister by the Queen. Ministers are selected by the Prime Minister and reflect the political makeup of the government. The civil service is independent of the party in power. After a general election the government may change, but the civil servants remain the same. Their task is to advise ministers and carry out the decisions which the politicians have made.

Judicial power is exercised by the judges sitting in courts. The United Kingdom has three different legal systems – for England and Wales; Scotland; and Northern Ireland. The system in England and Wales will be looked at in more detail in Chapter 4.

Some countries have a federal structure, in which local and national governments are independent of each other and have defined limits. Britain, however, is a unitary state. Parliament is regarded as sovereign and can vary the powers of local government, or even abolish them altogether.

Plans for Scottish and Welsh parliaments will transform the political geography of the United Kingdom. Devolution of powers will reverse a centralising tendency which has increased during this century. However, at this stage, Westminster will retain its sovereign powers.

Parliament

The Westminster Parliament is sometimes called 'The Mother of Parliaments'. It has evolved over many centuries. Its roots may be found in the nobles who advised the kings during the Anglo-Saxon period. Over time the practice of consulting these important nobles became formalised into a body we would recognise as the House of Lords. In the thirteenth century larger assemblies, known by the title 'parlamentum' met. Knights of the shires first joined these assemblies in 1254 and in 1265 Simon de Montfort also invited representatives of the towns to attend. The House of Commons traces its roots to that 1265 Parliament.

It was under the Tudor and Stuart monarchs that Parliament gained in power and importance. The Civil War which began in 1642 was a struggle between the King and Parliament. When the monarchy was restored in 1660, it was at the invitation of Parliament. Its new position as the Supreme Power was confirmed when James II went into exile and Parliament made William II and Mary the new monarchs. The rules which govern who will be monarch are now set down in an Act of Parliament (the Act of Settlement 1701).

The government takes office on the basis that it has the support of the House of Commons. If it loses that support, as Callaghan's government did in a key vote in March 1979, it falls. The doctrine of parliamentary sovereignty is still recognised, though membership of the European Union may have modified the position that:

1 Parliament can pass any law it wishes.

2 No Parliament is bound by the decisions of its predecessors and

3 No court may question the validity of an Act of Parliament.

After each general election a new 'Parliament' begins. Its term must not exceed five years, and prime ministers usually call new elections before the five years is completed. A 'Session' of Parliament lasts for a year, though the first session may be longer. All bills must pass both Houses within a session, or they automatically lapse. A Session begins with the Opening of Parliament, which includes the Queen's Speech.

The House of Commons

The House of Commons is made up of 659 representatives, each elected by a single constituency. It is the practice in the House of Commons that members do not refer to each other by name, but by the constituency they represent. The Chamber retains the original shape of the Commons' first permanent meeting place – the Upper Chapel of St Stephen's in the Palace of Westminster. MPs sit on two opposing benches, which were originally the choir stalls of the chapel. The altar was replaced by the Speaker's Chair. Supporters of the Government sit on the right-hand side of the Speaker and the front bench (sometimes called the Treasury Bench) is occupied by ministers. 'Backbenchers' are MPs who do not have a government (or opposition) post.

Table 2.1 Party membership in Parliament (June 1997)

	House of Commons	House of Lords
Labour	418	123
Conservative	165	482
Liberal Democrats	46	55
Ulster Unionists	10	
Scottish Nationalist Party	6	
Plaid Cymru	4	
Social Democratic & Labour	3	
Democratic Unionist Party	2	
Sinn Fein	2	
Others	3	
Cross-bench		313
Non-attenders		232
TOTAL	659	1205

Two major roles dominate the work of the House of Commons. The first is the task of making law. The legislative procedure will be looked at in greater detail later in this chapter. In addition to legislating, the House of Commons is active in scrutinising the work of the Government. On every day except Fridays, Question Time allows MPs to put oral questions to ministers about the work of their departments. In addition written answers can be submitted. These are published in Hansard (the record of everything said in Parliament, along with written questions and their answers).

Exhibit 2.2 Parliamentary questions

Monday 2nd June	14.30 Social Security
Tuesday 3rd June	14.30 Environment and the Regions
	15.05 Transport
Wednesday 4th June	14.30 Chancellor of the Duchy of Lancaster
	15.00 Prime Minister
Thursday 5th June	14.30 Trade & Industry

Source: Hansard, week commencing 2 June 1997.

Two types of committees meet in the corridors of the Palace of Westminster, Select Committees and Standing Committees. Their names may be slightly misleading, but each type has its own distinctive style. Standing committees meet as miniature

Houses of Commons, with the government supporters sitting on one side, and the opposition parties on the other. Select committees meet around a horseshoe-shaped table, facing the witnesses who appear before them.

Standing committees play an important role in the legislative process, which is described later in this chapter.

Departmental select committees meet to 'examine the expenditure, administration and policy of the principal government departments' (Standing Order 152). In addition other specialist select committees (such as the Committee of Public Accounts, Joint Committee on Consolidation) are also active in scrutinising the government's work. Inquiries are held, to which witnesses are summoned to give evidence. Reports are published by the Committee. The current system of departmental select committees was only set up in 1979. They have already proved to be an important means enabling MPs to hold the government to account, but criticisms have been made of the limitations under which they labour.

Members of Parliament have no formal job description. They can do as little or as much as they like. Only the electors of their constituency can remove them. Discipline within parties is maintained by the Whips. Each Saturday MPs receive from their whips a list of the business for the next week. Important business is highlighted by underlining. If only a single line is used ('a one-line whip'), their attendance is simply requested. Two underlinings ('a two-line whip') shows that a division is expected and that their presence would be desirable. A 'three-line whip' indicates that their attendance is required in order to give their party the necessary support.

In order to allow MPs to attend meetings or functions outside the House, 'pairing' can be arranged. These arrangements ensure that equal numbers of government and opposition Members do not vote, so the political balance is not upset. At times of great tension pairing arrangements can break down. A government with a small majority may find that it is in danger of defeat unless all its Members attend. To ensure that they do so, other meetings will be cancelled, ministers may be forced to fly home from European Union meetings, and sick MPs will be brought from hospital.

Further resources

The House of Commons

General

BBC Parliament broadcasts live from the House of Commons, and presents recorded highlights of proceedings in the House of Lords and the select and standing committees. Many cable operators provide this channel. Visits can be arranged to the House through your own Member of Parliament. Select and standing committees are usually open to the public.

Further reading

Hansard is available in print form in daily and weekly editions in most major libraries and Academic libraries. A CD-Rom version allows easy search by Member's name, constituency and subject. It is now available on the Internet.

Dod's History of Parliament (Dod's Parliamentary Companion) (1991).

Griffith, J.A.G. & Ryle, M. (1989) *Parliament: Functions, Practice & Procedures.* London: Sweet & Maxwell.

Silk, P. & Walters, R. (1998) *How Parliament Works.* Harlow: Longman.

The Times Guide to the House of Commons (May 1997) London: Times Books.

Internet address

http://www.parliament.uk

Pressure for reforms to procedures in the House of Commons has increased in recent years. A number of initiatives have been taken since May 1997 to review the effectiveness of parliamentary practices. Before the summer recess in 1997 the Select Committee on Modernisation of the House of Commons proposed a series of reforms to the legislative process.

The House of Lords

The upper chamber remains a vital part of Parliament. All bills must be passed by this House. Its less frantic nature, and the wealth of experience of its members, allows the House of Lords to act as a revising chamber. Many important changes to legislation have been made after consideration by the Lords. Because it does not enjoy the democratic legitimacy of the House of Commons, it rarely insists on changes when the Commons continue to oppose them. In the event of a dispute, the Commons will ultimately triumph. A bill which has been certified by the Speaker of the House of Commons as a 'Money Bill' (a bill which only contains provisions dealing with central government taxation or expenditure) can obtain the Royal Assent if the Lords have not passed it, without amendment, within one month of the Lords receiving it from the Commons. This procedure has never been invoked. Ordinary bills which have been passed by the House of Commons in two successive sessions but rejected in both sessions by the Lords can be sent for the Royal Assent despite the Lords' opposition. The only other requirement for the 'Parliament Act procedure' to be used is that one year must elapse between the 2nd Reading in the First Session and the passing of the bill by the Commons in the Second Session.

Approximately 1200 peers are entitled to sit in the House of Lords. In January 1997, 767 were hereditary peers who have inherited their peerage. Although some of these peerages are of great antiquity, (the title of Earl of Shrewsbury was granted in 1442), only 30 per cent date from before 1800 and 40 per cent were created earlier this century. There were 417 Life Peers, granted a title which cannot be passed on, for their contribution to the life of the country. The majority of these are former politicians but there are also composers, actors, businessmen and academics among their ranks.

Twenty-six peers are 'Lords Spiritual', the two Archbishops of the Church of England and the 24 most senior bishops. The country's most senior judges sit as 'Lords of Appeal in Ordinary' on the 'Appellate Committee of the House of Lords', which is the country's highest court.

The Executive

At a general election the candidate who wins the most votes in the constituency in which he stands becomes the Member of Parliament. The Queen invites the leader of the party with the most MPs in the new House of Commons to become her Prime Minister. He selects the members of his Cabinet and other ministers.

The Cabinet includes the most important members of the government. They meet at least once a week and together they are responsible for directing and co-ordinating the work of the government. In addition to meetings of the full Cabinet, ministers will attend meetings of Cabinet committees. These are set up by the Prime Minister and may be standing committees to oversee a particular area of policy or the progress of legislation, or *ad hoc* committees set up to deal with a particular problem.

The Cabinet of the Labour government under the Prime Minister, Tony Blair, formed in May 1997, contained the following office holders:

◆ Prime Minister

◆ Secretary of State for the Environment, Transport and the Regions (also Deputy Prime Minister)

◆ Chancellor of the Exchequer

◆ Foreign Secretary

◆ Lord Chancellor

◆ Home Secretary

◆ Secretary of State for Education and Employment

◆ President of the Board of Trade

◆ Minister of Agriculture, Fisheries and Food

◆ Secretary of State for Northern Ireland

◆ Secretary of State for Scotland

◆ Secretary of State for Wales

◆ Secretary of State for Defence

◆ Secretary of State for Health

◆ Secretary of State for Social Security

- ◆ Secretary of State for National Heritage

- ◆ Secretary of State for International Development

- ◆ President of the Council and Leader of the House of Commons

- ◆ Lord Privy Seal and Leader of the House of Lords

- ◆ Chancellor of the Duchy of Lancaster

- ◆ Minister of Transport

- ◆ Chief Secretary to the Treasury

Cabinet ministers have overall responsibility for the work of their department. They are assisted by 'junior ministers' (a term which covers 'Ministers of State' and 'Parliamentary Under Secretaries of State'). Ministers lay down the policy objectives for their departments, make the key decisions, steer departmental legislation through Parliament and respond to questions from MPs.

The work of central government is carried out by government departments. Very often the term 'Whitehall' is used to refer to these administrative bodies. Some are indeed in that particular road. Departments are under the political control of ministers, and are headed on the civil service side by the permanent secretaries. The most senior civil servants advise ministers on policy. They prepare proposals for ministers to decide upon. Other civil servants are involved in the day-to-day implementation of the policies adopted.

In recent years many of the administrative functions have been 'hived off' to executive agencies. The Benefits Agency (once part of the Department of Social Security) and the Driver and Vehicle Licensing Agency (Department of Transport) are just two examples. There are, at the time of writing, over 100 agencies. These have their own budgets and performance targets. Responsibility for the day-to-day work of the agency is in the hands of a chief executive. Although these agencies are formally still part of the civil service, they have a degree of independence from the department to which they provide support.

Further resources

Government departments

General

Most books on constitutional law include chapters on the Cabinet; ministers; and the civil service. Political autobiographies can be an interesting source of material about the workings of government. The BBC's television programmes, *Yes Minister* and *Yes Prime Minister*, are regarded as 'well informed'.

Further reading

Brazier, R. (1998) *Constitutional Practice*. Oxford: Oxford University Press.

Drewry, G. and Butcher, T. (1991) *The Civil Service Today*. Oxford: Oxford University Press.

Dynes, M. and Walker, D. (1995) *The Times Guide to the new British State*. London: Times Books.

Hennessy, P. (1986) *Whitehall*. London: Fontana Press.

Kaufman, G. (1997) *How to be a Minister*. London: Faber & Faber.

Internet Address

http://www.open.gov.uk

Table 2.2 Structure of a government department: Department for Education and Employment 1997

Office	Office holder
Politicians	
Secretary of State	David Blunkett MP
Minister of State (Employment and Disability Rights)	Andrew Smith MP
Parliamentary Under-Secretary	Alan Howarth MP
Minister of State (School Standards)	Stephen Byers MP
Parliamentary Under-Secretary	Estelle Morris MP
Minister of State (Education and Employment in the Lords)	Baroness Blackstone
Parliamentary Under-Secretary (Further and Higher Education)	Kim Howells MP
Civil servants	
Permanent Secretary	Michael Bichard
Directorates	*Headed by*
Personnel and Support Services	David Normington
Finance	Leigh Lewis
Strategy, International and Analytical Services (SIAS)	Graham Reid
Further and Higher Education and Youth Training (FHEYT)	Roger Dawe
Employment and Lifetime Learning	Nick Stuart
Operations	John Hedger
Schools	Peter Owen
Information	Jim Coe

The Judiciary

The third function of government – judicial – is carried out by judges. Independence from the Executive and Parliament is highly prized in the British system. To become a judge it is necessary to have 10 years' experience as a barrister or a solicitor with rights of audience in the High Court. The structure and work of the courts is covered in Chapter 4.

Local government

England has two frameworks for local government. Some authorities are 'unitary' – having responsibility for all local government functions. The metropolitan boroughs and some large cities and towns have a unitary authority. Elsewhere functions are shared between county councils (education, libraries, social services, emergency services, county roads) and district councils (housing, waste collection, planning). Some district councils have 'borough status'. This gives them no extra responsibilities but allows them to be called a 'borough council'.

Councillors are elected to represent districts (or 'wards') within the area of the authority. Elections are held on the first Thursday in May, and a full term lasts four years. Council meetings follow the completion of a cycle of committee meetings, in which most of the major decisions will have been resolved.

Local government is funded partly through grants from central government (80 per cent) and raises the rest through the council tax. In recent years councils have faced severe restrictions on the amount of money that they can spend. The government announces a 'standard spending assessment', which is its view of how much money the authority should spend. The assessment is not an indicator of need, but is a division of the total that the government wishes local authorities to spend, on the basis of a set of key factors.

Further resources

Local government

General

Most councils provide material about the services they provide. Council and committee meetings are open to the public.

Further reading

Bailey, S. (1996) *Cross on Principles of Local Government Law*. London: Sweet & Maxwell.

Internet addresses

http://www.hemming-group.co.uk

http://www.kable.co.uk

http://www.gold.net/users/fu30/localtext.htm

Types of legislation

Statutes, otherwise known as Acts of Parliament, are the most important form of law. Because of the volume of law required, governments often use secondary legislation – normally in the form of statutory instruments – to set out the detailed regulations. In the Education Reform Act 1988, some of the rules are set out in the Act itself. Section 22 says:

The Secretary of State may make regulations requiring, in relation to every maintained school, the local education authority, the governing body or the head teacher to make available either generally or to prescribed persons, in such form and manner and at such times as may be prescribed –

(a) such information relevant for the purposes of this Chapter (including information . . .); and

(b) such copies of the documents mentioned in subsection (3) below; as may be prescribed.

The detailed rules referred to were contained in a series of statutory instruments: Education (School Curriculum and Related Information) Regulations 1989 (SI 1989/954); Education (Pupils' Attendance Records) Regulations 1991 (SI 1991/1582); Education (Individual Pupils' Achievements) (Information) Regulations 1992 (SI 1992/3168); Education (School Performance Information) (England) Regulations 1994 (SI 1994/1420).

The making of legislation

Acts of Parliament begin life as Bills. These can start in either House, though by convention bills which involve taxation begin in the Commons. The stages are similar in both Houses

1 **1st Reading**: the purely formal introduction of the bill. The procedure takes a few moments as the short name of the bill is read out by the Clerk, and the Speaker orders that the bill be printed.

2 **2nd Reading**: generally this will take place after at least two weekends have passed since the 1st Reading. It is a debate on the principle of the bill and its major provisions.

3 **Committee Stage**: the bill now undergoes detailed examination. The text is considered clause by clause and amendments are discussed. Normally this is done in one of the standing committees which meet in special rooms on an upper floor in the Palace of Westminster. Some bills are so important that a 'Committee of the Whole House' is held in the Commons Chamber. However in the House of Lords most bills are considered by a Committee of the Whole House.

4 **Report Stage**: apart from bills which have been considered by a Committee of the Whole House and are not amended there, all bills come back to the Chamber for further consideration. Major amendments are debated and voted upon.

5 **3rd Reading**: this is a debate on the principles of the bill as finally amended. In the majority of cases this is a short formality.

Once a bill has passed all these stages, it is sent to the other House and undergoes the same procedure there. If amendments are made by the Second House these must be considered by the Originating House before the bill becomes law. In theory amendments could be shuttled between the two Houses indefinitely. However

Exhibit 2.3 Perceived defects in the present system of the House of Commons

4. Previous inquiries into the legislative process have consistently identified a number of defects in the way in which Parliament considers legislation. Criticisms are made not only of the procedures used but of the pattern and timing of legislative scrutiny during a typical parliamentary session.

5. The first criticism made is that there has hitherto been little, if any, consultation with Members or with the House as a whole before Bills are formally introduced. In recent years some draft Bills have been produced for prior consultation, and the present Government has specifically undertaken in the Queen's Speech to extend this process. The House itself has however made no attempt to undertake any systematic consideration of such draft Bills.

6. There has as a result been no formal channel to allow time and opportunity for Members to receive representations from interested parties. Consultations between Government and those outside Parliament with a legitimate concern in the legislation has also been criticised as patchy and spasmodic.

7. Once Bills are formally introduced they are largely set in concrete. There has been a distinct culture prevalent throughout Whitehall that the standing and reputation of Ministers have been dependent on their Bills getting through largely unchanged. As a result there has been an inevitable disposition to resist alteration, not only on the main issues of substance, but also on matters of detail.

8. The Committee stage of a Bill, which is meant to be the occasion when the details of the legislation are scrutinised, has often tended to be devoted to political partisan debate rather than constructive and systematic scrutiny. On Bills where policy differences are great, the role of Government backbenchers on a Standing Committee has been primarily to remain silent and to vote as directed. By contrast the Opposition has often set out to devise methods designed simply to extend debate. The Government has then been forced to bring in a guillotine which has often been draconian, as a result of which large sections of the Bill have not been considered.

9. Special Standing Committees, which were designed to encourage more informed discussion on Bills which were not highly politically controversial, have rarely been used. This has almost certainly been because of the perceived amount of extra time involved and the consequent pressure on the legislative timetable, although evidence from those concerned, including Ministers, suggests that such a perception is in fact misconceived.

10. Report stages have frequently been equally unconstructive. So far as the Opposition has been concerned, they have often been seen as an opportunity to debate on the floor of the House issues which they regard as of major political importance. Amendments and new clauses are tabled as a peg on which to hang a particular debate, not always closely related to the provisions of the Bill. By contrast the Government has frequently taken the opportunity to table literally hundreds of amendments, some very technical, some very long, possibly as a consequence of the Bill being, as First Parliamentary Counsel put it, 'produced too quickly to get the policy and drafting right'.

11. Turning to the pattern of legislation, critics regularly point to the marked imbalance in the legislative activity at different times in the session. Early on in a typical parliamentary year, the House is usually swamped with major Bills in Committee as Ministers seek to get a head start for their own measures. The recent change in the timing of the Budget and the subsequent Finance Bill has made this worse. By contrast the House of Lords is under extreme pressure at the latter end of the session as it receives the major Commons Bills.

12. This pattern, combined with the absolute cut-off imposed by prorogation, frequently makes the last few days of a session particularly chaotic as attempts are made to complete the Government's legislative programme. Bills go to and fro between the Houses, both of which are asked to agree (or disagree) usually with minimal notice to a large number of amendments. Few, if any Members, are able to know what is going on, and there is potential scope for error. The House has in the past even been asked to debate Lords Amendments of which there has been no available text.

Source: Select Committee on Modernisation of the House of Commons, *First Report* (1997).

compromises are usually reached quickly. A bill which has the approval of both Houses is sent to the Queen for her formal approval. Once she has given the Royal Assent the bill becomes an Act of Parliament. It could come into effect immediately, though most Acts make provision for a later commencement date.

Most successful bills are introduced by the Government – who have a large measure of control over the parliamentary timetable. Individual MPs have the chance to introduce their own bills, though few make it to the Statute book. Every session a ballot is held for Private Members' Bills and time is allocated on specific Fridays for consideration of these bills. Other Private Members' Bills can be introduced under Standing Order 23, which allows a short explanation to be given. These are popularly known as 'Ten Minute Rule bills'. They stand almost no chance of becoming law, and in fact the procedure is used as a way of drawing the House's attention to a particular issue.

Exhibit 2.4 presents extracts from the first report of the Select Committee on Modernisation of the House of Commons, which reported before the summer recess in 1997.

Players in the political process

Political parties are major players in the British political system. It is almost impossible to win election to the House of Commons without the endorsement of one of the major parties. Those who are independent of the major parties are also disappearing from local government. Each party has its own method for selecting candidates, though most allow some choice to the party members in the relevant electoral area (the constituency).

Since 1945 governments have been formed either by the Conservative or the Labour party. The Liberal Democrats have grown as the third party. Nationalist parties operate in Wales and Scotland. Northern Ireland has its own system of political parties, which unlike the rest of the United Kingdom is still based on a division along religious lines: there are currently three Unionist parties and two nationalist parties represented in the House of Commons. In May 1997 there were 418 Labour, 165 Conservative and 46 Liberal Democrat MPs out of a total of 659 (*see* Table 2.1). Once elected MPs can change parties without having to resign their seats. However such an action is extremely rare.

Political decisions can have a major impact on an industry or an individual business. In order to inform and persuade the decision makers, individuals and companies have become involved in lobbying. At its most basic, lobbying is writing a letter to one's MP. However recent years have seen the growth of a 'lobbying industry'. Specialists, with experience of government, Parliament or the civil service, will advise on the most effective way of influencing decision making, and assist in running a campaign. Pressure groups – ranging from Friends of the Earth to industry organisations – employ their own experts in 'lobbying'.

Chapter summary

Government is made up of the Executive (the Cabinet and the Government Departments of State), the Legislature (Parliament) and the Judiciary (judges and their courts). In this chapter we have seen how Parliament makes the law, whereas the Executive is involved in both promoting legal change and carrying out the tasks and powers set out in the legislation. In Chapter 4 we consider in more detail the work of the courts.

Assignment

Prepare a report outlining the steps necessary to turn into law the proposals outlined in the extract in Exhibit 2.4 from the Queen's speech 1997.

Exhibit 2.4

The Queen's Speech: Economic agencies to start by 1999

Regional development agencies will come into operation throughout England from April, 1999, under proposals announced in the Queen's Speech. The agencies' functions will include promoting inward investment, helping small businesses and co-ordinating regional economic development. Their budgets will be built up by redeploying existing programmes.

A bill to establish the agencies – which will broadly reflect the terms on which the Scottish and Welsh development agencies were founded in the 1970s – is expected to be introduced in parliament in the autumn. Between now and then, regional consultations will be held.

Although many local authority leaders and business representatives will welcome the establishment of regional development agencies – some have been campaigning for them for years – the consultation exercise will be more than a formality.

In parts of England it will be impossible for the consultation to move beyond square one – definition of what constitutes a region – without running into differences of opinion. The government's south-west regional office, for example, is responsible for an area from Cornwall to Wiltshire. Critics of this 'region' question whether Penzance, Bournemouth and Swindon have any more in common with each other than with the rest of the country. One of the most fundamental issues likely to be aired during consultations is the working relationship between the proposed new agencies and existing organisations involved in economic development.

The government will want the new agencies to work in close co-operation with non-statutory regional economic promotion partnerships involving local authorities, training and enterprise councils (Tecs) and other public and private sector interests which have been set up in recent years.

These have done a good deal to draw business leaders more actively into regional development issues than in the past. Representatives of local government, business and the Tecs are likely to stress the importance of the agencies doing nothing to undermine this type of partnership.

They will also emphasise that the creation of regional agencies must not divert attention from the need to undertake much economic development activity at local labour market level.

The new agencies fit into wider government plans to devolve decision making to the English regions. Chambers of councillors, drawn from existing local authorities, are to be established as a first step towards what could eventually become elected assemblies.

Source: Financial Times, 15 May 1997.

3

The European Union

Chapter objectives

By the time you have read this chapter you should understand:

◆ **the structure and work of the institutions of the European Union;**

◆ **the different types of EU legislation;**

◆ **the the legislative process in the EU.**

Introduction

Thanks to the European Communities Act 1972, European Union law is not a separate type of law, but is as much a part of English law as any Act of Parliament or English case law. Business is increasingly affected by law made in the European Union. It is not only exporters who are affected by European Union law. Firms and individuals operating solely within the United Kingdom are affected by legislation on the environment, health and safety and sex discrimination.

Britain joined the European Economic Community (EEC) (as it was then known) in 1973. There are currently 15 members. These are listed in Table 3.1.

Table 3.1 Member States of the European Union

State (Date of joining)	State (Date of joining)
Austria (1995)	Italy (1958)
Belgium (1958)	Luxembourg (1958)
Denmark (1973)	Netherlands (1958)
Finland (1995)	Portugal (1986)
France (1958)	Spain (1986)
Germany (1958)	Sweden (1995)
Greece (1981)	United Kingdom (1973)
Ireland (1973)	

Unlike the United Kingdom, which has no single constitutional document, the European Union is subject to primary legislation which defines the institutions, procedures and policy responsibilities of the Union. The European Community Treaty ('the EC Treaty') (which is the amended 1957 Treaty of Rome) and the Treaty of Economic Union 1993 (also known as the Maastricht Treaty) are the two major pieces of primary legislation. The Amsterdam Treaty (agreed in 1997 but not yet adopted) will, once it is signed and ratified by all Member States, become the latest piece of primary legislation.

Further resources

The European Union

General

A great deal of free information is produced by the European Commission and the European Parliament. Most libraries hold copies of these booklets. They are also available from European Commission Office, 8 Storey's Gate, London, SW1P 3AT (Tel: 0171 973 1992). Every quarter *Vacher's European Companion* is published. This gives detailed information about the Community institutions and their current membership.

The Europa web site is a useful source of information. Most towns and cities have a European Information Centre.

Further reading

Nugent, N. (1994) *The Government & Politics of the European Union*. Basingstoke: Macmillan.

Wallace, H. and Wallace, W. (1996) *Policy-Making in the European Union*. Oxford: Oxford University Press.

Craig P. and de Burca, G. (1998) *EC Law: Text, Cases, and Materials*. Oxford: Oxford University Press.

Tillotson, J. (1996) *European Community Law: Text, Cases and Materials*. London: Cavendish.

Edwards, G. and Spence, D (eds) (1995) *The European Commission*. Harlow: Longman.

Corbett, R., Jacobs, F. and Shackleton, M. (1995) *The European Parliament*. London: Cartermill.

Hayes-Renshaw, F. and Wallace, H. (1996) *The Council of Ministers*. Basingstoke: Macmillan.

Internet addresses

http://europa.eu.int

This is the home page of the European Union. This gives access to sites set up by each of the institutions, and allows you to obtain both general information and detailed documents. A copy of the Amsterdam Agreement, which if ratified, will amend the Treaty, can be found at:

http://ue.eu.int/Amsterdam/en/treaty/treaty.htm

Other useful sites include:

http://www.fco.gov.uk/eur

http://www.hull.ac/php/lbsebd/eia_html/access1.htm

The Commission

The term 'Commission' is used in two different ways. First, it is used to describe the College of Commissioners. It is this sense of the word which is used by the primary legislation. The key treaty articles are Articles 155 to 163. However the term is also popularly used for the European 'civil service' which assists the commissioners in their work.

The 20 commissioners, chosen by – but independent of – the Member States, make up the Commission. Although each commissioner has an area of responsibility, all decisions are taken on a collegiate basis. The Commission meets as a body on Wednesdays. Each commissioner is assisted by a cabinet made up of at least six members. These cabinet members are personally appointed by their commissioner, and a cabinet will normally contain a mixture of internal commission staff and outsiders from the commissioner's home civil service or the private sector.

Table 3.2 Members of the Commission, 1995–9

Commissioner	Areas of responsibility
Jacques Santer	President of the Commission. Shares responsibility for monetary matters (with Mr de Silguy), coordination of foreign policy and security policy (CFSP) and human rights (with Mr van den Broek) and institutional matters (with Mr Oreja).
Sir Leon Brittan	Vice-President of the Commission. External relations with North America, Australia, New Zealand, Japan, China (including Hong Kong), Korea, Macau, Taiwan, including aid and development matters. Common commercial policy. Relations with the OECD and the WTO.
Manuel Marin	External relations with southern Mediterranean countries, the Middle East, Latin America and Asia (except Japan, China, Korea, Hong Kong, Macau, Taiwan).
Martin Bangemann	Industrial affairs. Information and telecommunications technologies.
Karel Van Miert	Competition.
Hans van den Broek	External relations with the countries of central and eastern Europe and former Soviet Union, Mongolia, Turkey, Cyprus, Malta and other European countries. Common foreign and security policy (CFSP) and human rights (with the President). External diplomatic missions.

Table 3.2 *continued*

Commissioner	Areas of responsibility
Joao de Deus Pinheiro	External relations with African, Caribbean and Pacific countries and South Africa including aid and development matters, Lomé Convention.
Padraig Flynn	Employment and social affairs. Relations with the Economic and Social Committee.
Marcelino Oreja	Relations with the European Parliament. Relations with the Member States (transparency, communication and information). Culture and audiovisual policy. Publications Office. Institutional matters (with the President).
Anita Gradin	Immigration, home and judicial affairs. Relations with the Ombudsman. Financial control. Fraud prevention.
Edith Cresson	Science, research and development. Joint Research Centre. Human resources. Education, training and youth.
Ritt Bjerregaard	Environment. Nuclear safety.
Monika Wulf-Mathies	Regional policies. Relations with the Committee of the Regions. The Cohesion Fund (with Mr Kinnock and Mrs Bjerregaard).
Neil Kinnock	Transport (including trans-European networks).
Mario Monti	Internal market. Financial services and financial integration. Customs. Taxation.
Franz Fischler	Agriculture and rural development.
Emma Bonino	Fisheries. Consumer policy. European Community Humanitarian Office (ECHO).
Yves-Thibault de Silguy	Economic and financial affairs. Monetary matters (with the President). Credit and investments. Statistical Office.
Erkki Liikanen	Budget. Personnel and administration. Translation and in-house computer services.
Christos Papoutsis	Energy and Euratom Supply Agency. Small and medium-sized enterprises (SME). Tourism.

The term 'Commission' is also applied to the civil service of the Union. The administration is split into departments known as 'Directorates-General' (*see* Table 3.3). The DGs are referred to by their number (written in Roman numerals) – for example the Competition Directorate-General is popularly called DGIV (pronounced D.G.4). DGs are subdivided into directorates. In turn, these are made up of 'units'. The Commission employs around 15 500 people in permanent posts. As there are 11 official languages – into which all documents must be translated – it is not surprising that around 11 per cent of this workforce are in the language service.

Table 3.3 Directorates-General of the EU

Directorate-General	Responsibilities
DG I	External Relations: Commercial Policy and Relations with North America, the Far East, Australia and New Zealand
DGIA	External Relations: Europe and New Independent States, Common Foreign and Security Policy, and External Missions
DGII	Economic and Financial Affairs
DGIII	Industry
DGIV	Competition
DGV	Employment, Industrial Relations and Social Affairs
DGVI	Agriculture
DGVII	Transport
DGVIII	Development
DGIX	Personnel and Administration
DGX	Information, Communication, Culture, Audiovisual
DGXI	Environment, Nuclear Safety and Civil Protection
DGXII	Science, Research and Development
DGXIII	Telecommunications, Information Market and Exploitation of Research
DGXIV	Fisheries
DGXV	Internal Market and Financial Services
DGXVI	Regional Policy and Cohesion
DGXVII	Energy
DGXVIII	Abolished
DGXIX	Budgets
DGXX	Financial Control
DGXXI	Customs and Indirect Taxation
DGXXII	Education, Training and Youth
DGXXIII	Enterprise Policy, Distributive Trades, Tourism and Co-operatives
DGXXIV	Consumer Policy and Health Protection

Figure 3.1 presents in diagram form the structure of (part of) DGV, Employment, Industrial Relations and Social Affairs.

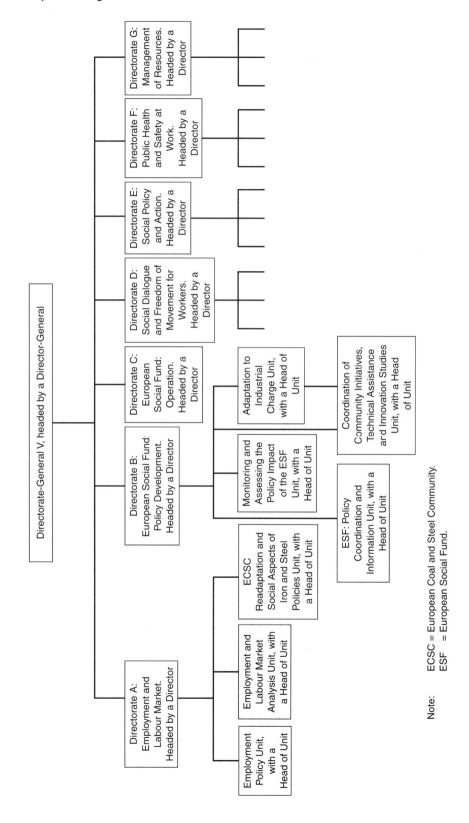

Note: ECSC = European Coal and Steel Community.
          ESF   = European Social Fund.

Fig. 3.1 Structure of DGV: Employment, Industrial Relations and Social Affairs

The Commission has three key roles:

1 **It is the initiator of action**. Only the Commission can table legislation. Legislation is drafted in the Commission by officials within the Directorates-General. They are responsible for preparatory work and consultation with government departments in the Member States and other interested parties. The draft legislation is approved by the Commission at its Wednesday meeting. Although other institutions cannot initiate legislation, Treaty Articles 138b (Parliament) and 152 (Council) allow them to ask the Commission to prepare legislation on a particular matter.

2 **It is the Executive of the Union**. Policies of the EU are prepared and implemented by the Commission. It is responsible for the operation of the Common Agriculture Policy (CAP), regional policy, Socrates and the many other programmes established by the EU. Sometimes the work is split between the Commission and national authorities. In regional policy the Commission has the overall responsibility for allocating funds, but management of projects is carried out at a national (or even sub-national) level.

3 **It is the Watchdog of the Union**. Responsibility for ensuring that Member States, other institutions, companies and individuals carry out their obligations under the Treaty rests with the Commission. If a Member State breaches the rules the Commission can bring Article 169 proceedings (*see* Exhibit 3.1). Actions have been brought against the Netherlands for failing properly to implement directives on the pollution of bathing water; against France for failing to repeal a provision in their Code du Travail Maritime which discriminated on the grounds of nationality; and against Britain for failure to implement directives on the quality of drinking water and on bathing water standards.

Exhibit 3.1 EC Treaty, Article 169

If the Commission considers that a Member State has failed to fulfil an obligation under this treaty, it shall deliver a reasoned opinion on the matter after giving the State concerned the opportunity to submit its observations.

If the State concerned does not comply with the opinion within the period laid down by the Commission the latter may bring the matter before the Court of Justice.

Source: EC Treaty, Article 169.

The procedure of an Article 169 action is presented in Figure 3.2.

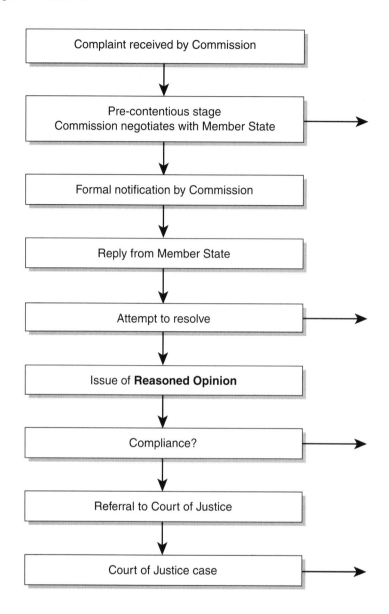

Fig. 3.2 Article 169 procedure

 ## The European Parliament

The voice of European citizens is heard in the European Parliament, which currently consists of 626 directly elected representatives of their home country. Elections are held every five years. Compared to Westminster, the European Parliament is very limited in its powers. Initially the Parliament was purely a consultative body, made up of delegates from National Parliaments. It has seen its powers increased in stages after the introduction of direct elections in 1979. Decision-making powers apply to non-compulsory expenditure of the budget and to accession and association agreements. There are varying degrees of involvement in the legislative process (*see* the section later in this chapter on the legislative process), and some degree of scrutiny over the other institutions.

Parliament meets for regular plenary sessions in Strasbourg. Committee meetings and some additional plenary sessions are held in Brussels. Most of the work of the Parliament is done in the committees. When a draft piece of legislation is sent to the Parliament it is referred to one of the 20 committees for a report. Other committees may be asked to supply the main committee with an opinion. Reports and opinions are delegated to a single MEP, known as the rapporteur, who prepares a draft for the committee. Although a rapporteur will be a member of a particular political group, it is the duty of this person to prepare a report which can win the support of the rest of the committee. The European Parliament is noted for being less confrontational than Westminster. After a series of meetings the Committee adopts a final report, which is submitted to the plenary session.

At the plenary session the full Parliament debates and votes upon reports. Regular statements are made to the Parliament by the Commissioners or the President of the Council and general debates are held. Time is also made available for oral questions to be put to the Commission or the Council.

MEPs sit according to political group. British Labour MEPs sit with the Party of European Socialists, currently the largest group in the European Parliament. Conservative MEPs are members of the European People's Party, a group which includes the Christian Democratic parties of other European states. The other groups are the European Liberal, Democratic and Reform Party; the Confederal Group of the European United Left and the Nordic Green left; the Union for Europe Group (dominated by Forza Italia); the Greens; European Radical Alliance; and the Europe of Nations Group.

The Council of Ministers

The European Union is not a superstate. Its most powerful institution is made up of ministers from national governments. No legislation can be passed against the will of the Council of Ministers.

The membership of the meeting will depend on the subjects for discussion. The General Affairs Council (GAC) brings together foreign ministers. It deals with general issues related to policy initiation and coordination, with the Coordination of Foreign and Security Policy, and other matters which are very sensitive politically. Specialist Councils include Ecofin (Economic and Finance Ministers), at meetings of which Britain will normally be represented by the Chancellor of the Exchequer or another Treasury Minister; the Agriculture Council; and the Budget Council. Other specialist committees meet less frequently: for example the Tourism Committee met just once in 1992.

Three main forms of voting are used by the Council. Simple majority voting is possible, though rarely used. Sometimes the Treaty requires a decision to be reached with unanimity. Examples of such decisions include the conclusion of agreements with one or more States or international organisations which establish an association involving reciprocal rights and obligations, common action and special procedure (Article 238 with Article 228); or secondary legislation proposed under Article 8a (Right of Movement and Residence). Unanimity means that no one votes against. An abstention does not prevent a 'unanimous' vote. Qualified Majority Voting (QMV) attempts to balance the interests of small and large countries (*see* Table 3.4). A measure requiring a qualified majority must gain 62 votes. To stop a measure it is necessary to have a blocking minority of 26. An abstention therefore has the same effect as a vote against. In practice there is a continuing reliance on consensus. Fiona Hayes-Renshaw and Helen Wallace discovered that 'only one in four decisions are contested; only one in seven attract negative votes as distinct from only abstentions; only one in sixteen attracts more than marginal opposition, and the topics are mostly esoterically technical.'

The Council is assisted by an array of other committees. The most important are the two COREPER groups, made up of senior civil servants who are permanently based in Brussels. (COREPER is a contraction of the French title of the committee, Comité des réprésentants permanents.) COREPER II is made up of the Ambassadors to the European Union whereas COREPER I consists of their deputies. In practice COREPER I members are specialists who concentrate on the more technical aspects of European law. Work is done by the COREPER meeting and issues sorted into 'A' or 'B' points. 'A' points are agreed at COREPER level and merely require the formal endorsement of the Council. 'B' points need to be thrashed out by the ministers themselves. Lower-level committees also assist the work of the Council. Immediately below the two COREPERS are the Special Committee on Agriculture (SCA); the Article 113 Committee which deals with negotiations for agreements with third countries; the Political Committee, which is composed of the Political Directors from the foreign ministries of each Member State, and prepares the work of the GAC on issues of foreign policy; and the K4 Committee which deals with justice and home affairs matters. These committees in turn are served by a number of working groups, which may be permanent or *ad hoc*. The Council is assisted by the general secretariat, which provides administrative support.

An important role in the work of the Council is played by the president. The country holding the presidency calls meetings, sets the agenda, chairs the Council and answers parliamentary questions. Presidencies last for six months and the rota is listed in Article 146 of the Treaty. To assist continuity, and to present a stronger face to the rest of the world, the Council can also be represented by the Troika. This involves the previous, current and next president of the Council. An extended form has recently appeared, known as the piatnika, which has five members.

In addition to Council meetings, ministers will meet in 'conferences', which are not as strictly bound by EU rules and codes of behaviour.

At least twice a year heads of government meet together, at 'the European Council'. These meetings have played an important role in the development and work of the EU. Leaders of the countries are able finally to resolve disputes between Member States and give new momentum to developments. The responsibility for preparing a European Council rests with the president of the Council of Ministers. Often the 'summit', as it is popularly known, is seen as the highlight of a presidency. Much effort is put into achieving a successful meeting.

It has become the normal practice for European Councils to meet over two days. A plenary session, involving heads of government and foreign ministers is held on the first morning after breakfast. The President of the European Parliament addresses this meeting. A further plenary session is held after a long lunch. These working lunches can turn out to be as important as any formal meeting. Informal discussions continue during dinner. In the evening session it used to be the practice that heads of government would hold informal 'fireside chats'. At some recent summits it has been necessary to convene an extra plenary session instead. While heads of government sleep their foreign ministers are often left to spend the night preparing draft conclusions. On the morning of the second day the draft 'Conclusions of the Presidency' are discussed further in plenary session until agreement is reached. Some summits have ended in the afternoon, whereas others have continued into the early hours of the next morning. The European Council has no power to make legally binding decisions. However the importance of the heads of government ensures that any decisions made guide the work of the Council of Ministers in the months that follow.

Table 3.4 Representation of Member States in the Council of Ministers

	Number of nominations for Commission	Votes when a qualified majority vote is held	Number of MEPs
Austria	1	4	21
Belgium	1	5	25
Denmark	1	3	16
Finland	1	3	16
France	2	10	87
Germany	2	10	99
Greece	1	5	25
Ireland	1	3	15
Italy	2	10	87
Luxembourg	1	2	6
Netherlands	1	5	31
Portugal	1	5	25
Spain	2	8	64
Sweden	1	4	22
United Kingdom	2	10	87
TOTAL	20	87	626

The courts

Fifteen judges, who sit in the European Court of Justice (ECJ) in Luxembourg, are responsible for ensuring that the institutions act in accordance with European law, and interpret the meaning of that law. Unlike the English courts, these judges do not give their own individual decisions, but the ECJ delivers a single judgement. This collegiate principle is so strong that it is not revealed whether a decision was agreed unanimously or whether there was only a bare majority.

As a result of the increasing workload of the ECJ, it is now assisted by the Court of First Instance (CFI). This junior court has increased its jurisdiction since it commenced work in 1989. It is now competent to hear all actions brought by natural or legal persons against measures taken by European institutions. The ECJ retains exclusive competence over cases brought by Member States and Article 177 cases. It can hear appeals from the Court of First Instance on points of law only.

These European courts should not be confused with the European Court of Human Rights. That court is an institution of the Council of Europe – a much larger body than the European Union – and it sits in Strasbourg. It is most unfortunate that media reports often fail to distinguish between these two very different courts.

The ECJ has 15 judges, which is the same number as in the CFI. In addition the ECJ is assisted by nine advocates-general. There is no English equivalent to the advocate-general, whose role is to deliver an independent opinion to the court, but who takes no part in the deliberation or voting of the judges.

The ECJ can sit in different formations depending upon the importance of the case. These are the Grand Plenum (15 judges); Petit Plenum (11 judges) and chambers of three, five or seven judges.

The ECJ is assisted by a registrar who is elected by the judges and advocates-general, and who is responsible for the administrative conduct, at all stages, of proceedings before the court.

Actions before the European Court of Justice

Figure 3.3 presents a classification of the actions heard before the ECJ.

The nature of the actions under the various Articles is as follows:

1 **Article 169** (Commission action against Member State). This action has been described earlier in this chapter.

2 **Article 170** (Member State action against another Member State). If the Commission has failed to take action against a Member State, another State may complain to the court. This action is only available **after** the Member State has complained to the Commission.

3 **Article 173** (actions to annul). Acts of Community institutions can be challenged under this action, which if successful will lead to the ECJ annulling the unlawful act. Privileged applicants (Member States, the Council and the Commission)

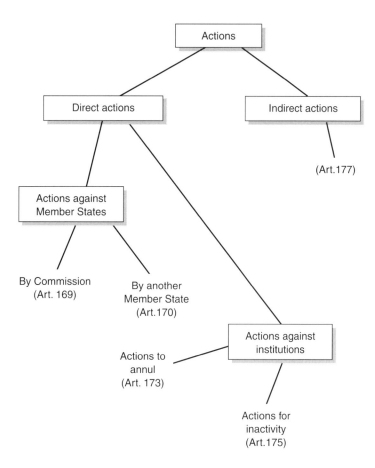

Fig. 3.3 Classification of ECJ actions

suffer no restrictions in bringing an Article 173 action. Parliament may only bring an action to protect its own prerogatives. Natural and legal persons must show that the act complained of is of 'direct and individual concern' to them. In practice this is a very difficult obstacle to overcome.

4 **Article 175** (Actions for inactivity). An action may be brought against an institution for failure to act.

5 **Article 177**. This indirect action allows courts in the Member States to refer a case to the ECJ in Luxembourg. It is not an appeal, but a request for interpretation. Once the case has been decided in the national court it is too late to seek a preliminary reference. The ECJ usually confines its ruling to the issue of interpretation, leaving it to the national court to draw the conclusion (which may be obvious) as to whether, in light of that interpretation, the national provisions should not be applied. This procedure has been very important in the development of European Union law. Exhibit 3.2 presents the text of Article 177.

Exhibit 3.2 EC Treaty, Article 177

The Court of Justice shall have jurisdiction to give preliminary rulings concerning:

(a) the interpretation of this Treaty;
(b) the validity and interpretation of acts of the institutions of the Community and of the ECB;
(c) the interpretation of the statutes of bodies established by an act of the Council, where those statutes so provide.

Where such a question is raised before any court or tribunal of a Member State, that court or tribunal may, if it considers that a decision on the question is necessary to enable it to give judgement, request the Court of Justice to give a ruling thereon.

Where any such question is raised in a case pending before a court or tribunal of a Member State against whose decisions there is no judicial remedy under national law, that court or tribunal shall bring the matter before the Court of Justice.

Types of legislation

The treaties are the primary legislation of the European Union. Secondary legislation comes in three main forms – regulations, directives and decisions. These are defined in Article 189 of the EC Treaty (*see* Exhibit 3.3). Many different legal systems exist within the European Union. Some rules can be written in a form which can apply irrespective of the differences in legal systems. These appear in the form of regulations. Other areas of law require a more individual approach. A directive sets the objectives, but each state needs to implement it in its own way. Decisions apply to named individuals, firms or countries.

Exhibit 3.3 EC Treaty, Article 189

A regulation shall have general application. It shall be binding in its entirety and directly applicable in all Member States.

A directive shall be binding, as to the result to be achieved, upon each Member State to which it is addressed, but shall leave to the national authorities the choice of form and methods.

A decision shall be binding in its entirety upon those to whom it is addressed.

The making of legislation

All legislation is prepared and introduced by the Commission. When legislation is proposed the Commission must specify the article in the Treaty which gives the Union the right to legislate on that particular matter. This is called the 'legal base'. There are a number of different legislative procedures laid down in the Treaty. The appropriate procedure is defined in the legal base. Often this leads to conflict between the institutions. A number of disputes arose in the late 1980s over the Commission's reluctance to use Article 100A. Instead the Commission used other bases which restricted Parliament's involvement. The most spectacular concerned a regulation laying down maximum permitted radioactivity levels for foodstuffs. It ended in delay and an action before the ECJ. There are currently three main legislative procedures – consultation, cooperation and co-decision. These are outlined in Figures 3.4 to 3.6. The consultation procedure has the smallest role in the European Parliament (EP). It has a right to be consulted, but the Council can ignore its advice. It was held in the *Isoglucose* case that a failure by the Council to consult would mean that the legislation would be invalid. In the cooperation procedure the Parliament has greater powers than in consultation, but the Council can still overrule it. However in the co-decision procedure Parliament can effectively veto proposed legislation.

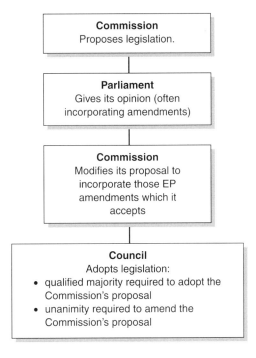

Fig. 3.4 Consultation procedure

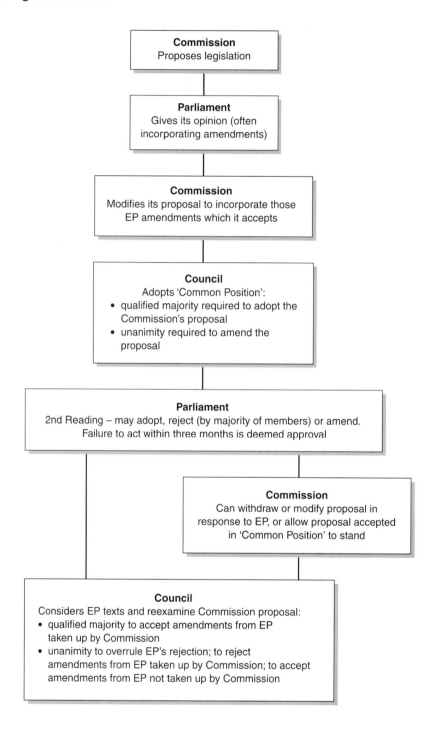

Fig. 3.5 Cooperation procedure

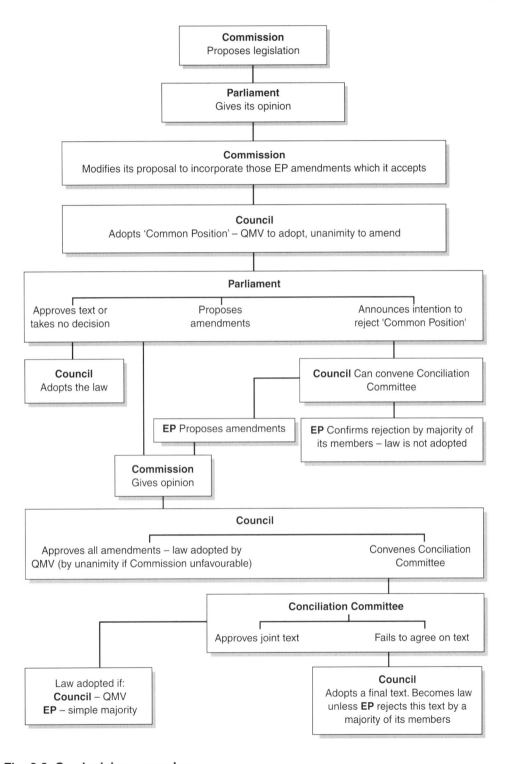

Fig. 3.6 Co-decision procedure

Note that the Amsterdam Treaty streamlines the co-decision procedure and will have the effect that most legislation will have to follow either the consultation or co-decision procedure.

 ## Chapter summary

The European Union and its institutions play an increasingly important role in British business life. This chapter has outlined the roles of each of the major institutions and described the law-making process. These will be changed as the European Union increases in both size and importance. The Amsterdam Treaty, once ratified and implemented, will mark the first stage in this development.

Assignment

Using the article reproduced in Exhibit 3.4, prepare a report on the potential influence that European law could have for a company. Explain the roles played by different EU institutions.

Exhibit 3.4

Business and The Law: Job agency ban ruled unlawful

An Italian law that banned private companies from acting as employment agencies was contrary to European Union competition rules, the European Court of Justice ruled.

The case arose out of an application in the Milan courts to confirm the necessary legal formalities for establishing Job Centre Coop, a co-operative society with limited liability.

In Italy the employment market was subject to a mandatory placement system administered by public placement offices and regulated by a law banning the pursuit of any activity, even unremunerated, as an intermediary between the supply of and demand for paid employment.

An earlier reference to the European Court had been made by the Milan District Court when Job Centre first applied for confirmation of the instrument under which it was established.

In the first case, the Court ruled it had no jurisdiction to rule on questions raised by the Italian court, as the national court was performing a non-judicial function.

Following that ruling, the Milan court dismissed Job Centre's application. Job Centre appealed and the Milan Court of Appeal stayed the proceedings and referred certain questions to Luxembourg.

The Italian court asked whether the provisions of the Treaty of Rome concerning the free movement of workers, freedom to provide services and competition, precluded national legislation under which any activity as an intermediary between supply and demand in employment relationships was banned unless carried on by public placement agencies.

In relation to free movement of workers the Court said it did not follow from the fact that workers were among the founding members of Job Centre that those provisions were applicable.

Once Job Centre had been set up and was running it would be an independent legal person, and the Court therefore ruled the provisions concerning free movement of workers had no relevance to the dispute.

The Court then turned to the compatibility of the Italian law with the EU competition rules.

The Court concluded that a body such as a public placement office could be classed as an undertaking for the purposes of the EU competition rules. The Court then analysed the competition rules concerned with state undertakings. It said any measure adopted by a member state that maintained in force statutory provisions that created a situation in which public placement offices could not avoid infringing the treaty provision prohibiting abuse of a dominant position, was incompatible with the treaty. An undertaking with a legal monopoly could be regarded as occupying a dominant position under the competition rules and the territory to which that monopoly extended (Italy) could constitute a substantial part of the common market.

The Court agreed with the European Commission that the market in the provision of employment services was both extensive and diverse. As the market was so extensive and differentiated and subject to enormous changes as a result of economic and social developments, public placement offices could well be unable to satisfy a significant portion of the requests for its services.

The Italian law created a situation where the provision of a service was limited contrary to the competition laws. The requirement under the competition rules that the abusive conduct had an actual or potential effect on trade between member states was fulfilled where the placement of employees by private companies could extend to the nationals or the territory of other member states.

The Court ruled, in the light of this ruling on the competition laws, that there was no need for it to rule on the treaty provisions on the free movement of services.

Source: *Financial Times*, 23 December 1997.

4

The law relating to business

Chapter objectives

By the time you have read this chapter you should understand:

◆ the classification of English law;

◆ the court structure of the English legal system;

◆ the meaning of key legal terminology.

Introduction

Ignorance of the law is no excuse. This maxim (in Latin, *Ignorantia juris neminem excusat*) means that it is no defence to say that you were unaware that your act was illegal. People in business cannot afford to ignore the law, since legal mistakes can be costly. Although lawyers can be employed for their specialist skills, a basic understanding of the legal system and major categories of law is invaluable in business.

Classification of law

The distinction between criminal and civil law

Perhaps the most important distinction in English Law is between criminal and civil law. Exhibit 4.1 sets out the major differences. A single act can have both civil and criminal consequences. The driver who causes a car accident may be prosecuted for dangerous driving, and be sued by the person injured for the injury and damage caused.

Exhibit 4.1 Differences between criminal and civil law

1 Terminology
- Criminal – 'Prosecute';
- Civil – 'Sue'.

2 Parties
- Criminal – Prosecution and Defendant;
- Civil – Plaintiff and Defendant.

3 Who can bring an action?
- Criminal – in general any citizen can bring an action, although there are some statutory exceptions to this rule. In practice private prosecutions are rare.
- Civil – only the person wronged may sue.

4 How are cases referred to?
- Criminal – an action is normally brought in the name of the Crown in trials on indictment. In a case cited as *R* v *Morgan* (referred to as The Queen and Morgan), Morgan is the defendant.
- Civil – the name of the plaintiff is given first, followed by that of the defendant, e.g. *Nicholson* v *Griffiths* (referred to as Nicholson and Griffiths).

5 Who can discontinue a case?
- Criminal – if the case is brought by the public authorities (Director of Public Prosecutions, Crown Prosecution Service), they decide whether to discontinue a case. It is not up to the victim. The Attorney General may end a prosecution by the issue of a *nolle prosequi*.
- Civil – the plaintiff may discontinue a case at any time, and the government is not able to put an end to a private civil case.

6 Is the Crown able to pardon a wrong?
- Criminal – yes;
- Civil – no.

7 What is the relevance of the victim's consent?
- Criminal – except for offences in which lack of consent is a key element in the nature of the crime (eg. rape), the consent of the victim is irrelevant;
- Civil – the consent of the victim will in most cases prevent that person from suing.

8 What courts are involved?
- Although some courts handle both civil and criminal cases, there is a distinct structure of courts for each type (*see* Figures 4.1 and 4.2).

9 What is the result of an action
- Criminal – sanctions (punishment);
- Civil – remedies (compensation, order prohibiting continuation of the behaviour complained of, instruction to carry out specific action).

10 What is the standard of proof required?
- Criminal – the prosecution must prove their case *beyond reasonable doubt*.
- Civil – the claims made must be shown on the *balance or probabilities* to be true.

Contract

A legal agreement between two parties is known as a contract. The existence of a body of law governing contracts is essential for a market system to work. In order to attract the protection of the law an agreement must fulfil certain conditions.

The first essential is the existence of an agreement. In most cases there is no requirement for this to be in writing, though a written contract is useful as a piece of evidence. English courts have sought to discover the existence of a contract by asking whether there has been an offer and an acceptance.

An offer has been defined as 'an expression of willingness to contract on specified terms, made with the intention that it shall become binding as soon as it is accepted by the person to whom it is addressed' (Treital 1995). It is distinguished from a mere 'invitation to treat'. The difference between the two is that an offer is expected to lead to a binding contract if it is accepted, whereas an invitation to treat is merely the opening of negotiations towards an agreement. In the case of *Fisher* v *Bell* (1961) a shopkeeper placed a flick knife in his window along with a price tag. It was at that time an offence to offer flick knives for sale. He was acquitted because, according to Lord Parker, 'It is clear that, according to the ordinary law of contract, the display of an article in a shop window is merely an invitation to treat. It is in no sense an offer for sale the acceptance of which constitutes a contract.' In general, displays in a shop window or in a self-service supermarket will be treated as invitations to treat, as will most advertisements. However as the manufacturers of a 'smoke ball' found out, if the advertisement is worded in such a way as to convey the impression that the offeror will be bound by any acceptance, then it is an offer. In that case (*Carlill* v *Carbolic Smoke Ball Co* (1893)) an advertisement claimed that their product was so good that anyone who used it properly and yet still caught influenza would be paid £100. The advertisement even stated that £1000 had been deposited in a bank as evidence of their sincerity. It was held that there was sufficient evidence to show that this was in fact an offer which could be accepted by following the instructions in the advertisement.

The agreement becomes binding once the offer has been accepted. Acceptance must be on the same terms as the offer, since proposing different terms will constitute a counter-offer. Sometimes this can lead to a 'battle of the forms', where each side sends its own standard terms. The courts could decide to recognise the last offer sent as the one whose terms govern the contract, or conclude that no agreement had ever been reached. A less rigid approach has been seen in recent years. In *Trentham Ltd* v *Archital Luxfer* (1993) the judge noted that the parties had acted as if a contract had been concluded and both sides expected that work to be done and paid for. He added, 'in this fully executed transaction a contract came into existence during performance even if it cannot be precisely analysed in terms of offer and acceptance'.

In addition to being conveyed by formal notification, acceptance can be achieved by conduct. Normally acceptance occurs when notification reaches the offeror, but a special rule applies to postal communications. In the case of *Adams* v *Lindsell* (1818) the postal rule was established which states that acceptance is complete when the reply is posted. The rule applies only to the post – it does not cover fax, telex or e-mail – and the offeror can avoid the rule by requiring that acceptance be made by use of a specified method, for example by fax.

An offer can be withdrawn at any time prior to acceptance being communicated. The postal rule does not apply to such revocation. An offeror can waive his right to communication of acceptance, but no one can be held to accept merely by their silence.

Not all agreements will be upheld by the courts. There is a presumption that agreements between members of a family, or between close friends, are not intended to be legally enforceable. Companies which deal together are presumed to intend that their actions have legal consequences. The second essential of a contract is that there is an intention to be legally bound. As a court cannot read people's minds it has to rely on the above presumptions. However evidence can be submitted to overturn the presumption. Mr Merritt promised to transfer the house he jointly owned into the name of the wife he had deserted, if she would pay off the mortgage. After full repayment he refused to honour his promise. He argued that an agreement between husband and wife was presumed to lack the required intention. The court ruled that in this case the presumption had been rebutted (*Merritt* v *Merritt* (1970)).

Consideration must pass between the parties. This was defined in *Dunlop* v *Selfridge* (1915) as 'An act or forebearance of one party, or the promise thereof' which is 'the price for which the promise of the other is bought'. Without this consideration a promise is legally unenforceable. Consideration need not be adequate but it must be sufficient. This famous legal maxim means that the court is not concerned with the amount of consideration – all the assets of a company could be legally sold for a penny, but there must be some economic value in the consideration. Performance of an existing obligation is not sufficient consideration. However the harshness of this rule has been mitigated by the development of the doctrine of promissory estoppel. Lord Denning laid down the principle that 'a promise intended to be binding, intended to be acted on and in fact acted on, is binding so far as its terms properly apply'. The doctrine of consideration remains since promissory estoppel only applies where there is an existing legal relationship, where the promisee has relied on the promise and it would be inequitable for the promisor to go back on the promise. Promissory estoppel may be used as a defence, but cannot be used to found an action.

Although most contracts can be made orally, some must be in writing. Contracts for the sale of land must be made in writing incorporating all the terms. Other transactions which must be wholly in writing include bills of exchange, consumer credit agreements and marine insurance contracts. Guarantees need not be written but they must be evidenced in writing.

In addition to rules which govern whether a contract exists, the law provides for ascertaining what is included in a particular contract, and what consequences will follow any breach. Express terms are stated by the parties and fall into three categories: conditions, warranties and innominate terms. A condition is a major term which, if broken, would allow the other party to treat the contract as ended. The breach of a warranty will give rise to a right to damages, but the contract will continue. Innominate terms are intermediate; their consequences will depend upon the results of the breach.

Implied terms are treated as part of a contract although express provision was not made by the parties. The courts will imply terms in an attempt to give effect to the parties' true intentions. Often the courts will refer to the 'officious bystander' test established in *Shirlaw* v *Southern Foundries* (1939). They will imply a term which is so obvious that, 'if while the parties were making their bargain, an officious bystander were to suggest some express provision for it, they would testily suppress him with a common "Oh, of course!"'. A term which is essential to make the contract work will also be implied. Parliament has also laid down some terms which will be implied into certain contracts. Examples can be found in the Sales of Goods Acts, described in Chapter 2.

Contract law also lays down rules to govern who has the capacity to enter a contract and the consequences which will follow a mistake or misrepresentation. When something happens which, without any fault on either side, prevents performance of the contract, the contract is said to be frustrated. Rules to cover frustration have been established by the courts.

When a contract has been broken remedies will be sought. These can include damages to cover the cost of losses incurred as a result of the breach. Sometimes the most appropriate remedy would be to require that the party in breach carry out the contract. This is known as 'specific performance'.

Agency

Sometimes agency is regarded as part of the law of contract. It covers the relationship between a principal and the person acting as agent for them. An agent's role is to bring the principal into a contractual relationship with a third party. Although many people describe themselves as agents, the law looks at the relationship not the label.

No special formalities are required to create an agency, unless the agent is to be given the power to execute a deed. The duties required of an agent have been developed by case law. These include an obligation to carry out instructions; to act with due care and skill; and not to delegate without the authority of the principal. The agent should not put himself in a position where he has a conflict of interest with the principal. If bribes are taken, or a secret profit made, the courts can order that the money be paid to the principal. In such circumstances the agent would be liable for any loss suffered by the principal in connection with the bribe.

Tort

Only a proportion of relationships are governed by contracts. In a crowded world the actions of an individual or a company may damage the person, property or interests of another. The behaviour which caused the damage may be accidental, reckless or deliberate. Tort law provides for legal redress for such wrongs. (The word comes from the French word for wrong.) There are a number of torts, each having its own set of rules.

Trespass

There are three kinds of trespass.

1 **Trespass to the person**. Three actions can give rise to this tort. **Assault** is defined as 'an act of the defendant which causes the plaintiff reasonable apprehension of the infliction of a battery on him by the defendant' (Winfield and Jolowicz 1994). Threatening words and actions, such as shaking one's fist or pointing a gun at someone will constitute this trespass. When contact is made the tort of **battery** is committed. **False imprisonment** is defined as 'any confinement of a person without lawful cause'. It is a defence if the 'victim' consented. This covers injuries sustained in sport, although the courts have been prepared to find that a player has exceeded that consent. Self-defence may be accepted, as long as the response is not disproportionate. Lawful arrest is a defence to a claim of false imprisonment.

2 **Trespass to goods**. Any attack upon the goods of another person may give that person the right to sue for damages. An attack may take various forms, ranging from withholding property from its rightful owner to scratching someone's car. It is possible to trespass against one's own goods. This will happen when goods are held until payment is made. An attempt to seize the goods back would be a trespass. Consent is a defence.

3 **Trespass to land**. This is defined as 'any unlawful entry of a person or thing onto land or buildings in the possession of another'. It can cover walking over someone else's property or throwing stones on to their land.

   Legal entry is recognised if the alleged trespasser had permission (Known as a 'licence'); or entered under authority of law (e.g. Police and Criminal Evidence Act 1984); or the person has a court order under the Access to Neighbouring Land Act 1992 to allow a person access to land to carry out 'alteration, adjustment or improvements necessary to preserve adjoining land'.

Defamation

Defamation involves making a statement about someone which tends to make reasonable and respectable people think less of that person. If this statement is made in a 'permanent' form, for example in writing or by picture or is broadcast on television or radio, it will be a libel. Slander is defamation by word of mouth or gesture. The defences are:

1 **Innocent publication**. An apology must be published for the court to accept this defence.

2 **Fair comment**. Any comments must be based on true facts and made without malice.

3 **Justification**. The ultimate defence is that the words are true.

4 **Absolute privilege**. This defence covers words spoken by an MP during proceedings in Parliament, or a fair and accurate report of judicial proceedings in a court in the UK, published contemporaneously.

5 **Qualified privilege**. This defence is only available if the report is fair and accurate; and is published without malice. The schedule to the Defamation Act 1952 lists the statements which attract qualified privilege.

Nuisance

Nuisance is any action which unlawfully annoys or damages another person. Private nuisance involves unlawful interference with one person's use or enjoyment of their land. Public nuisance materially affects a class of people, or indeed may affect everyone. The defences are:

1 **Rebuttal**. This involves claiming that the behaviour is not a nuisance.

2 **Prescription**. This involves a claim that the action has been carried out there for more than 20 years.

3 **Statutory right**. This may be invoked when the law grants an individual or company the right to carry out the action complained of.

4 **Act of God or Act of a stranger**. This defence is lost if the action was foreseeable.

5 **Consent**.

Negligence

In everyday speech negligence means carelessness. Legally it has a precise meaning and covers damage to a person or their property resulting from another person's inadvertence. To succeed in an action for negligence it is necessary to prove that a duty of care was owed to the plaintiff; this duty was breached; and the plaintiff suffered damage as a result. The leading case is *Donoghue* v *Stevenson* (1932), in which a woman was taken ill after discovering the ginger beer she had been drinking contained a decomposing snail. That case laid down the neighbour principle which says:

> You must take reasonable care to avoid acts or omissions which you can reasonably foresee would be likely to injure your neighbour. Who, then, in law is my neighbour? The answer seems to be – persons who are so closely and directly affected by my act that I ought to have them in contemplation as being so affected when I am directing my mind to the acts or omissions which are called in question.

The three defences are:

1 **Contributory negligence**. In this defence, the 'victim' contributed to the injury himself. This can provide a full defence, though in most cases will only result in the damages being reduced.

2 **Volenti non fit injuria**. This means that, if you agree to the risk, you cannot sue for any damage resulting.

3 **Ex turpi causa non oritur actio**. This is from the Latin, meaning no action can be based on a disreputable cause. In certain circumstances a court will dismiss a claim for negligence if the plaintiff was in the middle of committing a criminal act.

Administrative law

The actions of public authorities are regulated by this growing area of law. The most important development in administrative law is the growth of judicial review. Actions of ministers and local councils have been successfully challenged in court.

Property law

Property can be divided into real property (generally land) and personal property. Each has its own set of rules governing ownership and other rights over the property.

Company law

This term covers the law which relates to the formation, conduct and dissolution of companies. The main statutes are the Companies Acts of 1985 and 1989. European law has had an important influence in this area.

Exhibit 4.2 Key legal definitions

Court	A body established by law to exercise the judicial power of the state. ◆ Superior – unlimited jurisdiction (House of Lords, Court of Appeal, High Court); ◆ Inferior – limited jurisdiction.
Tribunal	A body established to adjudicate or arbitrate on a disputed question or matter. Governed by the Tribunals and Inquiries Act 1992. Regarded as administrative rather than judicial.
Plaintiff	The person who brings the civil case.
Prosecution	The party who institutes criminal case.
Defendant	The person sued in a civil action or charged with a criminal offence.

▶

Exhibit 4.2 continued

Appeal	Complaint to a superior court of an injustice done by an inferior one, on the merits of the case (as opposed to review of the legality of a decision). ◆ Against conviction; ◆ Against sentence.
Appellant	The person who takes a decision against him or her to a higher court.
Respondent	The person who is called upon to answer an appeal.
Case stated	A statement of facts prepared by one court for the opinion of another on a point of law.
Statute	An Act of Parliament. Requires approval of both Houses of Parliament (subject to the provisions of the Parliament Acts 1911, 1949) and the Queen.
Statutory Instrument	A comprehensive expression which describes all those forms of delegated legislation covered by the Statutory Instruments Act 1946 (which are subject to parliamentary control).
Regulation	EU legislation which is binding in its entirety and directly applicable in all Member States.
Directive	EU legislation which is binding, as to the result to be achieved, but leaves to the national authorities the choice of form and methods.

Sources of law

Custom

Although custom is of decreasing importance the courts will recognise local or trade customs as a source of law. Most customs have survived by being incorporated into law through judicial precedent.

Precedent

Most legal systems recognise the value of following previous decisions. However the doctrine of precedents plays a particularly important role in English law. The rule is that earlier decisions of courts at the same hierarchical level or above are binding on a judge faced with the same facts. The binding part of a judicial decision is the *ratio decidendi* (the reason for deciding), the principle of law on which the decision is based. Other comments by the judge are described as *obiter dicta* (remarks made in passing). These may be influential but are not binding. Legal reasoning involves discovering which parts of earlier judgments bind the case in hand. One lawyer will argue why the earlier case must be followed by the judge. The other side will try to 'distinguish' the earlier case by showing that a significant fact destroys its value as a precedent. Until the mid-1960s the courts were unwilling to overturn any precedents, believing that it was for Parliament alone to change the law. Since the House of Lords issued its 1966 practice statement (*see* Exhibit 4.3), the courts have become much less rigid in their approach to precedent.

Exhibit 4.3 House of Lords practice statement

> Their lordships regard the use of precedent as an indispensable foundation upon which to decide what is the law and its approach to individual cases. It provides at least some degree of certainty upon which individuals can rely in the conduct of their affairs, as well as a basis for orderly development of legal rules.
>
> Their Lordships nevertheless recognise that too rigid adherence to precedent may lead to injustice in a particular case and also unduly restrict the proper development of the law. They propose [to treat] former decisions of this House as normally binding, [but] to depart from a previous decision when it appears right to do so.

Source: House of Lords, Practice Statement, [1966] 3 All ER 77.

The practice statement expressly stated that this relaxation in the rules of precedent applied only to the House of Lords.

Exhibit 4.4 Precedent

House of Lords	Decisions bind all courts, except the House of Lords itself.
Court of Appeal	Bound by House of Lords decisions, even if the court feels the Lords were mistaken. It is bound by its own previous decisions except where: (1) there are conflicting earlier decisions; (2) the earlier decision is inconsistent with a House of Lords decision and (3) the decision was made *per incuriam* – literally, by carelessness or mistake. In practice the Criminal Division is less rigid in following precedent.
High Court	Bound by decisions of the House of Lords and the Court of Appeal. Divisional Courts are normally bound by their own previous decisions. The High Court itself is not bound to follow its earlier decisions, but in practice does so.
Crown courts, County courts and Magistrates courts	Bound by all higher courts but their decisions are not binding.

Legislation

Most modern law has been created by legislation. The best known form of legislation is Acts of Parliament, which are also referred to as Statutes. The procedure for creating Acts of Parliament is set out in Chapter 2. Statutes are regarded as the most important form of law. Parliament can overrule a precedent or custom but it has been a key principle of English law that the courts cannot challenge a statute. This is in contrast to the position in most countries, where the courts can strike down a piece of legislation which is contrary to a constitutional law. Since the *Factortame* case (1990) the courts have, however, been able to disapply legislation which is contrary to European Union law. The doctrine of implied repeal states that, 'if two inconsistent Acts be passed at different times, the last must be obeyed, and if obedience cannot be observed without derogating from the first, it is the first which must give way' (*Dean of Ely* v *Bliss* (1842)).

Secondary legislation has become increasingly important, and this is normally issued by the relevant government department.

Laws passed by the European Union – regulations, directives and decisions – may also be regarded as legislation. The European Court of Justice has ruled on many occasions since 1964 that European law is supreme over national law.

The legal system

The courts

The highest court in England and Wales is the Judicial Committee of the House of Lords. This deals with the most important cases. Leave to appeal to the House of Lords must be granted by the House of Lords or the Court of Appeal. Most cases get no further than the Court of Appeal, which is divided into the Criminal and Civil Divisions. All these courts are based in London.

Important civil cases are heard by the High Court. Claims in contract and tort are the responsibility of the Queen's Bench Division (QBD). The Divisional Court of the QBD deals with civil appeals from magistrates and crown courts. It also hears applications for judicial review. The Family Division deals with adoption, wardship and contested divorce cases. The Chancery Division covers cases involving property law. The High Court meets in London and in other major cities.

Crown, County and Magistrates courts can be found in most towns.

Legal personnel

Judges

Full-time professional judges preside over the most important cases. In the House of Lords the Judicial Committee is composed of Lords of Appeal in Ordinary. The most senior judge is the Lord Chancellor, who is also a member of the Cabinet.

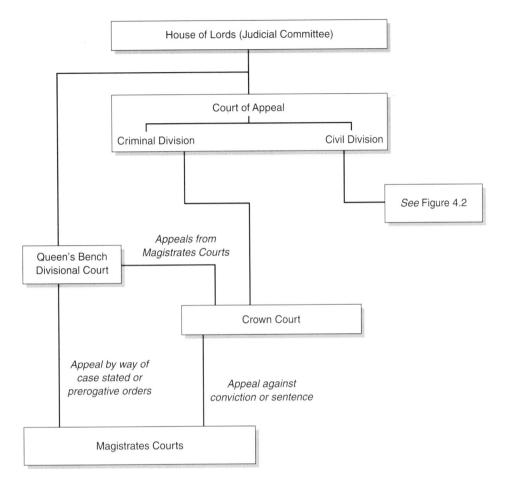

Fig. 4.1 The criminal courts

Judges in the Court of Appeal are known as Lord Judges of Appeal. The Civil Division is headed by the Master of the Rolls and the Criminal Division by the Lord Chief Justice.

High Court judges can also sit in crown courts. Circuit judges deal with lesser offences in the crown court and also sit in county courts.

Recorders and assistant recorders are part-time judges. All judges must be barristers or solicitors with rights of audience of at least 10 years' standing

In the magistrates courts cases are heard by lay justices of the peace or by a single stipendiary magistrate. Lay magistrates do not receive a salary, although they may claim expenses.

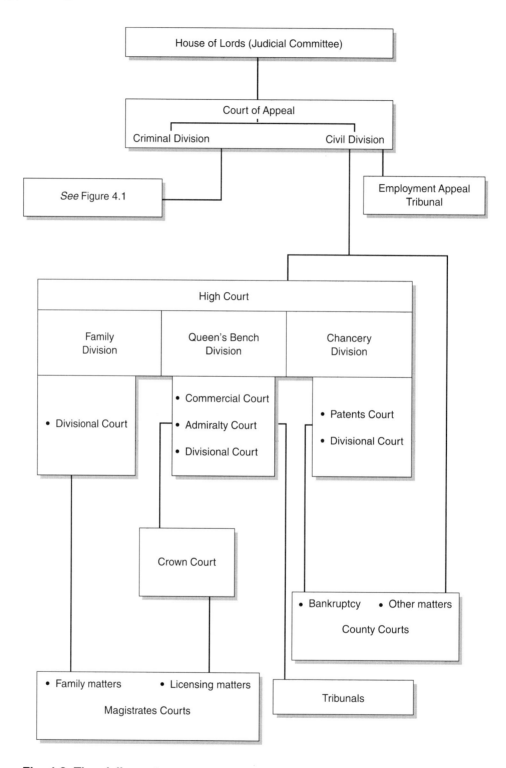

Fig. 4.2 The civil courts

Barristers

Barristers are the senior branch of the legal profession. In the past they were regarded as the specialist advocates. Some of the barriers which used to distinguish them from solicitors have been broken down. They are sometimes referred to as 'Counsel'. In court they wear wigs and gowns. Senior barristers may apply to become Queen's Counsel (QC). This title recognises their seniority but carries no duties.

Solicitors

Traditionally solicitors were the 'general practitioners' of the legal profession. They would, if necessary, engage a specialist barrister to act for their client. Today there is increasing specialisation within the ranks of solicitors, and individual solicitors can now apply for a higher courts qualification which will allow them to appear in all courts.

Further resources

The legal system

General

Any introductory legal textbook should outline the key features of the court structure, describe the personnel of the law and introduce the main areas of law. Specific textbooks deal in greater detail with particular areas of the law.

Further reading

Bailey, S.H. and Gunn, M.J. (1996) *Smith & Bailey on the Modern English Legal System*. London: Sweet & Maxwell.

Ingham, T. (1998) *The English Legal Process*. London: Blackstone Press.

Treital, G.H. (1995) *The Law of Contract*. London: Sweet & Maxwell.

Winfield and Jolowicz on Tort (1994). London: Sweet & Maxwell.

Internet addresses

House of Lords: http://www.parliament.the-stationery-office.co.uk/pa/ld/ldjudinf.htm

Courts: http://www.open.gov.uk/courts/court/cs_home.htm

Lord Chancellors Department: http://www.open.gov.uk/lcd/lcdhome.htm

Bar Council (Barristers): http://www.barcouncil.org.uk

Law Society (Solicitors): http://www.lawsoc.org.uk

Chapter summary

It can be seen that knowledge of the legal system is important for anyone wishing to be involved in modern business. An appreciation of the distinctions between the criminal law and the civil law aids understanding of the court structure and the language that is used by lawyers. Although specialist knowledge can be bought from the legal profession, successful business people understand the importance of the law in the defence of the interests of their business.

Assignment

On the basis of the article reproduced in Exhibit 4.5 prepare a report on the relative advantages and disadvantages of courts and tribunals for resolving disputes.

Exhibit 4.5 Courts and tribunals

Role of industrial tribunals called to account `FT`

The government is today expected to announce proposals to reform the industrial tribunal system, which has been criticised by businesses and unions alike.

The proposals, which follow an eight-month review, aim to improve the efficiency of a system in which the number of cases has increased by 150 per cent over the past five years. Tribunals dealt with a record 73,000 cases last year on 60 types of claim, from race discrimination to unfair dismissal.

The government has become increasingly concerned at the costs of tribunals, whose budget since 1988 has risen by 75 per cent to Pounds 26.6m this year. Launching the review in April, Miss Ann Widdecombe, employment minister, said the government would 'review the operation of the industrial tribunals with a view to identifying any changes which would help them to cope with an increasing volume and complexity of cases and reduce delays, while containing demands on public expenditure'.

Her announcement came just three weeks after a tribunal awarded record compensation of Pounds 300,000 to an army major who was forced to give up her career when she became pregnant.

The case, which paved the way for a series of armed service claims worth an estimated Pounds 100m, highlighted the increasing powers exercised by tribunals. The compensation followed last year's decision by the European Court of Justice to remove the ceiling on awards in sex and race discrimination cases.

Originally designed to deal with appeals against the training levy in 1964, tribunals have grown in response to a mountain of employment law. The 1971 Industrial Relations Act gave tribunals jurisdiction over unfair dismissal claims, and the caseload expanded again under the 1986 Wages Act. More recently the government transferred contractual disputes in England and Wales from the county courts to industrial tribunals.

The growth in employment law has undermined the informal nature of the industrial tribunal, which is led by a panel of two lay members sitting beside a legally trained chairman. One in three employers and one in five applicants are now legally represented at tribunal hearings, although legal aid is not available.

The Confederation of British Industry said: 'The whole process could be speeded up and made more efficient, but we would not want to see an increase in legalism. The informal structure would tend to permit less delay in most cases.'

The CBI is calling for tribunal chairmen to hear more cases on their own, without the help of lay members. At the moment chairmen have the power to sit alone in cases which revolve around legal issues.

However, the TUC argues that lay members have essential experience of the workplace, particularly in cases of sex and race discrimination.

Mrs Sarah Veale, senior policy officer, said: 'Industrial tribunals should see the use of lawyers, particularly by employers.'

The huge compensation awards to former servicewomen also highlight the legal anomalies in the tribunal system. While there is no limit to discrimination awards, the maximum compensation for unfair dismissal remains at just Pounds 11,000.

Mrs Janet Gaymer, chairman of the Law Society's employment law committee, said: 'We have been saying for a long time that it is totally illogical that you can have a limit on the amount of awards on an unfair dismissal and none on sex and race discrimination.'

One of the options open to the government is to expand the role of Acas, the conciliation service, which attempts to reach a compromise in all tribunal cases. However the proportion of cases resolved by Acas has fallen over the last five years from 58 per cent to 33 per cent. More than two thirds of Acas resources are now committed to individual conciliations. Another option is to prune administrative costs by taking a stricter line on delays. However, employment lawyers fear further efficiencies will ignore the logistical difficulties of mounting a case.

Mrs Gaymer said: 'A lot of the backlog of cases has reduced recently because of vigorous listing policies.

The concern that employment lawyers have is that tribunals are ignoring the requirements of both parties to a very large extent, over whether their representatives can attend or not.'

Source: Financial Times, 14 December 1994.

Part 2

THE ECONOMIC ENVIRONMENT

Introduction

After examining aspects of the politico-legal environment, it is now important to appreciate elements of the economic environment. Thus, this part is divided into three chapters:

◆ *Chapter 5* The United Kingdom microeconomic environment;

◆ *Chapter 6* The United Kingdom macroeconomic environment;

◆ *Chapter 7* The International economic environment.

Whereas the term microeconomics refers to the functioning of individual parts of the economy, the term macroeconomics refers to the functioning of the economy as a whole. In Chapter 5, therefore, we investigate the workings of the price mechanism as a means of determining the price of a product. Thus, we will examine the laws of supply and demand. The concept of elasticity will be introduced, with particular emphasis being given to elasticity of demand.

We will consider various market structures, such as monopoly and oligopoly, and how such structures influence the conduct and performance of firms that operate within them.

Finally, in Chapter 5, we will investigate why UK governments and the EU authorities have felt it necessary to intervene in markets in order to uphold competition.

When investigating the UK macroeconomy, in Chapter 6, a good starting point is to understand the circular flow of income and why the government needs to intervene in order to maintain the circular flow and manage aggregate demand. Thus, we will consider, in turn, the commitment to maintaining price stability, employment, maximising economic growth and maintaining a favourable balance of payments and a stable exchange rate.

Further, it is important to distinguish between various UK government macroeconomic policies, principally fiscal policy and monetary policy. The government employs a combination of both policies to manage the economy.

In Chapter 7 we will consider aspects of the international economic environment. A good starting point for this investigation is to ask why there is the need for trade between countries and what are the benefits of free trade for the world economy. Governments around the world have imposed restrictions to free trade and we will consider a number of these restrictions briefly.

In the world economy today, there are various economic groupings of countries, such as the European Union. It is important to have an appreciation of such groupings, and also of recent developments in central and eastern Europe.

Finally, in Chapter 7, we will briefly consider various international organisations such as the World Trade Organisation (WTO) and International Monetary Fund (IMF).

After reading Part 2, you should possess a broad understanding of the UK, European and world economic environment and of how various aspects of that environment impact upon business.

The United Kingdom microeconomic environment

Chapter objectives

When you have read this chapter you should be able to:

- understand the workings of the market mechanism;

- distinguish between various market structures;

- appreciate why some of the above structures need to be regulated by government.

Introduction

In this chapter we will consider how the laws of supply and demand operate in order to determine the price of a good. These laws allocate resources in a relatively simple economy and are characteristic of a market form known as perfect competition.

However, in more advanced economies there are various market imperfections, such as the domination of the industry by a few firms. This situation can lead to higher prices for the consumer and is known as an oligopoly. This, together with a monopoly, have been subject to government regulation. Furthermore, with the UK's accession to the European Union in 1973 company practices leading to imperfect market forms have been subject to scrutiny by the European Commission under the auspices of EU competition policy.

The market mechanism

Economists assume that society's needs and wants are unlimited, whereas there are limitations on the supply of resources. Therefore, consumers are faced with choices. Sacrifices have to be made in order to make these choices. Economists refer to the value of these alternatives foregone as **opportunity cost**.

One method of allocating scarce resources is through the market mechanism. Resources will be demanded by consumers and supplied by producers. It is therefore necessary to describe the law of demand and the law of supply.

Demand

First, it is necessary to illustrate the law of demand, this is shown in Table 5.1 and Figure 5.1.

Table 5.1 The law of demand

Apples	
Price	Quantity demanded
60	85
50	100
40	115
30	130
20	145

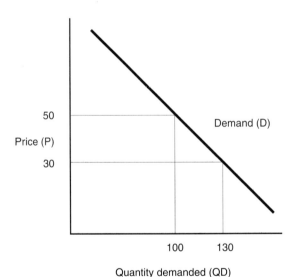

Fig. 5.1 The demand curve

Figure 5.1 shows that, all other things being equal, more will be demanded when the price is low than when the price is high. Thus, if the price of apples fell from 50 pence per kilo to 30 pence, there would be an increase in demand from 100 kilos to 130 kilos. This causes a movement along the demand curve. This must be distinguished from a shift in the demand curve from D to D1 or D to D2 which is shown in Figure 5.2. The shift from D to D1 represents an increase in demand whereas the shift from D to D2 represents a decrease in D.

Fig. 5.2 Shifts in the supply curve

The shift in the demand curve is caused by the following factors:

1 **The prices of other goods**. It is necessary to distinguish between substitute and complementary goods. Substitutes are said to exist when a rise in the price of one good is followed by a rise in demand for the other good. For example, if the price of butter rose, consumers would switch to margarine. When two or more goods are complementary in demand, an increase in demand for one generally results in an increase in demand for the other (for example, cars and petrol).

2 **Disposable income**. If the levels of disposable income of individuals rose, this would cause the demand curve to shift to the right;

3 **Tastes**. If consumer tastes changed to, say, a preference for eating red apples then, all other things being equal, demand for red apples would rise.

Supply

All other things being equal, more will be supplied when the price is high than when the price is low. This is illustrated in Figure 5.3.

An increase in price from 1 to 2.50 results in an increase in supply from 100 to 150.

Once again it is necessary to distinguish between a movement along the supply curve and a shift in the supply curve. The shift in the supply curve is illustrated in Figure 5.4, where S1 represents an increase in supply and S2 represents a decrease in supply.

Fig. 5.3 The supply curve

Fig. 5.4 Shifts in the supply curve

The shift in the supply curve is caused by:

1 **Changes in technology**. Improvements in production technology will lead to increases in the supply of such manufactured goods as cars.

2 **Acts of nature**. For example good weather conditions will cause an increase in the supply of agricultural products.

3 **Business expectations**. Good economic prospects will encourage manufacturers and suppliers to invest in new machinery and equipment, therefore leading to an increase in supply.

4 **Prices of resources**. A decrease in the cost of production, such as raw material costs, will lead to an increase in profits and therefore supply will be increased.

If the demand curve and supply curve are incorporated in one diagram an equilibrium price and quantity can be shown (see Figure 5.5).

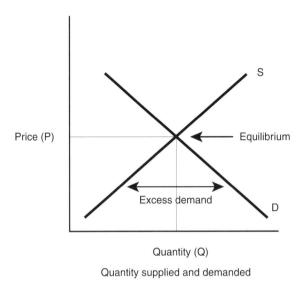

Fig. 5.5 **Equilibrium price and quantity**

If the price were set at a level above equilibrium, this would result in an excess of supply over demand, which forces suppliers to reduce their prices. Likewise, if the price were set at a level below equilibrium, pressure would be exerted by the market to force producers (suppliers) to raise prices.

In its purest form the market mechanism operates by allocating resources according to the laws of supply and demand.

Price elasticity of demand

Perhaps an easier and more realistic concept to understand than the allocation of resources according to the laws of supply and demand is that of elasticity of demand. This measures the responsiveness of demand to changes in price. Demand is said to be inelastic if the quantity demanded changes by a smaller percentage than does price. It can be illustrated by a steeply sloping demand curve (*see* Figure 5.6).

If the price of, say, a packet of cigarettes were raised from £2.80 to £3.00, there would be a minimal affect on quantity demanded.

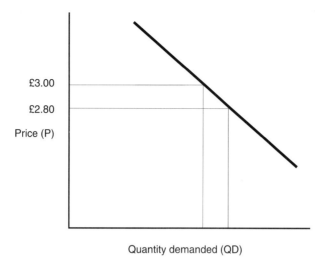

Fig. 5.6 Inelastic demand curve

On the other hand, if demand is elastic then demand changes by a larger percentage than does price. An elastic demand curve is shown in Figure 5.7.

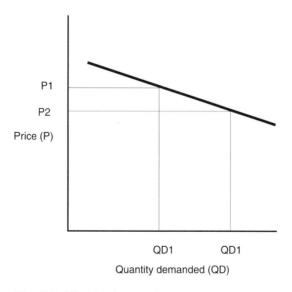

Fig. 5.7 Elastic demand curve

Price elasticity of demand is determined by the following factors:

1 The degree to which the good or service is considered to be a necessity. Tobacco is considered to be a necessity by some people, that is, for them, there is no close substitute for it.

2 The proportion that the good or service represents in relation to a household's total budget.

3 The longer the period of time, the more price elastic is demand for a product.

Elasticity of demand is calculated by using the following formula:

$$\frac{\text{Percentage change in quantity demanded}}{\text{Percentage change in price}}$$

Inelastic demand is indicated by an absolute value of less than one, whereas elastic demand has an absolute value of greater than one.

Of course the government takes advantage of the economic concept of elasticity of demand by raising excise duties on such goods as tobacco, alcohol and petrol. These goods are considered to be relatively inelastic in demand. Therefore increases in excise duty, and thus price, result in a marginal decrease in demand.

Income elasticity of demand

Income elasticity of demand measures the responsiveness of demand to changes in income, and is calculated by the following formula:

$$\frac{\text{Percentage change in quantity demanded}}{\text{Percentage change in income}}$$

Income elasticity occurs if the quantity demanded rises by a greater percentage than the rise in income, for example, if a 7 per cent rise in income results in a 10 per cent rise in demand. Income elasticity of demand is denoted by a value of greater than one.

Income inelasticity occurs where the percentage rise in demand is less than the rise in income, for example, where a 10 per cent rise in demand results in a 6 per cent rise in income. The value of income inelasticity lies between zero and one.

Cross-price elasticity of demand

Cross-price elasticity of demand measures the responsiveness of changes in the quantity demanded of good A to changes in the price of good B. It is calculated as follows:

$$\frac{\text{Percentage change in quantity demanded of good A}}{\text{Percentage change in price of good B}}$$

As we already know, substitute goods are those for which demand decreases when the price of another good decreases (for example, butter and margarine). In this situation cross-price elasticity is greater than zero.

Complementary goods are those for which demand increases when there is a decrease in the price of another good (for example, cars and tyres). In this situation cross-price elasticity has a negative value.

Elasticity of supply

Elasticity of supply measures the responsiveness of quantity supplied to changes in price. This is calculated as follows:

$$\frac{\text{Percentage change in quantity supplied}}{\text{Percentage change in price}}$$

Elastic supply is said to exist where the amount producers supply to the market exceeds the percentage change in price.

Inelastic supply occurs where the amount producers supply changes by a smaller percentage than the percentage change in price.

Having illustrated the operation of the market mechanism and introduced the concept of elasticity, we now investigate how markets are structured by considering various types of competition.

Market structures

In the last section we saw how price is determined by the operation of the laws of supply and demand. We now turn to a consideration of market structures. Economists consider that the structure of markets determines the conduct (e.g. pricing policy) and the performance (e.g. profitability) of firms within those markets. This is known as the Structure–Conduct–Performance (S–C–P) model.

There are basically four types of market structure:

a Perfect competition

b Monopoly

c Monopolistic competition

d Oligopoly

Perfect competition

If there are large numbers of business organisations and no single firm can influence the price, a market structure called perfect competition is said to exist. Other assumptions include the fact that each firm produces only a small fraction of the industry's total ouput; there are no barriers, such as high capital costs, preventing new businesses from entering the market; all firms produce an identical product, therefore there is no branding or advertising, and finally producers and consumers are assumed to have perfect knowledge.

It is difficult to illustrate this kind of market form in the real world but just think of a market in a town where there are many fruit and vegetable stalls. There are identical products, set-up costs, i.e. barriers to entry, are relatively low and each stallholder is said to be a price taker, that is, they have little say in the determination of prices. The price of fruit and vegetables is set by the operation of market forces, i.e. the laws of supply and demand.

In reality, however, perfect competition rarely exists, and most markets are said to be imperfect. It is now pertinent to outline the factors which make up imperfect markets and give some illustrations of each market form.

Monopoly

At the opposite end of the scale from perfect competition there exists a market form known as monopoly. We have all played the game of Monopoly where the object is to buy as many properties and streets as possible and therefore squeeze out the competition, i.e. other players, by making them pay ridiculously high prices and rents. Economists define a monopolist as the sole supplier to a market. Thus, there is only one business organisation and it is in such a dominant market situation, that it can set the price, that is, it is a price maker. Unlike the situation under monopolistic competition (which is considered below), in a monopoly there may be very little branding or advertising as the firm produces a single product. Such a market form existed in the gas, electricity and water industries before they were privatised in the mid-1980s. The government prevented new business entering these markets as they were considered, at the time, to be natural monopolies. Having several companies supplying a given area would result in a duplication of pipelines, cables, etc.

Somewhere between the two extremes of perfect competition and monopoly are market forms known as monopolistic competition and oligopoly. These are closer to how most market structures operate in the real world.

Monopolistic competition

With monopolistic competition there is a relatively large number of firms offering slightly differentiated products. If we go to our local out-of-town shopping centre, we are bound to find a retailer of electrical goods, such as washing machines or hi-fis. These are all similar products that are close substitutes for one another but because of product differentiation each firm possesses a monopoly over its own version of the general product. Thus, manufacturers of hi-fis or television sets create customer loyalty by allegiance to the brand. As a result each firm may set its own price but within limits imposed by the competition.

Oligopoly

Oligopoly is another form of imperfect competition where there are a few business organisations which dominate the market. If there are just a few producers then there is always the temptation on their part to get together or collude in order to fix prices. The best example to illustrate this market form is the practice followed by OPEC (the Organisation of Petroleum Exporting Countries), which met once a year in order to fix the price of oil. As production is concentrated in a few hands, there is very little the Western world could do to influence the price of a barrel of oil. In 1973, OPEC quadrupled the price of oil, which had near-devastating affects on the world economy. This type of price-fixing agreement is known as a cartel and the OPEC cartel lasted until 1986 when some producers in the cartel exceeded their production quota. Therefore, the market was over supplied with oil, and the result was a fall in prices. Cartels are declared illegal by UK, EU, and US competition authorities. Such authorities monitor this kind of anti-competitive behaviour as it is considered to be detrimental to the public interest to fix prices in such a way.

Before we consider how such authorities prevent such anti-competitive behaviour by monopolists and oligopolists it is necessary to consider why competition is good for consumers, producers and the economy as a whole.

Successive Conservative governments during the 1980s and 1990s have espoused the virtues of competition as being good for consumers in terms of lower prices and greater choice. Competition imposes pressures on producers to contain costs in order to maintain and improve efficiency. Competition is considered to be good for the economy as a whole as it promotes the more efficient use of scarce resources and seeks to redress such market imperfections as are outlined above. As a result, both UK governments and EU authorities have felt the need to develop a policy which promotes competition (*see* Exhibit 5.1).

The market structures outlined above are summarised in Figure 5.8.

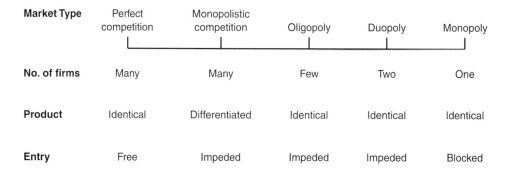

Market Type	Perfect competition	Monopolistic competition	Oligopoly	Duopoly	Monopoly
No. of firms	Many	Many	Few	Two	One
Product	Identical	Differentiated	Identical	Identical	Identical
Entry	Free	Impeded	Impeded	Impeded	Blocked

Fig. 5.8 Continuum of market structures

It is worth noting that, in the field of economics, an industry consists of firms, therefore, the oligopolistic market structure is said to exist where a few firms dominate the industry, for example in the world tyre industry (*see* Exhibit 5.2).

As can be seen from Exhibit 5.2, the production of tyres is in the hands of a few major manufacturers. Thus the industry is said to be concentrated. A further example of a high degree of industrial concentration is in the UK wines, cider and perry industry, where there are 51 firms. The five largest firms account for approximately 91 per cent of employment, and 94 per cent of output and net capital expenditure.

Exhibit 5.1

Switched on to competition

When Norman Askew, the gritty chief executive of East Midlands Electricity, joined the electricity company from managing aerospace businesses for TI, the engineering group, he found a company comfortable in its monopoly position. 'They'd never experienced a bad month,' Askew recalls of a business that had regular and predictable cash flows.

The same sort of comfort level existed when John Devaney, Chief executive of Eastern Group, biggest electricity supplier in England and Wales, took control of the Ipswich-based company. He found Eastern used to talk of consumers, not customers.

'What the company had to develop was new thinking that competition was good,' Devaney said. 'It didn't know what it meant, because it hadn't experienced any.'

All this is going to change in less than a year when the market supply Britain's 25m retail consumers of electricity will be opened to competition, ending the cosy monopolies the 14 public electricity suppliers in Great Britain have enjoyed since nationalisation in 1947.

The prospect of competition has forced the 14 to embark upon programmes of change that were inconceivable in the past. Many have invested in expensive and complex computer systems to help them manage customer calls and records; others have opted for low-tech solutions, modifying existing systems and putting more money into marketing.

All are trying to be more 'customer friendly', knowing that customer retention is, in the short term, the more profitable option than customer acquisition. For most of the utilities this entails training employees to use sophisticated telephone call management equipment so that customer inquiries get dealt with as quickly as possible.

But none can predict with any certainty how their approaches will reflect upon the shape of the market in five years' time.

'You have to take a medium to long term view of this market; there are no short term profits in it,' says Jim Forbes, chief executive of Southern Electric, based in Maidenhead.

Forbes believes that cost control will be a prime imperative of competition. 'Currently we spend £8 [a year maintaining] a customer. We're trying to get this to £6 a customer. If we can do that we'll increase supply profits by 20 per cent, and that's without doing anything to the customer base in terms of numbers.'

But, that said, Southern wants to be a successful contestant in the competitive market. It plans to link up with nationally known companies, outside its own area in the south-east of England.

'Marketing alliances are about cost sharing. For out-of-area marketing it's better to let the other guy [partner] get the customers and we can process them. We've recruited 250 to staff a call centre in Southampton.'

'Estimates for the cost of acquisition of new customers range from £100 to £130 a customer,' he says. 'If you can't get the acquisition cost down to £40 to £50 then it is hard to justify being in the business.'

Seeboard, an electricity company to the east of Southern, is also focusing on costs.

'The best profits do not necessarily come from the biggest market share,' says Jim Ellis, chief executive. 'Retention is the best way to make profits. To try to win a customer out of area can be very expensive. We have taken the view that you cannot give up the next five to 10 years of profit to win a customer.'

Seeboard will attack the competitive market with Beacon Gas, its 50/50 joint venture with Amoco, the US oil company. 'We want to make Beacon a national brand,' says Stephen Gutteridge, Seeboard's director of supply. 'You need a brand and image outside your area. Seeboard travels into London and into Southern Electric's area but not much further.'

Gutteridge questions whether the discounts available to electricity customers will be enough to induce many to change supplier. The marketing trials in the south-west and south-east England have seen consumers being offered up to £50 and £60 off annual gas bills. 'In electricity we're looking at price counting of £15 a year,' he says. 'My guess is that much less than 10 per cent will change.'

Devaney, however, is determined that Eastern Gas remains the biggest electricity company in Britain. 'We're born the biggest and we're going to stay that way,' he says.

Eastern has the most aggressive plans of any utility company and hopes to build its 'out of area' electricity business on the back of its retail gas operation. So far it has acquired 80,000 customers through the competition trials in the south-east and west of England.

Devaney says he wants 1m new gas and new electricity customers. 'The approach is to talk to people and explain what changing supplier means,' he says. 'It is a difficult concept for people to understand that you can buy gas from different companies but that it is delivered to them in the same pipes. Door-to-door is essential to get the message across.'

Unlike many of his peers, Devaney is confident that the money to be made in the competitive market. The contraction in retail margins, he maintains typical of a market in the stages of deregulation. Looking ahead, he believes margins have to grow to around the 4 cent to 5 per cent level. He says 'If the regulated supply margin stays at 1 per cent then there will be no new entrants.'

Source: Simon Holberton, *Financial Times*, 4 June 1997.

Exhibit 5.2

World tyre industry may face shake-out

Middle-ranking companies are squeezed between sector leaders and aggressive new entrants

After five years of consolidation, the world's tyre industry is likely to face another round of restructuring over the next decade, according to new research by the Economist Intelligence Unit.

Analysing the performance of the 12 largest tyre companies, accounting for more than 80 per cent of world sales, the EIU concludes that it is the companies rankign immediately below the 'Big Three' – Bridgestone, Michelin and Goodyear – which face the fiercest competition.

They lack the economies of scale of the biggest companies and are most at risk from aggressive emerging country producers, the EIU says, although its analysis is unlikely to go uncontested by the industry itself.

Continental of Germany, Sumitomo of Japan and Pirelli of Italy – ranked fourth, fifth and sixth – are all substantial businesses and themselves account for nearly a fifth of the industry's $70bn turnover.

However, they have many of the disadvantages of size without the compensating advantages, the researchers say. Because each has tyre sales of much less than half that of each of the 'Big Three', marketing and research and development costs have to be spread over much smaller production volumes.

'They have a world presence but typically they are significant players in only two or three regions and they do not dominate or lead in any region. In this situation it is difficult to earn the profit margins enjoyed by the industry leaders. And these companies show signs of being squeezed between the really large companies, which enjoy economies of scale, and the smaller, more focused companies which are growing through concentration on niche products or specific geographic areas.'

The point is made by reference to operating profit margins. The research shows that those of the 'Big Three' average 7.8 per cent last year, compared with 4.7 per cent for Continental, Sumitomo and Pirelli.

Nevertheless, it also shows that the three smaller companies have fared better than the top three in improving their margins over the past three years. The top three's 7.8 per cent is only marginally better than the 7.6 per cent achieved in 1994, whereas the three smaller companies have improved from just 3.7 per cent.

Pirelli, for one, says its improving margins show that its strategy of increasingly targeting high value-added, niche performance tyre business – while retaining a stake in more mainstream business – is paying off. And new flexible manufacturing technology, allowing commercially viable production of tyres in batches of as low as 150–200 units, means that 'Pirelli no longer feels particularly disadvantaged at the lack of scale economies enjoyed by the Big Three,' according to Mr Giuseppi Bencini, managing director of Pirelli Tyres.

Mr Bencini points to the company's exclusive supply contract, for Jaguar Cars' new XK8 sports car, of

World's leading tyre manufacturers 1995

Company	Country	Sales* ($m)
Bridgestone	Japan	13,000
Michelin	France	12,278
Goodyear	USA	10,105
Continental	Germany	4,938
Sumitomo	Japan	4,137
Pirelli	Italy	2,987
Yokohama	Japan	2,860
Toyo	Japan	1,524
Cooper	USA	1,267
Kumho	S Korea	1,147

*Tyre Sales   Source: EIU

Forecast of world car tyre sales

1996–2000 and 2005 (m units)	1996	1997	1998	1999	2000	2005
Western Europe	66.1	66.9	65.0	64.1	63.2	66.4
Eastern Europe & Russia	9.4	9.9	10.6	11.2	11.7	16.4
North America	63.2	64.9	67.8	67.7	69.1	75.8
Latin America	7.8	8.2	8.2	8.6	9.1	11.0
Asia	68.8	71.7	73.3	74.4	75.9	85.2
Others	2.6	2.7	2.8	2.9	3.0	3.8
Total	217.9	224.3	227.7	228.8	232.0	258.6

Source: EIU forecasts

▶

Exhibit 5.2 continued

a tyre developed with Jaguar engineers from scratch specifically for the XK8, as further evidence of the strategy working.

Like Germany's Continental, Mr Bencini maintains that collaboration between companies on specific projects is as likely a route to viability as further big takeovers.

One example is provided by Continental itself, which is collaborating with Michelin. Continental is providing Michelin with budget tyres from its low-cost plants in eastern Europe, while Continental has secured the right to use the Michelin-owned Uniroyal brand name for Continental-produced premium tyres throughout Europe.

However, the EIU says the big second tier companies also face a potential squeeze from below, in the form of aggressively expanding concerns from the Asia-Pacific region, notably Kumho and Hankook of South Korea. Kumho is already ranked tenth in the world with sales of $1.1bn. Hankook is only marginally behind in 11th place but has boasted of its intention to rank fifth within a few years.

The EIU warns that, just like South Korea's car industry, both are in danger of expanding too fast for their own resources. 'But providing they continue to survive they pose a real threat to the medium-sized players, particularly Sumitomo and to the other Japanese tyre makers such as Toyo and Yokohama.'

The industry and EIU research find common ground, however, in predicting that some competitive pressures should be offset by steady growth in demand for tyres as vehicle use increases in the emerging world.

Total demand, covering both original and replacement tyres is projected to rise by about 19 per cent between last year and 2005. However, only 8 per cent growth is forecast for the developed markets of Western Europe and North America, compared with a rise of 36 per cent for developing world markets.

The World Tyre Industry: A New Perspective to 2005. The Economist Intelligence Unit, 15 Regent Street, London, SW1Y 4LR. £595 / $945.

Source: John Griffiths, *Financial Times*, 14 March 1997.

Competition policy

Not only have recent Conservative governments advocated the benefits of competition but successive governments since the Second World War (both Labour and Conservative), have intervened by statutory means to deal with the various types of market imperfection, and to promote competition. These statutes are now outlined and their major purposes are explained.

Monopolies and Restrictive Practices Act 1948

The Monopolies and Restrictive Practices Act 1948 established the Monopolies Commission (now the Monopolies and Mergers Commission). It was given the power to investigate industries in which one firm, or a group of firms acting together, restricted competition by controlling one third of the market.

Restrictive Trade Practices Act 1956

The Restrictive Trade Practices Act 1956 regulated the custom whereby manufacturers jointly enforced the retail prices at which their products could be sold. This is known as Resale Price Maintenance (RPM). The Restrictive Practices Court was established to decide each case brought before it, on its merits. Further, restrictive agreements had to be registered.

Resale Prices Act 1964

The thinking behind the Resale Prices Act 1964 was that all resale price agreements were assumed to be against the public interest unless it could be proved otherwise in the Restrictive Practices Court.

Monopolies and Mergers Act 1965

The Monopolies and Mergers Act 1965 granted further powers to the Monopolies and Mergers Commission (MMC) to investigate mergers and acquisitions.

Fair Trading Act 1973

The Fair Trading Act 1973 established the Office of Fair Trading (OFT), headed by the Director General of Fair Trading (DGFT). Further, it defined a monopoly as 'a situation where a company supplies or purchases 25 per cent or more of all the goods or services of a particular type in the UK or a defined part of it'.

Resale Price Maintenance Act 1976

The Resale Price Maintenance Act 1976 further prohibited the practice of resale price maintenance.

Restrictive Practices Act 1976

The Restrictive Practices Act 1976 is concerned with agreements between people or companies that could limit their freedom to act independently.

Competition Act 1980

The Competition Act 1980 defined an anti-competitive practice as a course of conduct which restricts, distorts or prevents competition in the production and acquisition of goods or services in the UK.

An example of a restrictive trade practice, which was recently lifted, was the Net Book Agreement (*see* Exhibit 5.3). This was a selective distribution agreement, that is, a refusal to supply bookshops if they discounted book prices below the publisher's recommended price. The idea of the agreement was to protect small bookshops from large chains and supermarkets which could heavily discount books, bestsellers in particular.

There are three regulatory agencies with respect to competition law in the UK:

1 **The Monopolies and Mergers Commission (MMC).** This is an independent administrative tribunal whose members are appointed by the Secretary of State for Trade and Industry.

2 **The Office of Fair Trading (OFT).** This is headed by the DGFT who is appointed by the Secretary of State for Trade and Industry.

Exhibit 5.3 The ending of the Net Book Agreement

Book price pact finally declared illegal by court

The Net Book Agreement, which until recently enabled publishers to fix minimum prices, was finally declared illegal yesterday.

The Restrictive Practices Court ruled the NBA's prevention of discounting was against the public interest and that its abolition would not lead to the book-reading public suffering.

The ruling marks the final end for the agreement which collapsed in practice in September 1995 when the Publishers Association decided it could no longer be enforced.

Several publishers and WH Smith, the retailer had withdrawn support for the agreement and were swiftly followed by others afraid of losing market share.

The court case was brought by Mr John Bridgeman, the director-general of fair trading, to ensure the agreement could not be resurrected in future.

However, the agreement retained considerable support within the booktrade and the OFT was opposed in court by Mr John Calder, an independent publisher, and Ms Jenny Glayzer, chairman of the National Acquisitions Group, a body representing the library sector. They said discounting would make high quality books more expensive and so fewer of them would be published.

Giving judgment, Mr Justice Ferris said the court had identified no ways in which the public would be deprived of any benefits by the ending of the agreement.

Prices of mass-market paperbacks had increased in recent years at about twice the general rate of inflation. This occurred largely during the time the agreement was being enforced, he said.

'It is an example of the way in which resale price maintenance can fail to keep down prices – not of a tendency for prices to rise in the absence of resale price maintenance,' he said.

The court agreed with the OFT that the book industry had changed since 1962 when it had ruled the agreement was legal. Printing technology had changed, wholesaling had grown and booksellers ordered fewer books before publication to reduce their risks and were buying more books on a sale or return basis. Mr Bridgeman said afterwards: 'Modern production and distribution methods have removed the need for a price fixing agreement between publishers.'

Source: John Manson, Law Courts Correspondent, *Financial Times*, 14 March 1997.

3 **The privatised utilities 'watchdogs'**. These are: the Office of Telecommunications (OFTEL), the Office of Gas Supply (OFGAS), the Office of Water Services (OFWAT) and the Office of Electricity Regulation (OFFER).

Telecommunications, gas, water and electricity supply were formerly all owned by state monopolies. Because of the lack of competition and therefore choice for consumers, the above 'watchdogs' were set up in the mid to late 1980s.

The Monopolies and Mergers Commission cannot initiate enquiries but, when asked, will investigate specific markets or the behaviour of companies or mergers, and report recommended actions to the Secretary of State. Referrals to the MMC emanate from three sources:

a the OFT;

b the appropriate regulator for the privatised industries;

c the Secretary of State for Trade and Industry.

The bus and coach operator Stagecoach has been investigated by the OFT 25 times in recent years, leading to nine referrals to the MMC. Eight of these were found to be against the public interest and twice Stagecoach was forced to sell a stake of nearly 20 per cent in two bus operators.

In May 1997, for the first time in seven years, the Secretary of State made a referral to the MMC against the advice of the DGFT. This referral was over the award of two rail franchises to the coach operator National Express (*see* Exhibit 5.4).

Exhibit 5.4 Award of rail franchises to National Express

City concern as rail deals are sent to MMC

Mrs Margaret Beckett, the trade and industry secretary, surprised the City yesterday by referring to the Monopolies and Mergers Commission – against the advice of the Office of Fair Trading – the award of two rail franchises to National Express.

The highly unusual move drew sharp criticism from competition policy lawyers and was widely seen as a signal from Mrs Beckett that she would take a tough line on such decisions.

City analysts said the references made it more likely that Mrs Beckett would block other deals, including the proposed acquisition by Bass of rival brewer Carlsberg-Tetley.

Shares in National Express fell 28½p to 490½p after the referral of the coach group's acquisitions of the ScotRail and Central Trains franchises. The share prices of other transport companies with rail interests also fell sharply, on City fears that the government intends to intervene in the process of rail privatisation.

Mr Colin Child, finance director of National Express, said he was surprised at the decision, particularly as Mr John Bridgeman, director-general of fair trading, saw no competition problems in the Central Trains acquisition. In the ScotRail case, the Office of Fair Trading said the deal could go ahead if National Express sold Scottish Citylink Coaches, its Scottish express coach subsidiary.

But Mrs Beckett said she had decided that both acquisitions 'should be referred immediately to the MMC for a thorough investigation'. She said they raised competition concerns in the public transport markets in the West Midlands and Scotland.

Competition policy specialists were taken aback. It was the first time in seven years that an industry secretary has referred an acquisition against the advice of the OFT.

'This looks like a decision taken on political rather than competition policy grounds and introduces a very damaging new element of uncertainty into the system,' said one senior competition lawyer.

He suggested it was significant that the deals involved railway privatisations, which were fiercely opposed by Labour in opposition.

But Mrs Dorothy Livingston, partner at City lawyers Herbert Smith, cautioned against reading too much into one judgment. She also pointed to Mrs Beckett's statement that her decision had been made on competition grounds.

Mrs Beckett said: 'My decisions . . . do not in any way prejudge the question of whether or not they would be against the public interest. It is for the MMC to decide on this after investigation.'

Mr Child said National Express was 'confident' the MMC would recommend the acquisitions go ahead.

Last December National Express had to guarantee it would not raise coach fares or cut timetables to win MMC approval for its acquisition of the Midland Main Line.

Source: David Wighton, Charles Batchelor and Charis Gresser, *Financial Times*, 23 May 1997.

Competition policy also includes law on mergers. A merger takes place when two or more companies 'cease to be distinct'. A merger is subject to investigation by the MMC if it involves 25 per cent or more market share or the takeover of assets valued at £30 million or more.

European Union competition policy

The EU has also developed its competiton policy in order to promote freer competition. It is the responsibility of Directorate-General IV (DGIV), Competition of the Commission of European Communities. EU competition policy is aimed not only at regulating collusion and price fixing between firms and controlling the size to which firms grow through mergers and acquisitions, but also at introducing cross-border competition in the area of public procurement. An example of a situation where cross-border competition could be introduced is that where UK police forces may be placed under pressure to buy UK-built cars or motorcycles, instead of foreign ones. Further, EU competition policy aims to restrict state aid to indigenous firms. Such aid was widespread in the UK in the 1970s when billions of pounds were given to such industries as steel and shipbuilding and firms such as British Leyland.

The principal EU legislation is contained in Articles 85 and 86 of the Treaty of Rome (the EU Treaty), as discussed in Chapter 1. Article 85 gives the European Commission the power to regulate restrictive practices, such as market sharing and price-fixing agreements between firms. Article 86 (*see* Exhibit 1.4) is aimed at preventing firms abusing their dominant positions.

Further, Articles 92–94 are aimed at restricting the use of state aid to firms and industries through government grants, low-interest loans or tax concessions.

Further resources

The UK microeconomic environment

General

Quality daily and Sunday newspapers: *The Times*, *Financial Times*, *Guardian*, *Independent*, *Sunday Times*, *Observer*, *Independent on Sunday, The Economist* (published weekly).

Further reading

Begg, D., Fischer, S., Dornbusch, R. (1991) *Economics*. Maidenhead: McGraw-Hill.

Economic Review

Economics and Business Education.

Lipsey, R.G. and Crystal, K.A. (1995) *An Introduction to Positive Economics* (8th edn). Oxford: Oxford University Press.

Internet addresses

UK competition policy: www.open.gov.UK/oft/ofthome

EU competition policy: europa.eu.int/pol/comp/en/comp.htm

Chapter summary

This chapter has examined how the market mechanism works through the operation of the laws of supply and demand, distinguished between the various types of market structure and shown why the UK government and the EU authorities have dealt with market imperfections to increase competition.

We next consider the workings of the national economy as a whole, that is, the macroeconomic environment.

Assignment

Read the article reproduced in Exhibit 5.5 and answer the following questions:

1 Briefly outline the respective positions of McDonnell Douglas, Boeing and Airbus.

2 Why did the European Union Commission become involved in the merger between McDonnell Douglas and Boeing?

3 What were the Commission's objections to the merger and why was it unsuccessful in preventing it?

Exhibit 5.5 The EU competition commissioner

Van Miert's finest hour

When Mr Karel Van Miert became European competition commissioner in 1993 there were plenty who suspected that his socialist past would ill equip him for the battles that lay ahead.

But with all the zeal of a convert he has proved his critics wrong. In a crusade to enforce fair competition in the European Union, he has busted cartels, forced liberalisation upon closed sectors and taken a fairly tough line on government subsidies.

Yesterday, came his apogee. The last-minute climbdown by Boeing over its merger with McDonnell Douglas and Mr Van Miert hailed in Brussels as the little guy who took on the US giant – and won.

'You have to hand it to him,' says one Commission official. 'He took them on and he won. He showed that the European Commission is a force to be reckoned with.'

Mr Van Miert has been credited with placing the European Commission at the top of US news bulletins for the first time anyone can remember. 'The Boeing case shows that we are just as serious as the US competition authorities, and some would say have done a better job,' says one official.

But for all the glory of his victory over Boeing, Mr Van Miert's strategy of pushing the champion US aircraft manufacturer to the limit

was risky. There were times when it looked as if he had miscalculated.

He also faces criticism for having tainted the credibility of the EU's Merger Regulation by publicly voicing his concerns about the Boeing deal in what should have been a confidential procedure. After lambasting elements of the merger on a tour of the US earlier this year, it was not long before politicians on both sides of the Atlantic were rushing forward with their views on the deal.

'This case has politicised the Merger Regulation which is the one bit of competition policy that should be kept in an iron cask sealed off from the politicians,' says one Commission official. 'It has undone a lot of the efforts that have been made over the last few years to give credibility to the Commission's handling of mergers, even if the result is not too bad.'

This politicisation could play into the hands of supporters of an independent competition authority for Europe, along the lines of Germany's Bundeskartelamt. But Mr Van Miert's supporters defend his actions in the name of transparency.

'He is a man who believes in accountability and some of us do get nervous,' says a Commission official. 'But he believes in explaining to people what he is doing and why.'

Among those listening – and contributing – to the argument was the French government, chief champion of Airbus Industrie. Some suspect Mr Van Miert of courting favour with Paris, ahead of potentially bruising battles over the restructuring of state-owned bank Credit Lyonnais, the liberalisation of telecoms, energy and transport networks and subsidies to Air France.

But trying to buy favours from the French is a 'waste of time', according to one Commission official. 'You can secure any number of victories for the French in competition and trade matters, but they are always totally, and unrepentantly ungrateful,' he says.

Whatever Mr Van Miert's motivation, there is no disguising his enthusiasm for a good punch-up. Some fear that, fresh from his Boeing triumph, he will turn his energies to other contentious cases: a prospect which bodes ill for companies such as British Airways, which is still awaiting clearance for its proposed alliance with American Airways.

'I was rather hoping he would get a bop on the nose over this Boeing case,' says one airline industry expert. 'Now he will probably charge ahead and make unreasonable demands.'

It is also unclear how the fallout

▶

Exhibit 5.5 continued

from the Boeing case will affect relations between the EU and the US when it comes to co-operating on competition affairs.

'We were prepared to address the merger on the basis of concerns for customers, which is the traditional US approach to anti-trust law,' says Mr Richard Albrecht, Boeing's executive vice-president. 'The approach by the European Merger Task Force seems to be much more concerned with the effect on competitors.'

Some fear the Commission's clear defence of Airbus will lead to reprisals. The US authorities also have to clear the BA-AA alliance and are examining the planned merger between Guinness and Grand Metropolitan.

But the potential damage should not be exaggerated. 'This was such a hard case that to draw any general conclusions from it is probably dangerous,' says one competition lawyer in Brussels. 'I think both parties are mature enough to realise that and to recognise that they have got far more in common than separates them.'

Source: Emma Tucker, *Financial Times*, 24 July 1997.

6

The United Kingdom macroeconomic environment

Chapter objectives

By the time you have read this chapter you should be able to:

◆ understand the structure of the UK economy;

◆ appreciate the workings of the national economy by explaining what is meant by the circular flow of income;

◆ understand the importance of various government macroeconomic objectives;

◆ distinguish between various macroeconomic policies.

Introduction

The word macro is of Greek origin and means whole. It is therefore relevant for the business student to understand the workings of the whole economy as well as focusing on certain constituent parts of it such as those explained in Chapter 5.

First, we examine the structure of the UK economy, which is divided into primary, secondary and tertiary sectors, and also look at shifts in the size of these sectors which have occurred over the last 20 years.

Second, we illustrate a theoretical economic concept known as the circular flow of income. In order to maintain the circular flow, governments become involved with the workings of the national economy and our investigation of this leads us to a consideration of several UK government macroeconomic objectives. One such objective is the maintenance of a stable price level. In examining how this is achieved we consider in turn various government macroeconomic policies, for example, monetary policy.

Finally, this chapter considers the workings of the UK financial system, in particular the changed role of the Bank of England in that system since the coming to power of the present Labour government.

The structure of the UK economy

The economy is broadly divided into three main sectors which, together with examples of industries in each sector, are listed below.

1 **The primary sector**, which consists of such extractive industries as coal mining, oil exploration and agriculture.

2 **The secondary sector.** This consists of manufacturing industry, for example, the production of motor cars and consumer goods.

3 **The tertiary sector.** This comprises such service industries as banking, insurance and tourism.

In general, there has been a decline in both primary and secondary production in the UK, which has resulted in a contraction of the manufacturing base. This trend has partly been compensated for by the increase in services.

The circular flow of income

The circular flow of income is a simple model of the workings of the national economy. It is illustrated and explained in Figures 6.1, 6.2, 6.3 and 6.4.

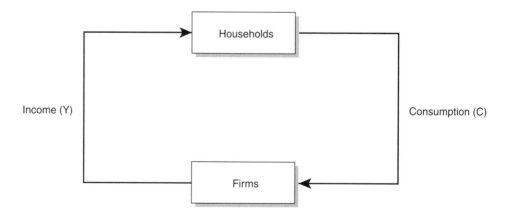

Fig. 6.1 The circular flow of income

At a basic level the economy consists of firms which produce goods and services and utilise the factors of production: land, labour, capital and enterprise. The reward to labour is a wage or income ((Y) in Figure 6.1). This income is used by households to consume (C) the output (goods and services) of the firm. Thus, the circular process is complete.

However, the circular flow ignores what are termed leakages and injections. Figure 6.2 shows an example of each of these.

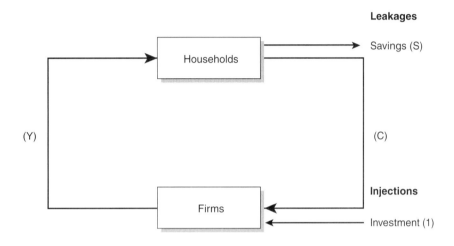

Fig. 6.2 The circular flow of income: leakages and injections

In Figure 6.2 savings are added to the model. Households not only consume goods and services from their income but they may save a proportion of it. This then represents a leakage from the circular flow. Firms may also invest, in capital equipment for example, and this therefore represents an injection into the circular flow.

So far we have ignored the influence of government in the workings of the national economy. Even in a free enterprise economy there is likely to be some government intervention. Its effect on this model is shown in Figure 6.3.

Government intervention in the form of fiscal policy affects the circular flow. The government levies taxes such as income tax on households. These are known as leakages. It also injects income through government spending, on such projects as road building.

Finally, the effect of foreign trade needs to be added to the model (*see* Figure 6.4).

As far as households are concerned, a proportion of their income may be saved, another proportion may be taken by government in the form of taxation, and finally a proportion may be spent on imported goods, such as cars and television sets. Firms, on the other hand, may not only invest and benefit from government expenditure but also inject money into the economy from export earnings.

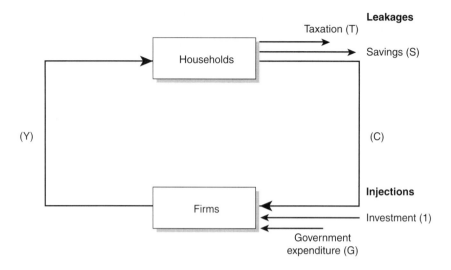

Fig. 6.3 The circular flow of income: expenditure and taxation

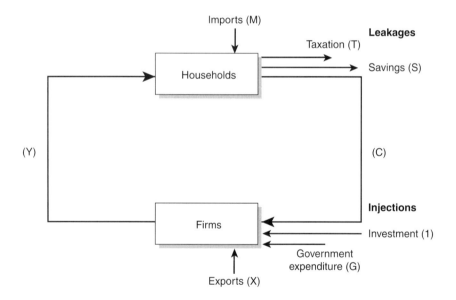

Fig. 6.4 The circular flow of income: the effects of foreign trade

The steps outlined above and depicted in Figures 6.1 to 6.4 complete the model of the national economy. However, as the leading economist, John Maynard Keynes, noted in the 1930s, the economy is not self-regulating in the way the circular flow assumes. Therefore the government needs to intervene to manage aggregate monetary demand (the total demand for goods and services in the economy).

It is useful, at this point, to introduce and explain what is meant by the terms 'multiplier' and 'accelerator'. The multiplier is a measure of the effect on total national income of a unit change in some component of aggregate demand. For example, if the government embarked upon a major road-building project, this would entail employing more labour, who would in turn earn more wages which would help boost consumer spending in the economy. The accelerator is a change in investment spending by firms as a result of changes in consumer spending. If, as just described, consumer spending rose, firms would have to invest in more stock and capital equipment in order to meet that demand.

The business cycle

Where injections into the economy exceed withdrawals, economic activity is said to be increasing. On the other hand, where withdrawals exceed injections, activity is in decline. These fluctuations in the output of the economy are known as the business or trade cycle.

This is illustrated in Figure 6.5.

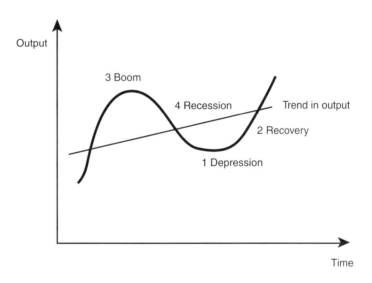

Fig. 6.5 The business cycle

As Figure 6.5 shows, there are four aspects to the business cycle:

1 **Depression**. This is characterised by high unemployment, low consumer demand and low business profits.

2 **Recovery**. At this stage of the business cycle, employment rises, as do consumer spending and company profits.

3 **Boom**. In these conditions labour shortages become evident, consumer spending rises fast and business profits are high.

4 **Recession**. Here employment and consumer spending fall and business profits decline.

In order to maintain the circular flow of income in the economy and in an attempt to alleviate extreme fluctuations in the business cycle, the government has several macroeconomic objectives. These are listed below.

1 Maintaining price stability by controlling the rate of inflation.

2 Maintaining employment.

3 Maximising economic growth.

4 Maintaining a favourable balance of payments.

5 Maintaining a stable exchange rate.

Macroeconomic objectives

We now examine and explain each of the macroeconomic objectives listed above.

Maintaining price stability

Governments believe that price stability leads to sustainable economic growth and thus higher levels of employment in the long run. By price stability is meant a low and stable rate of inflation, usually 2.5 per cent per year or less. Inflation may be defined as an upward and persistent movement in the general level of prices and is measured by the government by the Retail Prices Index (RPI). This measures the prices of a representative 'basket' of goods and is published once a month by the Office for National Statistics (ONS). The RPI is a measure of inflation that does not include the cost of mortgages, i.e. mortgage interest payments.

Economists are divided between the Keynesians and the monetarists as to the causes of inflation. The Keynesians (named after John Maynard Keynes) contend that inflation occurs 'when the total money demand in the economy exceeds the available or potentially producable output, then an inflationary gap develops and that generates rising prices'.

According to the monetarists, their most famous exponent being Milton Friedman of Chicago University, 'inflation is always and everywhere a monetary phenomenon'. Their theory as to the cause of inflation is based upon the quantity theory of money developed by Irving Fisher in 1911.

Exhibit 6.1 The retail price index

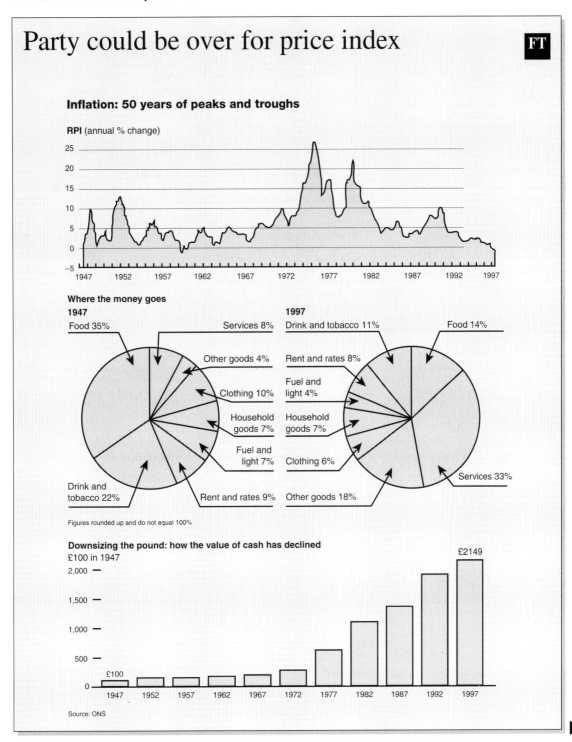

Party could be over for price index

FT

Inflation: 50 years of peaks and troughs

RPI (annual % change)

Where the money goes

1947
Food 35%
Services 8%
Other goods 4%
Clothing 10%
Household goods 7%
Fuel and light 7%
Drink and tobacco 22%
Rent and rates 9%

1997
Drink and tobacco 11%
Food 14%
Rent and rates 8%
Fuel and light 4%
Household goods 7%
Clothing 6%
Other goods 18%
Services 33%

Figures rounded up and do not equal 100%

Downsizing the pound: how the value of cash has declined
£100 in 1947

£2149

£100

Source: ONS

Exhibit 6.1 continued

The Retail Price Index today celebrates its 50th birthday as the headline measure of inflation – but this may be one of its last chances to blow out the candles.

RPI is currently used by the government as the target measure for monetary policy.

While sterling remains outside monetary union, the RPI retains its ability to hold of London analysts in thrall

The City is interested in the RPI because it gives you some idea of what government policy may do next – that is very important to most people,' says Roger Alford an economist at the London School of Economics.

The RPI was established by the Labour government in 1947 and represented an important shift in the relationship between the government and the economy.

Its predecessor was the Cost of Living Index for the Working Classes, a list of 14 was established in 1914. While the 1914 index was a crude attempt to measure the price of 'essential' goods the working class, the index that replaced it was much more sophisticated.

The compilers of the new index actually asked people what they bought and used the results of that survey to estimate the costs of running a typical household.

In 1947 the survey was still based around the working class, then defined as a household earning £250 a year or less, a situation that did not change until 1956.

The result is a fascinating portrait of changes in fashion and tastes – the original basket of goods included items that now seem comical, such as tram fares and unskinned rabbits.

And there are some surprising omissions: working class women in 1947 were less likely to wear the new-fangled bra, so the original index included corsets instead.

The RPI also shows how spending patterns have shifted, as a result of increasing wealth and altered lifestyles. In 1947, spending on services took up only 8 per cent of consumer spending. Food was responsible for over a third of working class household incomes.

Drink and tobacco accounted for 22 per cent of household expenditure – a remarkable figure considering the category consisted of just beer, whisky, cigarettes and pipe tobacco.

By 1997, smoking and drinking have sunk to just 11 per cent of average household spending. One reason is that the two goods involved have also shown the largest increases in cost.

A pint of beer was 7p (1s 4d) in 1947 – the same as a half-pound bar of chocolate. But 50 years later, the Office for National Statistics says the average pint costs £1.65.

The chocolate is now only half the price, at 79 pence.

Opinions are still divided 50 years later over whether measuring inflation is useful. The Bundesbank, Germany's central bank and the model for the future European bank, uses a broad measure of money supply as its target instead.

Recent academic studies in the US have argued that conventional measures such as the RPI can overstate the rate of inflation, because it cannot easily measure changes in productivity and quality.

The price of computers, for example, has barely changed, but their capacity has greatly increased.

Roger Bootle, cheif economist at HSBC Markets in London and a leading author on inflation, said 'It works pretty well – it is impossible to have an index that works perfectly. But by and large it does a good job.'

Source: Richard Adams, *Financial Times*, 29 August 1997.

The quantity theory may be expressed by the following equation:

$$MV = PT$$

where   M = the stock of money in the economy;

V = the velocity of circulation, that is, the number of times the money supply changes hands over a period of time, e.g. a year;

P = the price level, the average price of each transaction;

T = the output of goods and services, the total number of transactions in an economy.

According to the monetarists, as both the velocity of circulation (V) and the output of goods and services (T) are fixed in the short term, an increase in the money supply (M) leads to a directly proportional increase in the level of prices (P).

Therefore, it is thought that a key economic objective for the government, in order that it may maintain UK firms' competitiveness in relation to foreign firms, is controlling the rate of inflation by maintaining stable prices. If prices are rising faster in the UK than, say, in France, UK exports will become less and less price competitive. Inflation means also that people living on fixed incomes, such as savings, will suffer as prices rise. Furthermore, very high rates of inflation (hyperinflation) may lead to political upheaval and the breakdown of ordered society as it did in Germany in the early 1920s.

Maintaining employment

After the Second World War and during the 1950s and 1960s, successive governments were committed to trying to maintain full employment. This is a situation in which everyone who is willing to work, at the market rate for their type of labour, has a job, except those that are switching from one job to another. However, after the oil crises in the mid-1970s and early 1980s, when the OPEC oil producers sharply raised the price of oil (thus causing economic depression among the developed nations), it became increasingly difficult for UK governments to maintain full employment.

Unemployment refers to the situation of a member of the labour force who is without a job but who is registered as willing and available for work.

There are various types of unemployment:

1 **Cyclical unemployment**, which results from the trade cycles. These are regular oscillations in the level of economic activity over a period of years. Downswings in the level of economic activity in the economy create unemployment, which will be eliminated in the upswing.

2 **Structural unemployment**, created by some basic long-term change in the demand or technological conditions in an economy, such as has occurred in the coal-mining industry in South Wales and the ship building industry in the North-East of England (*see* Exhibit 6.2).

3 **Frictional unemployment**. This exists where workers are unemployed for short lengths of time between jobs.

High levels of unemployment not only have disastrous social consequences for the individuals affected, but also result in increased government expenditure on unemployment and social security benefits.

Maximising economic growth

In maximising economic growth, the aim of government is to achieve steady and sustained levels of export-led growth in the economy. This growth is often taken as a sign of rising living standards in an economy. It is measured by increases in gross domestic product (GDP). This is the total value of all final goods and services produced in the economy over a 12-month period. Gross National Product (GNP) is GDP plus net property income from abroad (i.e. net profits, dividends, rent and

Exhibit 6.2

The spring of recovery

FT

To Europe's 18.5m unemployed, the rosy prospects for the world economy may seem depressingly distant.

The latest forecast from the Organisation for Economic Co-operation and Development in Paris predicts that unemployment in the European Union will have declined from 11.3 per cent of the workforce this year to 11 per cent in 1998. It is a step in the right direction, to be sure; but a very small one compared with the mountain to climb. If EU unemployment were the same proportion of the workforce as it now is in the US (or as it was in the EU in 1976) the number of Europeans on the dole would be 10m fewer.

A reduction on this scale cannot be achieved quickly, because, as the OECD points out, a very large proportion of EU unemployment is now structural. Many people could not find jobs even if the economies were running at full throttle. The OECD emphasised this gloomy predica-ment by talking of a 'jobless recovery'. Companies continue to replace over-expensive labour with machines. So even if the new socialist government in France were to succeed in pumping up the economy, without structural reforms, the results would be dispointing.

On the other hand, the recent economic performance in the US shows what can in principle be achieved with a flexible labour market. The OECD forecasts that strong growth of 3.6 per cent this year will be combined with unemployment of only 5 per cent and inflation of 2 per cent, although with some slowing down in 1998.

Similarly, the UK, which has liberalised its labour and product markets, is expected to achieve an unemployment rate of 5.6 per cent next year, close to that of the US and only about half the rate in France and Germany. The moral should be clear, especially as the OECD calculates that every 1 per-centage point cut in structural unemployment could reduce government deficits by up to 0.5 per cent of GDP. In other words, if France could get its jobless rate down to that of the UK, it could be heading for a budget surplus without taking any other painful measures.

Of course, deregulating labour and product markets is not easy. It may mean, in the short term, that wages fall and workers in feather-bedded state industries lose their jobs.

But the latest forecasts from the OECD and the International Monetary Fund show that now is the time to do it. The world is set for a comparatively golden period of steady growth, low inflation and buoyant trade. In Europe, the prospect of monetary union has also brought exchange rate stability and convergent interest rates. These also can only be preserved by one thing – structural reform.

Source: Financial Times, 16 June 1997.

interest). Net national income or national income is GNP minus depreciation of the country's capital stock. Thus, economic growth may be defined as an increase in a country's productive capacity, identifiable by a sustained and continuous rise in real national income over a period of years.

Levels of growth may be determined by: the size of the workforce, the accumulation of productive equipment, technological progress and the size of the economy. High growth rates are associated with a highly motivated, skilled and productive workforce together with innovation, quality capital investment and a high level of skill training and education.

Although there are costs (negative externalities) associated with high levels of growth, in terms of environmental damage, growth nevertheless brings many benefits (positive externalities) that are required by society. These benefits take the form of improved real incomes and the ability to provide goods and services to all sectors of the economy without having to resort to high levels of taxation in order to redistribute incomes. Externalities are an external cost. Externalities in consumption exist when the level of consumption of some good or service by one consumer has a direct effect on the welfare of another consumer. These costs or benefits are not reflected in market prices.

We now examine several of the macroeconomic policies used by the UK government to pursue the various objectives explained above. We consider, first, what is known as fiscal policy and, second, monetary policy.

 ## Macroeconomic policies

Fiscal policy

The government receives revenue mainly through the taxation system, both from direct taxes, such as income tax, and indirect taxes such as Value Added Tax (VAT). In turn, the government is committed to expenditure on social security, health and education. Particularly in times of economic recession the expenditure will exceed revenue, resulting in a deficit. Normally, the government will need to borrow in order to finance this deficit; this is known as the public sector borrowing requirement (PSBR).

Monetary policy

Monetary policy means influencing the economy through the supply and price of money, the price of money being the rate of interest. An increase in the rate of interest will discourage borrowing, thus restricting aggregate demand, whereas a decrease will encourage borrowing, thus stimulating the economy.

It is useful at this point to consider various definitions of money used by the UK government, i.e. M0, M2 and M4.

M0 refers to notes and coins in circulation plus commercial banks' operating balances at the Bank of England. It is the government's 'narrow' definition of money.

M2 equals M0 minus bankers' balances at the Bank of England plus private-sector non-interest-bearing sight deposits with banks and private-sector interest-bearing retail bank and building society deposits.

M4 equals M2 plus other private-sector sight and timed deposits at banks and building societies and private sector holdings of bank and building society certificates of deposit. It is often referred to as the 'broad' definition of money.

In June 1997, the Bank of England Act 1946 was amended and the Bank was given operational responsibility for the setting of interest rates. It therefore acts independently of government (The Treasury), although it must meet the inflation target set by government. A Monetary Policy Committee was set up, consisting of the Governor of the Bank of England, the Deputy Governor and six other members. All decisions are taken by a vote. If there is no majority, the Governor has the casting vote. This Committee meets once a month. Thus, the Bank of England now has the key responsibility for implementing monetary policy in the UK.

The government and the Bank of England use a combination of fiscal and monetary policy to manage demand, maintain the circular flow of income and achieve the government's macroeconomic objectives.

We now consider two further macroeconomic objectives in relation to our foreign trading partners, namely, maintaining a favourable balance of payments and maintaining a stable exchange rate.

Maintaining a favourable balance of payments

The balance of payments is a summary record of all the transactions that occur between residents of a country and foreigners over a specified period of time. The balance of payments account, as it is known, is published every month. The balance of payments account consists of a current and capital account. The current account may be divided into the import and export of goods (visible trade) and the import and export of services (invisible trade – banking, insurance, tourism). The capital account is the balance of transactions in financial assets.

Maintaining a stable exchange rate

What is meant by exchange rate is the price at which one currency is exchanged for another, that is, how many Deutschmarks are needed to buy £1, e.g. £1 = DM2.95. The sterling exchange rate is determined in the foreign exchange market (FOREX). The Forex market is the market where buyers and sellers of currencies meet and the price of the currency (exchange rate) is determined by the laws of supply and demand. Thus, when the number of buyers exceeds the number of sellers the exchange rate will rise, and when sellers exceed buyers the exchange rate will fall.

It is important to distinguish between fixed exchange rates and floating exchange rates.

Fixed exchange rates

Exchange rates are fixed when governments or international agreements seek to maintain the exchange rate at a fixed value over a relatively long period of time. The International Monetary Fund (IMF) was set up in 1946 following the conference held in the New Hampshire, USA, town of Bretton Woods, to manage a system of fixed world exchange rates. Fixed exchange rates provide certainty for business in that long-term contracts can be entered into. Further, if the balance of payments is in deficit a fixed exchange rate regime imposes disciplined fiscal and monetary policy.

From 1946 to 1971, exchange rates were relatively stable and the US dollar was the major trading currency. In 1971 the UK authorities ceased to intervene in Forex markets and the pound was allowed to 'float'.

Some indicators of macroeconomic objectives and policies are shown in Exhibit 6.3.

Exhibit 6.3

Brown's first budget – the economy **FT**

A tight labour market . . .

Unemployment

% of labour force

Earnings*

Annual % change

In underlying average earnings index

*Whole economy

. . . and a consumer boom

House prices

Annual % change

In Halifax House Price index

Retail sales volume

Annual % change

bring dangers for inflation . . .

Inflation

Annual % change in RPI*

*Excluding MIPS

Money supply M4

Annual % change

. . . and higher interest rates

Real GDP growth

Annual % change

Base rate

%

◆ Gordon Brown yesterday presented his first budget against a backdrop of a more than usually divided economy, *writes Wolfgang Münchau*. Parts of the UK economy are on the verge of a potentially inflationary consumer boom, while large sections of manufacturing industry experience little growth.

◆ The gulf between an overheating service economy – mostly concentrated on the south east of the country – and a depressed manufacturing economy intensified during the past year through a policy mix that combined a relatively loose fiscal and a moderately tight monetary stance. This mix led to high real interest

rates, which in turn contributed to the stength of the pound. Against the D-Mark sterling appreciated by 25 per cent since last August.

◆ The rising pound put increased pressure on exporters, resulting in lower profit margins, although export volumes have so far been holding up surprisingly well.

Exhibit 6.3 continued

Imports have been rising fast to a record during April. Retailers report that the benefits of the strong currency were mostly passed on to consumers, a consequence of strong competition. The strength of sterling put pressure on import prices and helped keep the underlying rate of consumer price inflation close to the government's target of 2.5 per cent.

◆ Concerns about the sustainability of current economic growth were corroborated by a series of recent economic statistics. Last week's upward revision in gross domestic product gave the clearest indication yet of above-trend economic growth. Other statistics suggest that growth is now to a large extent driven by consumer spending: a rise in retail sales growth to levels last seen in 1988; an increase in M4, a measure of broad money, to outside its monitoring range; a rise in M0, a measure of liquid money balances available for immediate spending; a rise in bank lending, especially in consumer credit.

◆ The housing market and the windfall profits from building society flotations are among the main driving forces behind the boom. House prices have gone up by a national average of about 10 per cent over the past year, but on a highly uneven pattern, stretching from virtually zero to almost 50 per cent in certain parts of central and west London. Economic forecasters believe that the building society windfalls – including those that are yet to come – may have further boosted consumer confidence. Base rates have already gone up by 0.5 percentage point to 6.5 per cent since May 1. The market is expecting the Bank of England to raise interest rates further to 7 per cent or above during the next 12 months to keep a lid on consumer spending.

Source: Financial Times, 3 July 1997.

Floating exchange rates

There is a floating exchange rate when the laws of supply and demand determine the value of the currency, and the rate of exchange rises and falls. This is known as 'clean floating'. The pound was allowed to float between 1971 and 1990.

Managed floating exchange rates

There is a managed floating exchange rate when a country's Central Bank takes a more active role on the foreign exchange market and the currency is allowed to float within certain limits. This was the principle behind the setting up of the European Monetary System (EMS) of the EU in March 1979. In this system, currencies within the Exchange Rate Mechanism (ERM) are fixed against the European Currency Unit (ECU), (the common currency of the EU), and therefore fixed against each other. Sterling joined the ERM in 1990 at a central rate against the Deutschmark of £1 = DM2.95, with wide margins of fluctuation allowed, namely 6 per cent either side of the par (£1:DM2.95) value. Sterling was suspended from the ERM, along with the Italian Lira on what is known as 'Black Wednesday', 16 September 1992, and allowed to 'float'. Since then the pound has fallen in value against the Deutschmark. On 16 September 1997, the pound stood at DM2.83.

Recent UK governments have been committed to maintaining a stable exchange rate as this makes trading more certain. Further, a depreciating currency is often taken as a sign of economic weakness.

The UK financial system

Before we leave the explanation of the macroeconomy, it is necessary to provide a brief description of the workings of the UK financial system. As a starting point, it is useful to distinguish between borrowers and lenders. Individuals, business and government all borrow and lend money. Individuals borrow to finance, say, the purchase of a house or car. We also lend money by placing money in a bank or building society. The bank or building society then lends that money to other individuals, at a higher rate of interest, thus making a profit.

Businesses borrow money to finance the purchase of new capital equipment or new plant. A business that is a limited company may issue shares in order to do this.

Governments also borrow in order to finance the PSBR. They do this by, for example, issuing National Savings Certificates.

To facilitate the borrowing and lending process, financial institutions have developed. It is useful to distinguish between financial institutions and financial markets. Financial institutions include banks, and building societies and other financial institutions.

Banks

There are different types of bank, as the following list shows:

1 **Clearing banks**. Examples include Barclays and Lloyds. Both are part of the clearing system, that is, the system whereby payments are settled by cheque.

2 **Retail banks**. This category includes the clearing banks and also building societies. They all offer current and deposit accounts and advance loans and overdrafts, mainly to individuals.

3 **Merchant banks**. Examples include Rothschilds and Schroders. Merchant banks, sometimes known as wholesale banks, offer banking services to corporate customers.

4 **Central banks**. These are the central bank of a country, such as the Bank of England and the German Bundesbank.

Building societies

Building societies were originally Friendly Societies which attracted deposits and advanced loans (mortgages), mainly for house purchases. Several building societies have changed their legal status to become public limited companies (PLC). Examples of those which have made this change are Abbey National (1989) and Halifax (1997).

Other financial institutions

The final category of financial institutions includes insurance companies, pension funds, unit trust companies and investment trust companies. They collect vast sums of money from individuals, invest it over a long term in, say, government stocks and shares in limited companies, and then pay the money back, with interest. They form part of the capital market.

Financial markets

Financial markets include the capital market – the market for medium and long-term capital, e.g. the Stock Exchange – and the money market – the market for short-term capital.

Further resources

The UK macroeconomic environment

General

Quality daily and Sunday newspapers. *The Economist*. Several publications from the Office for National Statistics (ONS) give trends in the UK economy, for example, *Economic Trends*, *National Income and Expenditure* ('The Blue Book'), *The UK Balance of Payments* (known as the 'Pink Book').

Further reading

Artis, M.J. (ed.) (1994) *Prest & Coppock's The UK Economy: A Manual of Applied Economics* (13th edn). Oxford: Oxford University Press.

Dunnett, A. (1992) *Understanding the Economy* (3rd edn). Harlow: Longman.

Economic Review

Economics and Business Education

Griffiths, A. and Wall, S. (eds) (1995) *Applied Economics: An Introductory Course* (6th edn). Harlow: Longman.

Internet addresses

www.hm-treasury.gov.UK/pub/htmi/www.ft.com

www.bankamerica.com/capmkt/brief-intl.htmi

Chapter summary

In this chapter we have considered the workings of the national economy by reference to the circular flow of income and have explored government economic objectives and policies. Maintaining a favourable balance of payments and a stable pound in relation to other foreign currencies leads us to a consideration of the UK's economic relationship with the rest of the world. This is the subject of the next chapter.

◆ ## Assignment

Read the article reproduced in Exhibit 6.4 and answer the following questions:

1 Explain what is meant by a central bank. How is it different from a UK High Street bank?

2 Contrast the relationship of the Bank of England and that of the German Bundesbank with their respective governments, before 1997.

3 Outline the 1997 reforms of the Bank of England with regard to monetary policy.

Exhibit 6.4 Central banks

Chancellor's proposals fall short of overseas standards

The government's decision to grant 'operational responsibility' to the Bank of England over interest rates leaves the UK lagging and other developed countries in terms of central independence.

The legislation promised the Queen's Speech will enable the Bank's new monetary policy committ to set base rates, and removes Bank's responsibility for issuing government debt. But the proposals from Mr Gordon Brown, the chancellor fall short of matching independence enjoyed by modern central banks.

Germany's Bundesbank is a model of central bank independence most often set up as an example. The Bundesbank sets its own interest rate policy, with an obligation to protect the value of the German currency as its only legislated aim. The Bundesbank is also directed to support the general economic aims of the German government, but under the Bundesbank is also directed to support the general economic aims of the German government, but under the Bundesbank Act it is fully autonomous from instruction by the government.

The Bundesbank's central council,

which is made up of officers of the federal bank and the heads of the regional government banks, sets an annual target for the broad money supply measures M3, and a long-term target of 'price stability', which the bank defines as between 0 per cent and 2 per cent annual inflation. In contrast, the Bank of England's monetary policy committee will be bound to observe the inflation targets set for it by the Treasury, which remains firmly under the authority of the chancellor.

Most of Britain's European Union partners possess central banks with power over inflation or monetary policy targets. In the Group of Seven major industrialised nations, the central banks of the US, Italy and France are alongside Germany in having the freedom to set both interest rates and policy targets.

The Bank of Italy, in particular, has taken great strides in recent years, to the point where it is as independent as the Bundesbank. Since the early 1980s, it has taken care to distance itself from Italy's central government. No government representatives take part in the bank's decision's on monetary policy, which do not require government

approval. Even in Germany, the Minister of Finance has the right to participate in Bundesbank council meetings, although he cannot vote.

More recently, the other popular model for central bank independence has been the New Zealand Reserve Bank, cut free from government by a Labour party that occupied the 'radical centre' in the manner of New Labour.

In 1990 the Reserve Bank was granted independence, although the country's target rate of inflation is enshrined in legislation by parliament. The target rate subsequently became a major issue during the New Zealand general election last year, with opposition parties campaigning on their policies for widening the inflation band.

New Zealand's structure has been suggested for the tenure of the governor of a truly independent central bank. Mr Don Brash, the popular and influential head of the Reserve Bank, is guaranteed his position, so long as inflation remains within its legislated target band. If it misses the band, he can be dismissed. An earlier proposal, to dock the governor's pay if he failed to hit the target, was not adopted.

Exhibit 6.4 continued

Mr Eddie George, the governor of the Bank of England, is appointed by the government, and employed on fixed-term contract. He enjoys only the same job security as any other employee of the government.

The Bank of Italy, in contrast, is able to select its own governor. The appointment needs only to be confirmed by the president of Italy. The governor's term is indefinite.

The governing board of the Swiss National Bank, by reputation one of the world's most independent banks, has three members, nominated by an independent committee and elected by the Swiss parliament.

The world's most powerful central bank head, the chairman of the US Federal Reserve System, is an appointee of the US president. The chairman is nominated by the president for four-year terms, and must be approved by Congress, a procedure that has overturned presidential nominees for other senior posts in the federal government.

The central bank that the 'new' Bank of England most closely resembles is the Bank of Japan.

Central Banks: more or less independent

Central Bank	Sets interest rates	Can intervene in foreign exchange market	Sets intrest or monetary targets
Bank of England	✔	✗	✗
US Federal Reserve	✔	✔	✔
New Zealand Reserve Bank	–	✔	✗
Swiss National Bank	✔	✔	✔
European Central Bank	✔	✔	✔
Bundesbank	✔	✔	✔
Bank of France	✔	✔	✔
Bank of Italy	✔	✔	✔
Bank of Japan	✔	✗	✗

Under the 1942 Bank of Japan Law, the bank's policy board has the authority to formulate and carry out monetary policy. But ultimate responsibility for monetary policy rests with the Ministry of Finance – just as monetary policy will be controlled by the UK Treasury. Like the reformed English central bank, the Bank of Japan has authority over setting official interest rates.

But the most independent central bank of them all looks likely to be the European Central Bank. It comes into existence at the end of 1998 ready for the European single currency and is designed to be completely free of political interference.

Source: Richard Adams, *Financial Times*, 7 May 1997.

7

The international economic environment

Chapter objectives

By the time you have read this chapter you should be able to:

◆ understand the benefits of free trade (i.e., the theory of comparative cost advantage);

◆ understand the main regional trading blocks within the 'Global Triad';

◆ appreciate recent economic developments in central and eastern Europe;

◆ understand key international agreements and major international organisations.

Introduction

The law of comparative advantage helps us to understand how free trade benefits all economies and consumers in the international economic environment. In reality, however, governments use a number of restrictions to free trade. In addition, they have formed a number of economic groupings in what is known as the Global Triad. The Triad is a term used to describe three important areas in the world economy – the USA, western Europe and the Pacific rim of Asia. Several important regional groupings in the Triad will be considered, including the European Union (EU) and the ASEAN Free Trade Area (AFTA).

It is important also to consider the changing economies of the countries of eastern Europe such as Poland and Hungary. These have become increasingly receptive to EU and US influence and investment in recent years.

Finally, this chapter describes a number of international economic organisations, such as the World Trade Organisation (WTO), formerly known as the General Agreement on Tariffs and Trade (GATT), which are important in the promotion of free trade.

Free trade theory

It is relevant to begin this chapter with a review of the theory of comparative advantage and the benefits of free trade. Free trade enables firms and countries to specialise in the activities that they perform best. The law of comparative advantage states that under free market conditions, countries specialise in the production of goods and services which can be manufactured at a comparatively lower cost than that at which they can be made in other countries. Its operation is illustrated in Table 7.1.

Table 7.1 Unit labour requirements

	Country A	Country B
Cars	50	110
Textiles	20	30

The law of comparative advantage was developed by the nineteenth-century economists Adam Smith and David Ricardo. They found that it was not necessary for one country (A in Table 7.1) to have an absolute cost advantage in the production of goods, for it to find a partner willing to trade. Although Country A possesses absolute advantage in the production of cars and textiles, it possesses comparative advantage in the production of textiles. Therefore, Country B can specialise in textiles.

Restrictions to free trade

A number of restrictions to international trade have been developed by nations over the years. These may take the form of tariffs, quotas and what are known as non-tariff barriers. Tariffs are taxes imposed on imports by the importing country. Quotas are a quantitative limit placed on the importation of a good. Non-tariff barriers include national controls on trade, for example, certificates of origin, anti-dumping duties, voluntary export restraints (VERs) and health and safety, technical and product standards.

Certificates of origin

A certificate of origin names the place where the good underwent its last major transformation. Local content rules are of interest in this connection. Such rules relate to the amount of a component input sourced from local manufacturers. For example, in 1995, at the Toyota factory in Derby, 80 per cent of components were sourced from local suppliers.

Dumping

Dumping may be broadly defined as the exporting of goods at prices below the cost of production.

Voluntary export restraints

Voluntary export restraints (VERs) are imposed when an importing country asks the exporter to agree quota restrictions. Voluntary export restraints were used extensively in the car industry in the early 1980s. This was before Japanese car manufacturers set up factories in Europe, including Nissan, Honda and Toyota in the UK.

The reasons for the imposition of non-tariff restrictions, and thus the limitation of free trade, include the need to protect key industries, to protect a new industry and to counter the practice of dumping. The WTO defines dumping as 'Any sale in an export market at a price below the price charged in the supplying firm's own country (plus transport and foreign distribution costs) whatever the motivation.' An obvious motive would be to penetrate markets.

Since the early 1990s, the EU has been reviewing the import of D.RAMS (Dynamic Random Access Memory chips) from Japan and South Korea and sold in the European market at below cost price. There was, in June 1997, an industry solution to this problem, with the setting up of a system of voluntary agreements between the major manufacturers of D.RAMS (*see* Exhibit 7.1).

Exhibit 7.1

EU poised to strike price pact over chips

European Union, Japanese and South Korean semiconductor makers are poised to begin talks on a 'gentleman's agreement' on minimum prices that could lead to the lifting of EU anti-dumping measures on computer memory chips.

The European Commission announced in March it was reintroducing minimum price undertakings on imported Japanese and South Korean D-Ram chips, after a 21-month suspension, when it found evidence that manufacturers were again selling below cost price. That decision pleased European D-Ram manufacturers, but caused concern in the electronics industry.

D-Rams, or Dynamic Random Access Memory chips, are the basic building block for all kinds of intelligent electronic devices from video recorders to personal Computers. The EU market is estimated at Ecu5bn (£3.39bn) a year, of which

Japan and South Korea manufacturers have around 80 per cent. Brussels is nearing the end of a review of the measures – one of the EU's largest and most complex dumping cases – which date back to 1990 for Japan and 1993 for South Korea. It is expected to make recommendations to EU ministers soon on future action, prompting growing speculation among industry analysts.

But the European Electronic Component Manufacturers' Association (EECA) representing EU semiconductor manufacturers, is poised to begin talks with its Japanese and South Korean counterparts on an industry-to-industry agreement on minimum prices. The talks, backed by the Commission, could lead to the replacement of EU measures with a voluntary price-monitoring framework.

The Electronic Industries Asso-

ciation of Japan and the Korean semiconductor Industry Association have both demanded EECA drops its long-standing complaint about dumping by the two countries in return for an agreement. EECA, in turn, is seeking guarantees from the European Commission, before it enters talks, that anti-dumping duties would immediately be imposed on any manufacturers found to be breaching a future agreement.

'We want a very strong signal from the Commission that it will take action if dumping is found,' said Mr Eckehard Runge, EECA's secretary general. 'It is showing signs of moving that way. It recognises semi-conductors are a strategic industry, and EU investment must be protected.'

The industry agreement would be modelled on that already operating between Japan, South Korea and

Exhibit 7.1 continued

the US on so-called flash Eproms, and various types of D-Rams. It would involve a voluntary framework, whereby manufacturers agreed to sell above minimum prices, and would store production cost and pricing information on disks which could be checked at any time by the European Commission.

Mr Eckehard said preconditions for talks to begin could be met within the next two weeks. The existing anti-dumping measures were reintroduced in phases from April 1 – a gradual approach designed to avoid turmoil in a market in which over-capacity and intense competition drove prices down 80 per cent in 1996. Prices, which were already showing signs of having 'bottomed out' earlier this year, have stabilised since the measures were re-introduced.

EU measures against Japan involved minimum price undertakings from 11 manufacturers – Toshiba, NEC, Hitachi, Mitsubishi, Fujitsu, Matsushita, Sharp, Oki, Sanyo, Minebea and Texas Instruments Japan – according to a formula based on cost price plus a 9.5 per cent profit margin. Catchall anti-dumping duties of 60 per cent were imposed any other manufacturers, to avoid new market entrants circumventing the measures.

The measures against South Korea involved similar price undertakings from Goldstar, Hyundai and Samsung, with catchall duties on other manufacturers of 24 per cent.

European semiconductor manufacturers including Siemens, SGS Thomson and Philips would like to see tariffs removed, as long as an anti-dumping agreement can be worked out and with the proviso that breaches of 'fair trade' are punished quickly and effectively.

An agreement between European and Far Eastern semiconductor manufacturers endorsed by the EU would also be welcomed in the US, which sees the lifting of EU tariffs as a precondition for European chip companies to join the US–Japan Semiconductor Council

Source: Neil Buckley and Paul Taylor, *Financial Times*, 30 June 1997.

The global triad and regional economic groupings

Trade is concentrated in three main areas of the world, more commonly known as the Triad. These three areas are: North America, Europe and the Pacific rim of Asia. The trade arrangements in the Triad account for nearly one-half of world trade. The economic groupings of countries in these areas are known as:

1 The European Union, consisting of 15 Member States. Total population approx. 400m.

2 The North American Free Trade Association (NAFTA). This consists of the USA, Canada and Mexico. Total population 360m.

3 The ASEAN Free Trade Area (AFTA). This was formed on 1 January 1993 and consists of the Association of South East Asian Nations (ASEAN), established in 1967, plus other nations. ASEAN originally included Brunei, Indonesia, Malaysia, Singapore, the Philippines and Thailand, and these were later joined by Vietnam. The ASEAN nations were joined by Burma and Laos in July 1997. Cambodia's invitation was, however, frozen due to political repression there. AFTA has a potential total population of 466 million people.

It is relevant to consider briefly the significance of NAFTA and AFTA, but more importantly the European Union as this has a major bearing on the UK and its position in the European and international business environment.

The European Union

The European Economic Community (EEC) as the European Union was once known, has its origins in the customs union of the Benelux countries (Belgium, Luxembourg and the Netherlands), which was established in 1948 with the aim of facilitating free trade between the three countries while simultaneously establishing a common external tariff barrier.

In 1957 the Treaty of Rome established the EEC which consisted of the Benelux countries (Belgium, Netherlands and Luxemburg) plus France, Italy and the Federal Republic of Germany (the then West Germany).

The UK made several attempts to join the EEC although it was a member of the European Free Trade Association (EFTA). This consisted of Austria, Finland, Iceland, Liechtenstein, Norway, Sweden and Switzerland. During the 1960s the UK still had close trading links with the Commonwealth and former Commonwealth countries. Eventually the UK joined the EEC in 1973 along with Ireland and Denmark. A referendum held in 1975 confirmed Britain's membership.

Further widening of the European Community (EC) took place in 1981 when Greece joined. Spain and Portugal joined in 1986, making a total of 12 countries. In 1995 these 12 countries were joined by Sweden, Austria and Finland.

As a result of the widening of the EU, membership of EFTA declined. However, the EU maintained close links with the remaining countries in EFTA (Norway, Switzerland, Iceland and Liechtenstein). This free trade area became known as the European Economic Area (EEA) and came into force on 1 January 1994, with the aim of creating the world's largest common market. It extends to all member countries the four freedoms offered by the EU's internal market – freedom of movement of goods, services, labour and capital.

The major issues facing the EU, as it became known in 1991, after the Treaty of European Union (TEU) signed at the Dutch town of Maastricht, involved converting it from a common market to an economic and political union.

At this stage in our explanation it is useful to distinguish between various levels of economic integration. Distinction must be made between a free trade area, a customs union, a common market, economic union and economic and political union.

Free trade area

In a free trade area there are no internal tariffs, quotas, etc. Therefore there are no trading barriers between member countries.

Customs union

A customers union possesses the characteristics of a free trade area but also has a common external policy on trade with non-members.

Common market

A common market exists at the next stage of economic integration and involves promoting the freedom of movement of goods, services, labour and capital. The removal of all restrictions on competition is also encouraged.

Economic union

The establishment of economic union involves each individual member state forgoing unilateral economic control. Thus control over fiscal and monetary policy is relinquished and a single central bank is created.

Economic and political union

In an economic and political union, member states forgo political as well as economic sovereignty and a common form of central government is established.

The progressive stages outlined above, in the context of the EU, are known as 'deepening'. The main areas of interest as a result of the Maastricht Agreement are the formation of the Single European Market (SEM) on 1 January 1993, and the creation of Economic and Monetary Union (EMU), set for 1999. It is necessary to consider these in turn.

The Single European Market

The Single European Act 1986 (SEA), which amended the Treaty of Rome, defined a single, or common market, as 'an area without internal frontiers in which the free movement of goods, services labour and capital is ensured'. These became known as the 'Four Freedoms'. The Single Economic Market (SEM) was scheduled to commence on 1 January 1993.

The Cecchini Report (*The Cost of Non-Europe*, 1989) set out the benefits of creating a common market, such as the creation of 1.8 million new jobs and a reduction in consumer prices by approximately 6 per cent as a result of increased competition. By June 1995, approximately 90 per cent of the internal market measures had been adopted. These included, for example, the ending of VAT controls at national frontiers, equal recognition of national academic qualifications in all member countries, and the freedom for individuals to live anywhere in the EU provided they can support themselves.

Economic and Monetary union

Economic union implies the creation of a single market, as discussed earlier, whereas monetary union means the irrevocable fixing of exchange rates, a single common currency and the creation of one monetary authority to manage, among other things, interest rate and exchange rate policy.

The three stages towards Economic and Monetary Union (EMU) were laid down at Maastricht in 1991 and were based upon the Delors Plan (1989). (Jacques Delors is the former President of the European Commission.) The three stages towards EMU are discussed in turn below.

Stage 1

Stage 1 involved the completion of the internal market and increased macro-economic co-ordination (July 1990 – 31 December 1994). This was successfully achieved.

Stage 2

Stage 2 was a transitional stage during which a European system of central banks was established with the aim of introducing a common monetary policy. This stage commenced on 1 January 1994 and is still going on. It is preparing the way for transition to Stage 3. Further macroeconomic co-ordination is to be achieved by adherence to five convergence criteria. The criteria are as follows:

1 Inflation rates to be not more than 1.5 per cent above those of the three member states with the lowest performance.

2 A budget deficit not to exceed 3 per cent of GDP.

3 National debt not to be in excess of 60 per cent of GDP.

4 Nominal long-term interest rates to be not more than 2 per cent above the level in the three states with the best performance.

5 The Member States' currency to have respected the normal fluctuations of the ERM for at least two years.

Entrance into EMU will be decided during 1998 on the basis of the actual performance, against the criteria, of the EU economies in 1996 and 1997. At the time of writing, all EU countries, except Greece, meet the key condition of the Maastricht Treaty, i.e. a ratio of budget deficits to GDP of 3 per cent or less. Only Luxembourg, Finland, France and the UK complied with the debt to GDP ceiling of 60 per cent, however this is likely to be interpreted more flexibly than the other convergence criteria.

Stage 3

Stage 3 involves the irrevocable fixing of exchange rates against each other and the common currency (the euro, a basket of common currencies). It also involves devolving full responsibility to the European system of central banks and the European Central Bank for carrying out monetary policy (beginning in January 1999).

Thus the EU has developed from a customs union, in which free trade was encouraged between member states and a common external tariff wall was erected against other trading nations, through to a common market where the four freedoms are encouraged. At the time of writing, the EU is developing into an economic union with moves being made towards a single currency, a central bank and a unified monetary system. The major topic of debate concerns whether it will attain the next level of integration i.e., political union. Further 'deepening' of the EU is at the time of writing taking place.

The European Union

General

Quality daily and Sunday newspapers. *The European* newspaper.

Further reading

Bennett, R. (1996) *European Business*. London: Financial Times Pitman Publishing.

Dawes, B. (ed.) (1995) *International Business, A European Perspective*. Cheltenham: Stanley Thornes

Eurobusiness

European Business Journal

European Business Review

Welford, R. and Prescott, P. (1996) *European Business*. London: Financial Times Pitman Publishing.

Internet address

EU: europa.eu.int

We now consider the three free trade areas which make up the Global Triad, namely NAFTA, AFTA and APEC.

North American Free Trade Area

The North American Free Trade Area (NAFTA) linked the United States and Canada in 1989. Mexico joined in 1994, making it a total market of 365 million consumers. The aim is to eliminate all trade barriers between the three countries over a period of 15 years (*see* Exhibit 7.2). Furthermore, it seeks to link North America in a process of co-ordinated economic development. In Canada, 80 per cent of export earnings stem from the USA. In Mexico, 70 per cent of exports go to the USA. However, in the USA only 25 per cent of exports go to Canada and a fraction to Mexico. The benefits accruing to each of the member states of NAFTA are as follows:

1 **USA and NAFTA**. The benefits of NAFTA, as far as the USA was concerned, was that it gave access to Canadian and Mexican raw materials, for example, Mexican crude oil, and markets, for example, electronics and cars.

2 **Canada and NAFTA**. For Canada the need was to secure the benefits from the 1989 Free Trade Agreement with the USA and to target Mexican export markets.

3 **Mexico and NAFTA**. Mexico needed to penetrate the North American market and safeguard itself against volatile US trade policies in the Americas.

NAFTA is purely a free trade area as there is no unifying institutional infrastructure, unlike the EU.

ASEAN Free Trade Area

There are inherent difficulties with the ASEAN Free Trade Area (AFTA) because of the contrast between the export-promoting countries of Malaysia and Singapore and the poorer protectionist countries like Indonesia. Relatively high internal tariff

Exhibit 7.2 NAFTA

Old wounds to reopen

FT

Which of the following have been caused by the North American Free Trade Agreement?
1. The loss of 500,000 US jobs.
2. A 2m rise in Mexican unemployment.
3. The peso crisis.
4. More hepatitis and chronic diarrhoea in Mexico.
5. Two armed uprisings south of the Rio Grande.
6. Malfunctioning toilets at the office of the US Trade Representative.

Answer: None or all of the above, depending on whom you ask.

US trade officials call it the 'fly-paper syndrome': throw any criticism at Nafta, and it sticks. Nafta-bashing has become such a popular game that even Trade Representative officials engage in their own facetious version of it. When the toilets stopped working in their office recently, they were sure Nafta was to blame.

But tomorrow the US administration will fight back, releasing a report to Congress on the first three years of the trade accord between the US, Mexico and Canada, in effect since January 1, 1994. The report will not only reopen old wounds over Nafta; it could have a big effect on trade policy in President Bill Clinton's second term. The short history of Nafta could help determine the near-term future of American trade with Latin America, as the president gears up to ask Congress for 'fast track' authority – the right to negotiate trade agreements without having to submit them to a line-by-line veto by legislators.

It is hard enough to separate fact from fiction in any trade dispute and that has proved particularly to be the case with Nafta. But American protagonists of Nafta seldom seem to try. The debate has become a proxy for a battle over much larger issues: globalisation, economic dislocation, job insecurity, ethnic paranoia and even the future of the American middle class. Politicians have proved adroit at using Nafta as a lightning rod for fears about economic life in the 21st century.

'It's not so much the details of Nafta, but just this [feeling that] "we've got to do something about all these jobs that are going to other places around the world",' says Mr William Daley, the US commerce secretary, who shepherded the agreement through Congress in 1993. That makes it easy to use the agreement to 'touch on a nerve of fear'.

And, in the US, that nerve remains exposed despite conditions of near-full employment and an economic resurgence of historic proportions. The Department of Labour has ruled that 125,000 people have lost their jobs because of Nafta. Although Nafta opponents say this is an underestimate, as Mr Sidney Weintraub, a US expert on trade, says, it is equivalent to the number of jobs created by the US economy every fortnight.

But what matters to the political debate is not facts but public perceptions: many Americans believe their jobs are insecure, badly paid and under threat from cheap-labour states such as Mexico where – according to Mr Dick Gephardt, the Democratic party leader in the House of Representatives – 'people can match our productivity for pennies'.

Many Americans believe hundreds of thousands of jobs have been lost as US companies shift operations to Mexico; they say employers use the threat of relocation to depress wages paid to US workers. Many believe jobs have been lost and wages cut in Mexico too. A popular perception is that, under Nafta, everybody loses.

US administration officials admit they bear some of the blame for that poor image: strategically, they erred by selling the deal in 1993 on the basis that it would create, in the words of a State Department official, 'jobs, jobs, jobs'. Mr Daley admits this, too. The 'positives and negatives may have been over-stated; the expectations may have been too high,' he says.

Anti-Nafta legislators such as Mr Matthew Martinez, Democratic congressman from California, say the Mexican government – beset since 1994 by a currency crisis, two armed rebellions, drug scandals and corruption – is not a reliable partner for the US. Others, such as Mr Bob Clement, a Democrat from Tennessee who backed Nafta in 1993, believe the US got a raw deal beause of the trade deficits it has with both partners. 'We have a $16.2bn (£10.1bn) trade deficit with Mexico and a $22.8bn deficit with Canada. That doesn't look much like a partnership to me.' Strip emotion from the debate, though, and there are some underlying truths:
• It is too soon to tell whether or not Nafta is working. Three years into a process that will see the elimination of tariffs within 15 years, it is hard to assess fundamental structure change.
• The economies of both the US and Mexico have been influenced by forces far stronger than those unleashed by Nafta. The peso crisis cost 1m Mexican jobs and led to a 25 per cent fall in Mexican wage rates. The US economic boom has pushed US unemployment down by 1.4m since 1994. The effect of Nafta,

▶

Exhibit 7.2 continued

on jobs or even wages, is difficult to isolate and is likely to be marginal.

• Though national pride may be offended by trade deficits, the overall volume of trade matters more than which country is running a surplus, economists argue. Nafta has helped expand trade between the US, Mexico and Canada by 45 per cent (according to the Nafta commission).

• The environmental problems associated with Mexico's *maquiladora* industries, or assembly plants clustered along the border, have probably got worse as migration into these zones has increased. But this is because employment has grown and long-standing tax benefits for operating near the border have yet to be phased out. Still, almost everyone agrees that the environmental provisions of Nafta have not worked, at least so far.

• Nafta may have helped 'lock in' Mexico to a non-protectionist reaction to its financial crisis. According to Mr Weintraub, US exports to Mexico rose 11 per cent from 1993 to 1995. In a previous crisis in 1982, US exports fell 50 per cent as Mexico closed its borders.

• The 'great sucking sound' of jobs and investment heading southwards, forecast in 1992 by Mr Ross Perot, then a presidential candidate, has yet to be heard. Foreign direct investment in Mexico almost doubled in the three years since Nafta came into force to nearly $8bn a year, says Ns Nora Lustig of the Brookings Institution. However, US and Canadian direct investment in Mexico is less than 1 per cent of plant and equipment expenditures at home.

In the end, politics – rather than economic facts – is likely to determine the course of the debate over Nafta and, more importantly, the question of granting fast track authority to extend free trade agreements to all of Latin America, starting with Chile. Already, anti-Nafta sentiment has forced a delay in the fast track debate. President Clinton believes he will need to expend a significant amount of political capital on Capitol Hill to get fast-track authority. He does not want to spend it at least until the autumn, when the battle over the balanced budget is over.

No one believes it will be easy for Mr Clinton to get fast-track authority from the Republican Congress unless he presents a bill that does not seek to enforce standards on labour and the environment, as was the case with Nafta. 'President Clinton could have fast track today if he wanted it, by not asking to have labour and environmental standards added,' says Doug Bereuter, a Republican congressman from Nebraska. But this would be unacceptable to much of the president's own Democratic party. 'People are feeling burned by Nafta', says a Democratic congressional aide, adding that the momentum in 1993 for trade expansion has evaporated.

Democratic congressmen display pictures of new electronics plants in Mexico alongside grim images of the cardboard shanty-towns where employees live. These, they say, are the true fruits of Nafta. Meanwhile, the side accord on labour has been ineffective at guaranteeing Mexican workers the right to organise in trade unions.

They demand that future trade agreements should force US companies to do more to raise the living standard of their non-US employees and that foreign trade partners be compelled to enforce fair labour laws and prevent negative environmental consequences. That will be the crux of the debate over fast track: whether social policies on environment and labour rights are part of future trade agreements. And, even this year, that debate will fall foul of the presidential election politics of 2000: the two most likely contenders for the Democratic presidential nomination, Vice-president Al Gore and Mr Gephardt, have much at stake over fast track. Mr Gore portrays himself as the Green candidate and Mr Gephardt looks like the candidate of labour.

If President Clinton's fast-track proposals shortchange the environmentalists, Mr Gore may pay the price in 2000. Trying to find a way to avoid this could easily lead to further delays over fast track – perhaps well into next year. That would give Mr Clinton a weaker hand next March at a summit meeting of western hemisphere leaders in Chile.

This in itself would not derail the Free Trade Agreement for the Americas which Mr Clinton and the others have agreed to negotiate by 2005. The process has a strong momentum of its own, says Mr Robert Devlin of the InterAmerican Development Bank. However, it would reduce the ability of the US to influence the process. In the end, the fate of fast track – and of further integration of the North American market – will probably depend on how strongly Mr Clinton wants history to judge him as a 'free trade' president. No one knows how much he is willing to pay for that legacy or whether it can be bought at any price.

Source: Nancy Dunne, Stephen Fidler and Patty Waldmeir, *Financial Times*, 30 June 1997.

walls therefore remain. Further there has been controversy concerning the admission of Cambodia and Burma to the group because of the political repression present in those countries which detracts from the key objective of economic liberalisation. Nevertheless, Burma (together with Laos) was admitted in July 1997 and given ten years from January 1998 to comply with the tariff-reduction schedule. Other members have until 2003 to reduce tariffs on 98 per cent of traded items, except for Vietnam, which has until 2006. Intra-ASEAN trade has grown from $27 billion in 1990 to $70 billion in 1996.

At this stage, mention must be made of the four 'Asian Tiger' economies of Singapore, Hong Kong, Thailand and South Korea. Until recently, these countries enjoyed very rapid economic growth. However, during 1996/97, they experienced a slowdown in economic growth, a declining exchange rate against the dollar and rising current account deficits on their balance of payments (*see* Exhibit 7.3).

Exhibit 7.3 Asian economies

The real lesson from Asia

FT

Is the Asian 'miracle' over? Despite the turmoil in the region's stock markets, which has driven the FT/S&P Pacific Basin (ex-Japan) index down 9 per cent in the past week, the short answer is no. That reply will disappoint many in Europe and North America – all those, that is, who dislike boasts of 'Asian values', fear Asian competition or detest the triumph of these outward-looking market economies.

Yet disappointed they will almost certainly be. Their only hope is for the governments of the countries concerned to lose their heads, as did the Brazilians after the first oil shock in the 1970s. Mistaken policies then ended a period of growth that had been comparable to that of the Asian tigers.

What happened in east Asia over the past few decades was never a miracle and, for that reason, is unlikely to vanish overnight. The present upheaval may be painful, not least to the *amour propre* of such leaders as Mahathir Mohamad, Malaysia's prime minister. But it will pass.

The starting point for any understanding of Asian success is the gap between the output per person in the tiger economies and that in the most advanced economies in the world. This gap defines the opportunity for catching up.

Catching up is precisely what east Asian economies have been doing. Between 1970 and 1995, the gross national product per head of South Korea rose almost elevenfold, of Hong Kong four-fold and of Thailand three-and-a-half-fold. In 1970, Korea's real income per head (at purchasing power parity) was some 15 per cent of that level. By 1995 it was over 40 per cent of the US level. Thailand's income per head has risen from some 11 per cent to 28 per cent of US levels over the same quarter of a century. This is convergence at work. Japan, Hong Kong and Singapore have already caught up.

Inevitably, the opportunity for rapid growth is a function of the size of the remaining gap. On average, argues Jeffrey Sachs of Harvard University, a doubling of real income per head reduces the underlying growth rate by 1.4 percentage points. If US real income per head will grow sustainably at 1½ per cent a year, Japan's would be expected to grow about as fast,

South Korea's at a little over 3 per cent and Thailand's at about 4 per cent.

Yet these are merely tendencies. Individual countries can do better. Hong Kong, South Korea, Singapore and Taiwan have done so. As if to prove there is nothing geographically determined about east Asian performance, the Philippines has, until quite recently, done far worse.

What is striking about the region, however, is how many countries have managed to seize available opportunities to import modern technology and managerial skills and converge on the incomes enjoyed by advanced countries. They have done so because of their limitation of one another. This is neither a miracle nor the fruit of uniquely Asian virtues: Chile has already demonstrated that it is possible to learn from east Asian countries, despite being an ocean away.

Policy is what matters: successful countries have made economic growth a priority; they have followed prudent macroeconomic policies; they have generated extraordinarily high savings rates; they

▶

Exhibit 7.3 continued

have removed obstacles to trade, particularly to exports; they have kept real exchange rates at competitive levels; they have intervened so in directions encouraged by the market; and they have promoted mass literacy.

The question raised by the present turmoil is whether such fundamental forces for rapid growth have become irrelevant. There are three arguments:
• That the opportunities for catch up are rapidly diminishing.
• That even though these opportunities are not diminishing quickly, east Asian countries have lost the capacity to exploit them;
• That a hostile world environment will prevent the countries from exploiting their potential, as happened in the 1930s.

Take these three arguments in turn. In the first place, the countries most affected by the market turbulence – Thailand, Malaysia, Indonesia and the Philippines – still possess substantial room for catching up. Maybe the exceptionally rapid growth of the first half of the 1990s will not be sustained. But sharp reductions in past rates of growth seem far more plausible for Singapore or Hong Kong, which have been relatively untroubled by the markets, than for Indonesia, Malaysia or Thailand.

In the second place, those worried about the loss of the capacity to deliver fast growth can point to clear signs of hubris in Mahathir's Malaysia, the late-regime decay of Suharto's rule over Indonesia or the declining authority of the technocrats in Thailand. Yet, except conceivably for Thailand, it is far from evident that the others have lost the policy threads binding them to past successes.

Finally, there is nothing in the global environment to suggest continued rapid growth is infeasible.

True, east Asian countries have to adjust to the rising competition of China, but the latter's growth also creates opportunities for them, as the US has done for Canada. On balance, the underlying global environment is more liberal than at any time since the early part of the century and more stable than since the 1960s.

If there is no reason to believe rapid growth is at an end, how does one explain what is happening? Part of the answer is that market economies never proceed in straight lines. Before the first world war, the US economy was notoriously unstable, which hardly prevented it from growing explosively. The chances of failing to match capacity with output, or demands for loans with the ability of financial institutions to lend sensibly, are particularly high in dynamic but immature economies.

Fortunately, in the case of the east Asian countries, there is also a perfectly good short- to medium-term explanation for the turmoil. It lies in the gyrations of the dollar, particularly against the yen, set against the background of heavily managed exchange rates and immature and inefficient financial systems.

The story can be told most easily of Thailand – the epicentre of the earthquake. During the dollar weakness up to spring 1995, east Asian economies with currencies closely linked to the dollar enjoyed superb competitiveness, not least against producers based in Japan. This helped trigger exceptional growth: the Thai economy expanded at an average rate of 8.4 per cent a year between 1990 and 1995.

Rapid growth, combined with the emerging market euphoria, stimulated huge capital flows. Thailand was able to run a current account

deficit averaging close to 7 per cent of GDP between 1990 and 1995. If the exchange rate had been floating, such capital flows would have driven up the currency. Under Thailand's fixed rate, they helped stimulate inflationary excess demand. They did so by keeping interest rates low and stimulating borrowing, particularly for investment in property. Monetary policy could do little about this, given the commitment to the fixed exchange rate.

Things as good as this have to come to an end. With the appreciation of the dollar, they did. The effects on Thailand's exports were exacerbated by the global slowdown in electronics. Also important was the emergence of supply constraints in an economy that had been running flat out for years.

A great deal of what then happened was the result of a foolish resistance to overwhelming market pressure for devaluation. Even now, the decline in east Asian exchange rates against the resurgent dollar is not extraordinary by global standards. Over the past 12 months, the depreciation of the D-Mark has been bigger than that of the Malaysian dollar and not all that much smaller than of the Thai baht.

So would all have been well if the baht had been allowed to float fairly freely throughout? The answer is that things would have been far better. At the least the transmission of external pressures on to the domestic economy would have had far milder effects.

Should all be well now that the baht is floating? Alas no. Policy errors leave long shadows. In this case Thailand's mistakes have hurt its neighbours, partly because they must be concerned about their competitive position and partly because of the contagion that is now infecting the region.

▶

Exhibit 7.3 continued

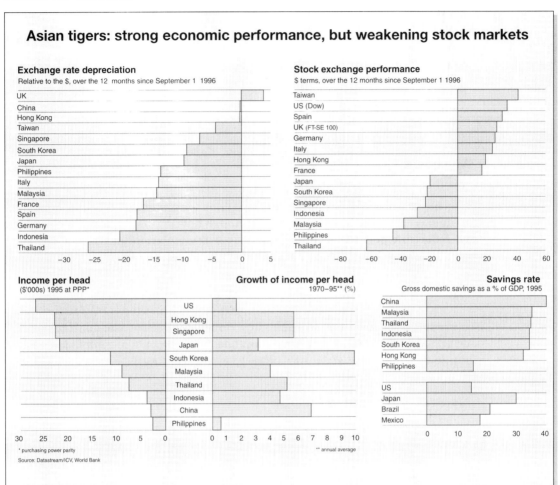

Asian tigers: strong economic performance, but weakening stock markets

Exchange rate depreciation
Relative to the $, over the 12 months since September 1 1996

Stock exchange performance
$ terms, over the 12 months since September 1 1996

Income per head
($'000s) 1995 at PPP*

Growth of income per head
1970–95** (%)

Savings rate
Gross domestic savings as a % of GDP, 1995

* purchasing power parity
** annual average

Source: Datastream/ICV, World Bank

Yet the deepest shadows are always at home. In the defence of the exchange rate the central bank has laid out over $23bn of Thailand's reserves, while high interest rates (to defend the currency) have damaged the solvency of the private sector. Still more seriously, the fixed exchange rate encouraged the private sector to run up short-term foreign debts of around $50bn. An exchange-rate commitment that fails is, in short, a machine for destroying a private sector's solvency.

The legacy of the episode is serious. The current consensus is that the Thai economy will grow by less than 2 per cent this year and by not much more in 1998. This is disappointing. But after years of growth at 8 per cent, it is hardly a catastrophe.

In the region as a whole, the devaluations will be helpful. For the rest, what matters is to take advantage of the opportunity to put their houses in order. It is precisely because the performance of the region has not been a miracle that

this is possible. But, for the same reason, growth does depend on sustaining the right policies. Opportunities can be thrown away, as the history of Latin America repeatedly shows.

The east Asian model has not collapsed. Rather, the combination of fixed exchange rates with distorted financial systems is inconsistent with stable growth. That is the true lesson of the Asian turmoil.

Source: Martin Wolf, *Financial Times*, 2 September 1997.

As ASEAN did not satisfy the regional investment interests of countries like Australia and Japan, nor the USA, the Asia Pacific Economic Co-operation group (APEC) was formed in 1989.

Asia Pacific Economic Co-operation group

The Asia Pacific Economic Co-operation group (APEC) comprises the six ASEAN countries plus Australia, Japan, Canada, South Korea, New Zealand, the USA, the People's Republic of China, including Hong Kong, and Taiwan.

Mercosur

A further economic and trading group, outside the Global Triad, is Mercosur, which consists of the South American nations – Argentina, Paraguay, Brazil and Uruguay – and was formed in 1991. Although outside the Triad, it has close links with the USA, and it was hoped that the Free Trade Area for the Americas (FTAA) would begin in March 1998 (*see* Exhibit 7.4).

Furthermore, Mercosur and the EU are due to sign a Free Trade Agreement in 1999 (*see* Exhibit 7.5).

Before we go on to describe the roles of several of the major economic international organisations, it is necessary now to outline developments in central and eastern Europe (CEE) in the last decades of the twentieth century.

Central and eastern Europe

We referred in Chapter 5 to the market mechanism as being a means of allocating scarce resources. The history of the countries of central and eastern Europe during the twentieth century provides a clear illustration of the workings of a system which lacked free markets.

In the early part of the twentieth century, the Soviet Union or Union of Soviet Socialist Republics (USSR), was established under the leadership of Russia. The USSR was characterised by communist ideology which was very opposed to the operation of free markets, regarding these as leading to inequities in income and wealth. Thus, resources in the USSR were allocated by central state planning. This meant that all the means of production, distribution and exchange were placed in state hands. As a result there was no efficiently functioning markets. For example, instead of allowing the market mechanism to allocate food, rationing was used to ensure that everybody received their allocation. Queues developed at food stores as a consequence. Labour was directed into jobs, and there was no unemployment. Large state-owned enterprises were set up with designated suppliers and customers.

After the Second World War a number of countries in central and eastern Europe (CEE), such as Poland, Czechoslovakia and Hungary became satellites of the Soviet Union and therefore central state planning pervaded their economies. (We will refer to the above countries as the CEE states.)

Exhibit 7.4 Free Trade Area for the Americas

Americas free trade talks get green light

Trade ministers from 34 countries in the Americas have agreed that detailed negotiations over the creation of a free trade zone for the region should start next year, but failed to decide on how the talks should proceed.

Following a compromise between the US and the Mercosur trade grouping, the ministers agreed that talks to set up a Free Trade Area for the Americas (FTAA) 'should' begin in March 1998, but left open the 'objectives, approaches, structure and venue' of the negotiations.

Mr Luiz Felipe Lampreia, Brazil's foreign minister, described the declaration as a 'partial agreement'.

'We have not solved a number of issues, but some very important topics have been agreed upon,' he said, after the meeting in the Brazilian city of Belo Horizonte.

'No one's position has been prejudiced,' said Mr Peter Allgeier, associate US trade representative.

However, diplomats also said the agreement would give momentum to the FTAA talks. A senior US trade official said that the process was now 'irreversible' and pointed to the creation of so-called 'preparatory committees' for the negotiations, which he said were a crucial stage in the Uruguay Round of trade talks.

The FTAA talks have been held up by the disagreement between the US, which wants to begin discussions on reducing tariffs next year, and Mercosur, whose members are Brazil, Argentina, Uruguay and Paraguay, which want to start with talks on making business easier and only move to discussions about tariffs at a later date.

Trade ministers have now given themselves until their next meeting in Costa Rica in February next year to reach an agreement on a schedule for negotiations, which are then due to start after a heads of state summit in Santiago, Chile, the following month.

A senior Mercosur official said that negotiations on substantial issues could not start before the US government had received so-called 'fast track' approval from Congress, which would prevent legislators from amending any final treaty.

However, Mercosur diplomats said that the declaration had been worded to show a strong commitment to the FTAA from Latin American countries, in order to persuade doubting members of the US Congress about their seriousness.

The US position at the Belo Horizonte meeting was complicated by the admission last Wednesday by the White House that it would be very difficult to get 'fast track' approval this year.

However, the US government argues that 'fast track' should not be a precondition to beginning the talks.

Diplomats also admitted that the meeting showed the growing confidence of the Mercosur trade grouping, which is now holding membership talks with Peru and the Andean Community of countries. Chile and Bolivia are already associate members of Mercosur.

Leaders from the 34 countries – Cuba is excluded from the group – agreed at a summit in Miami in 1994 to set up a hemispheric free trade area by 2005.

Source: Geoff Dyer, *Financial Times*, 19 May 1997.

In the late 1980s, revolution took place in the Soviet Union and the Communists eventually fell from power. The revolution quickly spread throughout central and eastern Europe. The USSR broke up and eventually the Confederation of Independent States (CIS) was formed. Of course, there were, within this new grouping, no openly competitive markets, no profit-motivated firms and no financial system. However, the CEE states were rather more economically advanced as they had not been taken over by the Communists until the late 1940s. They therefore possessed strong national identities and were located geographically near to the dynamic western European market economies, particularly the former West Germany.

Thus, during the 1990s these former centrally planned economies have moved towards the market mechanism as a means of allocating resources. In addition they have presented great investment opportunities for western European and US firms (*see* Exhibit 7.6). For example, the German car manufacturer Volkswagen took over the Czech manufacturer Skoda.

Exhibit 7.5 EU-Mercosur agreement

EU-Mercosur pact 'set for 1999'

The European Union and Mercosur, the South American trade grouping, will be in a position to sign a free-trade agreement in 1999, according to Manuel Marin, the EU commissioner responsible for relations with Latin America.

Negotiations would begin next year and heads of state of the 15 EU and four Mercosur nations – Brazil, Argentina, Uruguay and Paraguay – would sign the agreement at a summit in the second half of 1999, he said.

Speaking at the World Economic Forum's Mercosur summit in São Paulo, Mr Marin added: 'This will be the first time in the world … that we put on the table liberalisation between one region and another.'

Mercosur signed an agreement with the EU in 1995 to establish the model for negotiation of a trade pact. If the trade deal is signed in 1999, the new EU-Mercosur agreement would start well before the 34-country hemispheric free-trade zone, known as the Free Trade Area of the Americas (FTAA), by 2005.

However, Mercosur diplomats reacted with scepticism to Mr Marin's comments, arguing that a tariff reduction agreement with the EU could not be achieved without a significant reform of the EU's common agricultural policy. Agriculture is one of the Mercosur countries' strongest sectors. One Brazilian official said his comments reflected a growing rivalry with the US for closer relations with Mercosur.

However, Mr Marin also stressed the need to strengthen Mercosur before the creation of the FTAA.

The US and Mercosur have disagreed over the timing for negotiations on reducing tariffs and some South American diplomats fear that the US would like Mercosur to disappear after a FTAA is formed.

Earlier, delegates at the conference heard Thomas McLarty, the US's special envoy for the Americas, assure them that the US 'fully supports regional trade pacts among our hemispheric neighbours which create but do not divert trade'.

Source: Geoff Dyer, *Financial Times*, 15 September 1997.

Exhibit 7.6 EU and the countries of central and eastern Europe

No turning back from brave new Europe FT

Now there is no turning back. With the publication of Agenda 2000, the European Commission's 1,300-page blockbuster on enlargement, the historic process of admitting 10 former Soviet bloc countries into the European Union is finally underway.

Agenda 2000 marks the end of Old Europe, the intimate Club of Six built 40 years ago around France, Germany, the Benelux countries and Italy. The vision of an ever closer Union is shifting towards the looser confederation of nation-states favoured by Britain.

The new Europe will have a longer frontier with Russia as well as borders with Ukraine, Belarus and Moldova. It will enjoy direct access to the Black Sea and closer contacts with the Caucasus and Central Asia. The EU's own population will increase by one-third to nearly 500m people; but total gross domestic product will rise by barely 5 per cent.

'Europe's cultural diversity will be a source of creativity and wealth. The accession of new member-states will enhance the Union's weight and influence internationally,' says Agenda 2000, 'but the sheer number of applicants and the very large differences in economic and social development will present the Union with institutional and political challenges far greater than ever before.'

Moreover, the EU today is hardly at ease with itself. More than 18m people are out of work. Public support for further integration is fragile. Economic and monetary union looks within reach but is still not a done deal. Only last month, EU leaders ducked the very institutional reforms necessary to manage a Union of more than 20 members.

This is the background to the Agenda 2000 blueprint which Mr Jacques Santer, president of the European Commission, presented to the European Parliament in

►

Exhibit 7.6 continued

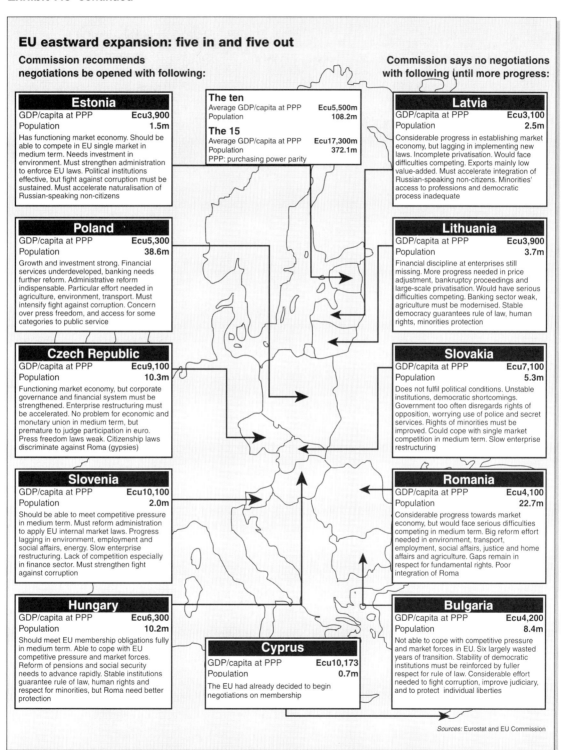

EU eastward expansion: five in and five out

Commission recommends negotiations be opened with following:

Commission says no negotiations with following until more progress:

Estonia
GDP/capita at PPP	Ecu3,900
Population	1.5m

Has functioning market economy. Should be able to compete in EU single market in medium term. Needs investment in environment. Must strengthen administration to enforce EU laws. Political institutions effective, but fight against corruption must be sustained. Must accelerate naturalisation of Russian-speaking non-citizens

Poland
GDP/capita at PPP	Ecu5,300
Population	38.6m

Growth and investment strong. Financial services underdeveloped, banking needs further reform. Administrative reform indispensable. Particular effort needed in agriculture, environment, transport. Must intensify fight against corruption. Concern over press freedom, and access for some categories to public service

Czech Republic
GDP/capita at PPP	Ecu9,100
Population	10.3m

Functioning market economy, but corporate governance and financial system must be strengthened. Enterprise restructuring must be accelerated. No problem for economic and monetary union in medium term, but premature to judge participation in euro. Press freedom laws weak. Citizenship laws discriminate against Roma (gypsies)

Slovenia
GDP/capita at PPP	Ecu10,100
Population	2.0m

Should be able to meet competitive pressure in medium term. Must reform administration to apply EU internal market laws. Progress lagging in environment, employment and social affairs, energy. Slow enterprise restructuring. Lack of competition especially in finance sector. Must strengthen fight against corruption

Hungary
GDP/capita at PPP	Ecu6,300
Population	10.2m

Should meet EU membership obligations fully in medium term. Able to cope with EU competitive pressure and market forces. Reform of pensions and social security needs to advance rapidly. Stable institutions guarantee rule of law, human rights and respect for minorities, but Roma need better protection

The ten
Average GDP/capita at PPP	Ecu5,500m
Population	108.2m

The 15
Average GDP/capita at PPP	Ecu17,300m
Population	372.1m

PPP: purchasing power parity

Latvia
GDP/capita at PPP	Ecu3,100
Population	2.5m

Considerable progress in establishing market economy, but lagging in implementing new laws. Incomplete privatisation. Would face difficulties competing. Exports mainly low value-added. Must accelerate integration of Russian-speaking non-citizens. Minorities' access to professions and democratic process inadequate

Lithuania
GDP/capita at PPP	Ecu3,900
Population	3.7m

Financial discipline at enterprises still missing. More progress needed in price adjustment, bankruptcy proceedings and large-scale privatisation. Would have serious difficulties competing. Banking sector weak, agriculture must be modernised. Stable democracy guarantees rule of law, human rights, minorities protection

Slovakia
GDP/capita at PPP	Ecu7,100
Population	5.3m

Does not fulfil political conditions. Unstable institutions, democratic shortcomings. Government too often disregards rights of opposition, worrying use of police and secret services. Rights of minorities must be improved. Could cope with single market competition in medium term. Slow enterprise restructuring

Romania
GDP/capita at PPP	Ecu4,100
Population	22.7m

Considerable progress towards market economy, but would face serious difficulties competing in medium term. Big reform effort needed in environment, transport, employment, social affairs, justice and home affairs and agriculture. Gaps remain in respect for fundamental rights. Poor integration of Roma

Bulgaria
GDP/capita at PPP	Ecu4,200
Population	8.4m

Not able to cope with competitive pressure and market forces in EU. Six largely wasted years of transition. Stability of democratic institutions must be reinforced by fuller respect for rule of law. Considerable effort needed to fight corruption, improve judiciary, and to protect individual liberties

Cyprus
GDP/capita at PPP	Ecu10,173
Population	0.7m

The EU had already decided to begin negotiations on membership

Sources: Eurostat and EU Commission

Exhibit 7.6 continued

Strasbourg yesterday. He trod carefully, well aware that EU governments have the last word on the Commission's recommendations.

The first area of contention is the proposal that five countries should join Cyprus early next year in the first wave of countries negotiating to join the Union. The favoured five are the Czech Republic, Poland, Hungary, Estonia and Slovenia.

Mr Hans van den Broek, Dutch commissioner in charge of eastern enlargement, resisted pressure from inside and outside the Commission to restrict the shortlist to the Czechs, Poles and Hungarians, who were invited last week to join the Nato alliance.

But the Danes, Finns and Swedes are pressing for accession negotiations to begin with all 10 applicants. This is a gesture to the two disappointed Baltic states of Latvia and Lithuania rather than to Bulgaria, Romania and Slovakia. France may be tempted to champion the cause of the new reformist government in francophile Romania; others may call for a negotiation with all 10 countries, knowing that this could be a recipe for delaying the process.

The second bone of contention is money. Net recipients from the EU budget such as Spain are sceptical about Commission claims that enlargement can be funded without any real increase in EU spending beyond the ceiling of 1.27 per cent of EU gross domestic product planned for 1999. 'We don't believe in the feeding of the five thousand,' said a senior Spanish diplomat. 'There are not enough loaves and fish to go round.'

Yet the British, French, Germans and Dutch are adamant that there should be no increase in national contributions to the next EU budget, which will run from 2000–2006. Indeed, the Germans and Dutch are threatening to copy Mrs Margaret Thatcher's successful campaign in the early 1980s to cut Britain's contribution.

Agenda 2000 proposes tighter rules on eligibility for Brussels funds. 'This rationalisation has nothing to do with enlargement,' said Mrs Monika Wulf-Mathies, EU regional affairs commissioner, yesterday. 'We would have to do it anyway.' But Mrs Wulf-Mathies has heeded Spain's warnings that it will not tolerate any tampering with the multi-billion dollar Cohesian Fund, set up in 1992 to reduce economic disparities between the poorer countries – Greece, Ireland, Spain and Portugal – and the rest of the Union.

Even if the last three join the elite Emu group in 1999, they still stand to draw on cohesion money as long as their average GNP per capita is below 90 per cent of the average. The British government yesterday said it would oppose interpretation.

Finally, the proposed reforms of the Common Agricultural Policy strike a balance between what the Commission considers is politically manageable rather than economically desirable.

Perhaps the hottest issue is how long the central and eastern Europeans must wait before they can enjoy the same rights and privileges as the existing members of the Club. Agenda 2000 devotes a mere paragraph to the question, declaring that transition periods may be necessary but should be limited in scope and duration.

Transition periods are indeed inevitable. Spain had to wait ten years before its tastiest farm products could circulate freely. All the central and and eastern Europeans face huge problems in meeting EU standards in social and environ-

mental policy. Poland, with a population of 40m bordering Germany and one-quarter of its labour force employed on the land, is in a class of its own.

Mr van den Broek said yesterday that too long transition periods add up to second-class membership. But limits on freedom of movement of people and agricultural goods will be the subject of much hard bargaining in the closing accession negotiations and will define full membership.

How long will negotiations last? The Commission's working hypothesis is that the first wave of new members will enter the Union in 2002. But this looks optimistic. Spain took seven years to conclude a deal. Some Spanish negotiators still smart from the experience. Enlargement is also hostage to the EU's internal agenda. The successful launch of Emu is almost certainly a precondition of expansion eastwards in the mind of France, if not Germany.

Constitutional reform, including a streamlined European Commission, a rebalancing of power between small and large member states and more majority voting, is necessary to prevent a paralysis in decision-making. The Commission wants another inter-governmental conference as early as possible after 2000, which could pose a hurdle to new membership.

Outside factors could also upset the Commission's plans. The proposed accession of Cyprus is a ticking timebomb in the absence of a settlement between the Greek and Turkish communities. Mr van den Broek brushed aside Turkish warnings about opening negotiations next year with the Nicosia government, preferring to stress how the prospect of membership could propel the old antagonist toward compromise.

Exhibit 7.6 continued

But it is a gamble. Nato's expansion eastward seems certain to influence EU enlargement, at least indirectly. The EU insists that Union membership cannot be compensated for Nato membership, but the pressures exist. Benign Russian attitudes may also change, especially as the EU proposes to extend its writ into the Baltic states, including Estonia with its big Russian minority.

Similar potential for friction exists in Romania and Slovakia, with their sizeable Magyar minorities. They will need every incentive not to backtrack on their commitments to neighbouring Hungary. As Mr Santer underlined yesterday, enlargement will only succeed if it appears to be an inclusive process where the prospect for membership is real.

Source: Lionel Barber, *Financial Times*, 17 July 1997.

International economic organisations

We now consider several international organisations which have important economic roles in the business environment. The first two are international bodies set up outside the framework of any other international organisation. The third, fourth and fifth are bodies which have economic roles within the United Nations.

1 World Trade Organisation (WTO).

2 The Organisation for Economic Co-operation and Development (OECD).

3 The International Monetary Fund (IMF).

4 The World Bank (the International Bank for Re-construction and Development).

5 United Nations Conference for Trade and Development (UNCTAD).

World Trade Organisation

The WTO is based in Geneva and was founded as the GATT (General Agreement on Tariffs and Trade) in 1947 to promote free trade throughout the world by restricting protectionist measures such as import controls by domestic governments. The motivation for founding the GATT was the intention to avoid a repetition of the Great Depression of the 1930s, when governments took protectionist measures to protect their home-based industries. It was these measures that severely curtailed trade and led to a major depression throughout the world.

The GATT became known as the World Trade Organisation (WTO) on 1 January 1995. Agreements by the WTO take the form of Rounds, the most recent being the Uruguay Round which involved discussions in the years 1986–94, when it was agreed that, for example, tariffs on industrial goods were to be cut by an average of 37 per cent and import quotas on textiles and clothing were to be phased out over the next ten years. In July 1997 India agreed to phase out import quotas on 2500 consumer electronics goods and textiles after heavy pressure from the WTO and the IMF.

Organisation for Economic Co-operation and Development

The OECD is based in Paris and was formed in 1948 with 24 members (known as G24). Its major initial purpose was to ensure that the western European countries operated a commom economic programme as a result of post-war economic reconstruction. In March 1990 the Centre for Co-operation with Economies in Transition (CCET) was formed. As a result, the OECD has been joined by the Czech Republic (December 1995), Hungary (April 1996) and Poland (November 1996).

The OECD also carries out impartial surveys of member countries' economies. It dispenses advice on its own behalf, unlike the IMF and World Bank (*see* below).

The major economic nations in the OECD are: the USA, Canada, the UK, Germany, France, Italy and Japan. These are known as the Group of Seven (G7) nations.

International Monetary Fund

The IMF consists of 181 members and is based in Washington. It was established in 1946 after the 1944 Bretton Woods Conference which sought to bring order to international trade by setting up a system of fixed exchange rates. The system for the fixing of exchange rates gradually broke down in the 1970s, with the result that in the 1980s the IMF largely became concerned with the debt problems of the Third World and it imposed austere economic adjustments on Third World countries. In the 1990s it has been involved in the freeing up of markets in the centrally state planned economies of the former Soviet bloc.

The World Bank (the International Bank for Reconstruction and Development)

The World Bank was also created under the Bretton Woods agreement and provided funds for the reconstruction for the world economies after the Second World War. From the mid-1950s it has provided funds for the Third World.

United Nations Conference on Trade and Development

The United Nations Conference on Trade and Development (UNCTAD) is a pressure group formed in 1964 to represent the economic interests of the Third World. Its major successes have been the stabilisation of prices of primary commodities and the duty-free treatment of exports of manufactured goods from the underdeveloped to the developed world. This is known as the general system of preferences.

International economic organisations

General

Quality daily and Sunday newspapers. *The Economist*.

Further reading

Bennett, R. (1996) *International Business*. London: Financial Times Pitman Publishing.

Griffiths, A. and Wall, S. (eds), (1995) *Applied Economics: An Introductory Course* (6th edn). Harlow: Longman.

Palmer, A. and Hartley, B. (1996) *The Business and Marketing Environment* (2nd edn). Maidenhead: McGraw-Hill.

Internet address

ASEAN: www.asean.or.id (ASEAN WEB)

faraday.clas.virginia.edu/~cepzt/asean.htmi

NAFTA: the.tech.mit.edu/Bulletins/nafta.htmi

www.iep.doc.gov/border

Chapter summary

This chapter has been divided into three main parts. The first part explains the law of comparative advantage and the benefits of free trade, however, there still exists a number of restrictions to free trade. In order to promote free trade and economic cooperation between countries, a number of regional economic groupings have developed. The EU is probably the most integrated grouping. The rest of the chapter focused on the economic development of the EU.

The second part of the chapter consides other less integrated economic groupings in the world economy, such as NAFTA and AFTA. The chapter also considered economic developments in Central and Eastern Europe since the fall of communism.

The final part considered several international economic organisations, the most important of which, is probably the WTO which has evolved from GATT, formed after the Second World War, to promote free trade among nations.

Assignment

1 From the knowledge you have gained in Chapters 6 and 7, list the main macro-economic indicators and briefly explain their application to the proposed EU Economic and Monetary Union (EMU).

2 Describe the advantages and disadvantages of EMU to business.

Exhibit 7.7 European Monetary Union

Emu: who's going to make it

FT

J P Morgan Calculator May 26 1997

	Yesterday	1 week ago	4 weeks ago
Germany	100%	100%	100%
France	100%	100%	100%
Belgium	100%	100%	97%
Portugal	83%	81%	75%
Spain	80%	80%	70%
Finland	79%	79%	76%
Ireland	75%	75%	59%
Sweden	63%	62%	56%
Italy	62%	64%	52%
Denmark	47%	51%	46%
UK	44%	52%	36%

The Emu calculator reveals, real time, the probability of individual countries joining Germany in a monetary union in 1999 implied by financial market prices. Market probabilities are derived from the interest rate swaps market, in which investors swap floating-rate interest payments for fixed-rate ones.
The implied probability of Italy participating in Emu in 1999 can be calculated looking at where the spread between post-1999 lira and D-Mark swap rate lies, between the zero level implied by Emu and the level we would expect if Italy is not in Emu. Italy's non-Emu spread is estimated by currency strategists at J.P. Morgan using the pre-1992 correlation of the lira-D-Mark swap spread with similar spreads outside Europe.

Source: Financial Times, 27 May 1997.

Part 3

THE SOCIOCULTURAL ENVIRONMENT

Introduction

Part 3 describes trends in society and discusses forecasts and the major implications of the trends. Never before has society been changing so rapidly.

First, Chapter 8 explains the origins and science of demography, sociodemographic trends and their vital importance for governments and businesses in planning and focusing their activities more effectively. The 'population explosion' is also discussed, and forecasts up to 2050 are given. The implications of these forecasts for our society in the coming decades are discussed.

As may be seen from Chapter 8, the current and projected rates of population growth are unprecedented. Alarmist predictions that this will lead the world into disaster appear to be outweighed by the arguments for more optimistic outcomes. The aim in this chapter is to present objective, balanced views of the forecasts and projections and to provide details of key sources for further research for readers interested and keen to look into such issues more deeply.

Chapter 9 also describes trends in society, specifically how living in the UK has been changing. Again, we include forecasts and analyse the implications of these for twenty-first-century society. Among the specific areas examined are: our ageing population; family life; spending and leisure activities; households and the impending need for at least four million new homes; changes and trends in employment, income and wealth.

Part 3 concludes with an in-depth review of another significant trend in society, that of people's expectations and their demands on businesses and, indeed, on all types of organisations, to act in a more socially responsible way. As a result of this trend, businesses are having to respond to pressure groups and the demands of consumers who, increasingly, believe that companies must play their part in benefiting society. One spin-off for those companies which are seen to be putting something back into society is that they tend to attract more loyal customers and are often more successful in commercial terms. Again, the pace of these changes and trends is unprecedented and cannot be ignored. The public's perception of and influence on the social responsibilities of business are further facets of the operating environment that today must be taken into account when managing a business.

8

Demography and sociodemographic trends

Chapter objectives

By the time you have read this chapter you should be able to:

◆ describe the precise meanings of (a) demography and (b) sociodemographic trends;

◆ explain why sociodemographic trends are studied and what sort of organisations use them;

◆ explain, using your own examples, how sociodemographic trends influence planning in business and government organisations;

◆ provide a few reasons why some sociodemographic forecasts turn out to be wrong;

◆ explain the difference between a forecast and a prediction.

 ## Introduction

The *Concise Oxford Dictionary* defines demography as *the study of the statistics of births, deaths, disease, etc., as illustrating the conditions of life in communities.*

This chapter describes the origins of modern demography and how important this topic is to forecasting in both business and government. An understanding of how demography and sociodemography evolved, and knowledge of the most notable trends, help us to anticipate the changes in society and, therefore, enable us to plan effectively for the future. Without this use of demographics there would be chaos.

The chapter also highlights the need for objectivity and a questioning, even sceptical, approach to interpreting sociodemographic statistics so as not to be misled by biased survey data or slanted presentations of survey results.

Areas of planning that stem from sociodemography include:

a in business, to assess the size of markets and the pattern of demand for different goods and services;

b in government, to determine levels of taxation and provision of schools, health care, housing and pensions.

Because of their importance, these and other related topics are also dealt with in further detail in Chapter 9.

How demography evolved

Demography has been considered a subfield of sociology but economists also came to appreciate the value of analysing demographic data, particularly in the study of population trends and in estimating future population size. Sometimes this has led to the fear of over-population, most notably in the work of Thomas Malthus, an English clergyman and economist who lived in the early nineteenth century, author of *Essay on Population*. Many regard this work as the beginning of modern demography.

Malthus started a controversy that still causes argument today. His theory is based on a simple formula, namely that the population would continue to grow in geometrical progression, doubling every 25 years, while the means of subsistence would increase in arithmetical progression, that is, far more slowly, over the same 25-year periods. Figure 8.1 presents a series of numbers that illustrates Malthus's thinking.

Geometric progression	1	2	4	8	16	32	64	128	256	Population growth
Arithmetic progression	1	2	3	4	5	6	7	8	9	Increase in the means of subsistence

Fig. 8.1 Geometric and arithmetic progression to demonstrate the thinking of Malthus

Figure 8.1 represents nine 25-year periods, i.e. 225 years, during which time, Malthus predicted, the population would grow 27 times more than the means of subsistence. In other words, the population would become unsustainable. Malthus described how insufficient nourishment would bring about not only hunger and death but also cannibalism, infanticide, slaughter of the old, war – fighting over land and food – and dreadful epidemics. He was a pessimist.

Malthus was taken seriously, partly because the population growth in some countries followed his predicted rates of growth. For instance, the population growth of the USA in the nineteenth century matched Malthus's predictions almost exactly, doubling roughly every 25 years from five million in 1800 to 80 million by 1905. However, when we look more deeply into the reasons for this growth we begin to see flaws in Malthus's theory, and we can begin to understand the complexity of the study of demography.

First, in Malthus's day, a family with six children was regarded as the norm. Child mortality and death from diseases were high so it was also normal to expect only four of the six children to survive to marriageable age. Malthus assumed that when they in turn became parents, the childbearing and survival trends would continue, giving his population growth rate that doubles every 25 years.

Immediately we can see that critical to the study of demography are the fertility or **birth rates** and the mortality or **death rates**, neither of which, for a variety of reasons, including social factors and medical advances, has followed Malthus's predictions (in most countries). Modern medicine has greatly reduced the risk of infant mortality, and improved diet and better housing conditions have enabled people to enjoy much healthier and longer lives. These and other social trends have led to smaller families. For parents to have as many as six children is unusual these days.

Why, then, did the population growth in the USA in the nineteenth century match Malthus's predictions? The main reason was **migration**, another critical factor in the study of demography. At that time the population growth in the USA resulted more from immigration than from a rising birth rate.

So we can now understand the complexity of demography, which requires the combined analyses of (a) birth rates (fertility), (b) death rates (mortality) and (c) migration. These are defined and described in more detail below. Adding to the complexity of this field of study is the influence of changes in society, religious and social customs, e.g. religious influences or social pressures to bear more (or fewer) children, which impinge on the three main elements of demography. Consequently, what has evolved is the study of sociodemographic trends – social trends and demographic trends being inseparable.

Before we look in more detail at how these various factors are interpreted and measured, it is useful to know why the study of sociodemographic trends is so important, for governments and businesses. But do not forget the legacy of Malthus. Despite the flaws in his theory he is generally regarded as the 'Father of the science of demography'. (It has been argued that his assumed rate of arithmetical progression for the 'means of subsistence' is also unsound as advances in agro-technology have changed the variety and ways in which much of our food is grown and produced – Malthus appeared to base much of his thinking on corn. Furthermore, our other sources of food, such as cattle, poultry and fish, actually reproduce at a much faster rate than humans do.)

The importance of sociodemography

The study of sociodemographic trends is vitally important to both government and business in order to forecast and plan for the future. Without planning, there would be chaos in society and wasted effort in business.

The importance for government

The government obtains revenue (its income) mainly from taxation. It also makes expenditures. Both are directly affected by sociodemographic trends. Examples include:

◆ **A falling birth rate**, requiring the government to plan for fewer schools (perhaps, to close schools) and for a decrease in the number of young people entering the labour force. A shortage of labour could hinder continuing economic growth.

◆ **A rising death rate** (meaning that people living longer), requiring the government to pay out more in state pensions, to provide more longer-term health care, nursing homes and so on.

◆ **Increases in divorce rates, single parent families and single aged surviving partners**, requiring the government and local governments to plan for more and smaller dwellings. Government housing policy must be changed accordingly.

The above are only a few of the major complex issues that governments need to tackle, but all stem from sociodemographic trends and forecasts. Planning for the future provision of pensions is a very serious issue, not confined to the UK, as illustrated by Exhibit 8.1.

The trends are even more pronounced in Japan, as indicated by the article reproduced in Exhibit 8.2. A long-term effect of these trends is that each member of the working population will have to support more non-working members than ever before. This is referred to as the 'dependency ratio'. Incidentally, in the Republic of Ireland the high birth rate, though it is falling, will delay the so-called 'pensions time bomb' for Ireland by about 25 years, leaving it well behind the rest of Europe.

The importance for businesses

Businesses, like governments, need to study sociodemographic trends in order to forecast and plan for the future. In particular, businesses will use sociodemography to:

◆ ascertain the size of a market;

◆ forecast market demand and changes in the pattern of demand for different goods and services;

Exhibit 8.1 Pensions

Pensions in Europe. What's the problem?

The European Commission seems to be getting very concerned about pensions provision within Europe. What's the problem?

The main problem is a falling birth rate. European pensioners get the bulk of their pension income from state schemes run on a pay-as-you-go (PAYG) basis. This means the money comes from taxation of people who are working. That is fine as long as the ratio of pensioners to workers is declining or static.

But longevity is increasing and birth rates are dropping, partly because generous state pensions support old people more comfortably than big families ever did. This means a shrinking number of working people have to support a growing number of elderly.

Currently there are four people of working age for every pensioner in the European Union. By 2040 it is estimated there will be just two. The result is a growing strain on some EU economies as the tax burden rockets.

Which countries are worst affected and why?

Those where birth rates have fallen, or are falling, from a relatively high base. The pain is intensified when a big proportion of pensioners' income is paid by state PAYG schemes. Countries in this group include Germany, Italy and France.

For example, Germany's state pension system was reportedly DM10bn (£3.5bn) in deficit in 1995, when contributions were increased to a steep 19.2 per cent of taxable earnings.

It may get worse. By 2030 pension payouts will have risen to a hefty 15 to 20 per cent of gross domestic product in all three countries if maintained at present levels.

Both France and Italy have cut state pensions and introduced measures to encourage more private provision. The cost was rioting in the streets and a watering down of the reforms.

Will the UK be affected too?

The bulge in the proportion of elderly in the population is not expected to strain the UK's public finances too badly. That is partly because the birth rate has not fallen heavily. Moreover state PAYG schemes account for a relatively small part of pensioners' income.

For example, the UK basic state pension is worth only 12 per cent of average adult male earnings. An equivalent German scheme is worth 60 per cent of average adult male earnings.

If state provision is so low, where do UK pensioners get their income?

Many get a big chunk of it from private funded pension schemes. The beauty of the schemes is that each new generation – typically with assistance from employers – provides for its own retirement by investing in tradeable assets, such as shares. These rise in value over time, reducing the amount of contributions required.

Bill Birmingham of the National Association of Pension Funds, a trade body, estimates the UK has £600bn in private pension assets, a huge bulwark against future needs. The Republic of Ireland and the Netherlands also have big funded pension systems, and are also thus relatively immune from the financial squeeze affecting some other EU nations.

What is the European Commission doing to sort out the problems of those states squeezed by big unfunded pension liabilities? The commission is making belated attempts to encourage them to increase funded provision. The greater the proportion of pensions that can be provided by this means, the lower the tax burden on future generations of workers to support pensioners. Are there any pitfalls? The snag of shifting from PAYG to a funded system is that one generation of workers has to pay twice: once through taxation used to pay pensions to their parents' generation; and once in contributions to their own retirement funds.

There is another difficulty with funded schemes. Governments can raid them – in a roundabout way – to finance public spending. The preferred method is to impose restrictions on pension funds' investments that force them to buy government bonds.

This captive market allows the government to lower its cost of borrowing at the expense of funds' long-term returns. Funded schemes can thereby become tributaries of a PAYG system.

For example, Belgium requires 15 per cent of pension fund assets to be in Belgian government bonds. Other states merely specify a percentage of assets that have to be held in the local currency, referred to as 'currency matching'. That has a similar effect, given the fondness of continental investment managers for sovereign bonds.

But isn't one of the main aims of the EU that capital should be able to slosh freely over national borders? Quite so. There are suggestions that the commission could challenge national investment restrictions through a test case in the European Court of Justice, in which it would argue they contravene the Treaty of Rome, on which the EU is founded.

Meanwhile, it has published a consultative document, which makes the case for freeing pension funds to seek the best rate of return on assets, both in the EU and outside it.

The paper suggests a system of prudential regulation for pension funds, with the aim of putting paid to member states' claims that investment restrictions are needed to protect funds from taking excessive risks. Legislation may follow.

Source: Guthrie, J. 'FT guide to: Pensions time bomb', *Financial Times*, 23 June 1997.

Exhibit 8.2

> # Elderly outnumber children
>
> Elderly citizens now outnumber children in Japan for the first time, the government said yesterday. A low birthrate and increased longevity were reflected in the number of Japan's elderly people exceeding the population of children under 15 by 50,000 from June 1, when there were 19.54m Japanese aged over 65, and 19.49m aged under 15.
>
> The trend is expected to continue and the number of elderly is likely to be double that of children by the year 2025, the official added.

Source: Financial Times, 27 June 1997. © Reuter.

◆ identify sources of labour supply and forecast changes in the labour market. For example, in the UK the number of young people entering the labour market is in decline whereas the number of those aged over 50 is increasing; thus many companies are changing their recruitment policies.

Marketing departments, in particular, use the categories used in demographic analysis as means of segmenting the market. Age is most widely used for segmentation purposes, but other variables that are used for identifying the segments of the market to target with particular products and services include sex (gender), family size, ethnicity, religion and family life cycle.

As you can see from examining advertisements for, say, clothes, cosmetics, breakfast cereals, alcoholic drinks, holidays, banking services, and so on, each product offering is carefully designed to suit the needs and wants of selected market segments, that is, particular groups of customers. Targeting enables companies to operate more efficiently and, invariably, customers are more satisfied – if not delighted – to find products that match their particular preferences.

Segmentation using demographic variables alone is rarely sufficient for understanding of a market. Market researchers combine the demographic variables with socioeconomic variables such as occupation, social class, income, education, etc. Indeed, some marketing academics and practitioners now include these variables in the field of demography. In addition, geographic location (such as, country, type of neighbourhood) and other methods of segmentation such as psychographic (which considers people's attitudes, opinions and interests) and in terms of behaviour are often used. However, the use of demographic variables remains popular, probably because of the ease of which demographic statistics can be obtained.

In the UK, the bases of demographic data are from the national census which compulsorily collects from every household such information as age, occupation, family size, etc. every ten years. National censuses have been carried out by the government since 1801 (with the exception of the year 1941). Some topics and questions change from census to census, e.g. those concerning migration, birthplace, journey to work, social class, ethnicity, etc. Questions concerning ethnicity have been omitted since 1981.

The government combines the data from each census with other records of births, marriages and deaths, etc., to conduct detailed analyses which are then published, mainly through the Office for National Statistics. Local governments use census data too, as illustrated in Exhibit 8.3.

In addition to the government's sociodemographic statistics, there are other useful (and sometimes alarming) sociodemographic statistics that are compiled and published by many independent research bodies. For instance, in 1997, the Joseph Rowntree Foundation published *Death in Britain*, which reveals that death rates in poorer areas are rising for the first time since the Victorian era, and that in the field of health, the inequalities gap is widening.

These findings highlight another valuable purpose of collecting demographic data and carrying out statistical analyses. New questions may be raised, prompting further research and revealing some startling findings, as illustrated by the article reproduced in Exhibit 8.4. Such findings can assist the government in formulating new health-care policies and effective preventative measures to improve the lives and life expectancy for all sectors of society.

In business, wherever there is change there are new business opportunities. Keeping up to date with the sociodemographic trends and forecasts is an essential activity not only in order to identify the new opportunities but also to avoid being surprised by a decline in current markets or other problems such as a shortage of labour.

Birth rates and fertility

The birth rate is the number of births for each 1000 persons in the population in a given year. Strictly speaking, it is an index and is the 'crude birth rate' – actually a measure of fertility. Demographers also refer to the 'general fertility rate' which is the number of children born for each 1000 women aged 15 to 44.

In demography, 'fertility' concerns the actual number of children born and not the potential capacity to bear children (that is 'fecundity'). Fertility is profoundly affected by numerous social and cultural variables, including:

◆ how widely contraceptives are used;

◆ the legality and acceptability of abortions when unwanted pregnancies occur;

◆ the extent to which sterilisation is performed;

◆ religious rules or customs that prohibit widows or divorced women from re-marrying;

◆ whether children are regarded as economic assets, as they often are in poorer countries where there are no state pensions;

Exhibit 8.3

Census figures revealed

Millions of facts about life in Leicestershire have been crammed into new information packs put together by County Hall.

The aim of the special packs is to put statistics from the 1991 national census at the fingertips of members of the public.

The easy-to-read summaries profile the county area by area and include figures on population size, age structure, ethnicity, employment and health.

Among the facts contained in the packs is that in Leicester, for example, some 1,851 households are without an indoor bathroom while countywide the total number is more than 3,500.

Other facts include

■ 45.4 per cent of households in Leicester do not have a car;

■ 1,008 single fathers countywide are bringing up their families on their own;

■ More than 72 per cent of Leicestershire households are owner-occupied. The national average is 67 per cent;

■ 89,837 men and women countywide suffer from long-term illness.

The county council uses the census data to define those parts of Leicestershire's population most in need.

Mr Keith Spilling, chief assistant of County Hall's research and information department, stressed the continuing importance of the census. 'It helps us to understand more about the county council's customers and therefore to better plan for their needs.'

The profile sheets are now available for reference at county libraries and the Leicestershire Record Office and can be bought for £5 each.

SINGLE PEOPLE

■ 5.7 per cent of households in Leicester and 3.3 per cent in Leicestershire are run by single parents.

■ 1,008 single fathers are bringing up their families on their own in Leicestershire, compared to 10,114 single mothers.

■ There are 2,098 pensioners aged 85 or over living on their own in Leicester, and 5,860 countywide.

AGE, OCCUPATION

■ THE largest age group countywide is between 30 to pensionable age, numbering 353,501.

■ Residents aged 75 plus make up the smallest age group, at 56,753.

■ Some 400,940 people are employed in Leicestershire.

■ There are 33,047 unemployed people in the county, of which 22,056 are male.

■ More women in Leicestershire (48,480) suffer a long-term illness, compared to 41,357 men.

AMENITIES

■ SOME 3,500 Leicestershire households are without an indoor bathroom.

■ Nearly 41,190 households countywide do not have central heating.

■ There are 134,034 households with more than six rooms in Leicestershire.

■ Some 12,455 households have just two rooms or less.

Source: Leicester Mercury, 27 October 1994. © Leicester Mercury, 1994; reprinted with permission.

Exhibit 8.4

Professionals 'lead healthier, longer lives'

People at the bottom of the social scale in the 1990s are still the most likely to suffer ill health and die young, according to a survey published yesterday.

Death rates for unskilled men are three times higher than for male professionals and managers. If working class men had the same death rates as those at the top, there would be 17,000 fewer deaths each year.

Although the gap in life expectancy between rich and poor is growing, we can all hope to live longer. Professioal men in England and Wales can expect to live to be 75 but labourers are likely to die five years younger.

Skilled women can hope to live to be 80 while unskilled women are expected to die at 77, says the Health Inequalities report from the Office for National Statistics.

The number of women dying from breast cancer has fallen significantly in the past 15 years. In the early 1980s, of every 100,000 women 74 professionals and 50 unskilled women died of breast cancer. Now there are 52 and 54 respectively.

Deaths from lung cancer are five times higher for men and three times higher for women in lower social classes. Unskilled workers are nearly three times more likely to admit to smoking than those with professional careers.

Among women, professionals consume on average more than twice as much alcohol as the unskilled. Men's propensity to drink alcohol does not seem to be related to their socio-economic status, as there are similar consumption patterns across classes.

But 11 per cent of unskilled men say they are non-drinkers compared with only 3 per cent of professionals.

As people at the bottom of the social scale tend to fall ill more often than others, they also visit their doctors more frequently.

But those at the top are more likely to take preventative measures. For example, 64 per cent of professionals regularly visit a dentist, compared with only 38 per cent of manual workers. There are similar patterns for eye tests.

The UK trend for longer life is repeated throughout western Europe. However, it is in stark contrast with many former Soviet countries, where life expectancy has started to fall.

Source: Simon Buckby, *Financial Times*, 9 September 1997.

◆ the existence of government policies, laws, tax exemptions or allowances which either encourage larger families or limit the number of children in each family as in the People's Republic of China.

Clearly, fertility, in demographic terms, not only concerns the biological facts but also is influenced by many social and cultural factors. So, when we examine birth rates, it is important to look at the facts behind the figures in order to put them in the context of the country or society to which they apply. The changes in cultural and social patterns should be identified. For instance, in Japan, there is a falling birth rate: one factor that is significant in this context is the growing trend for women to postpone marriage until their thirties. There is a similar trend in some other industrialised societies. Another factor that may significantly affect the birth rate is war. This causes a pause or a drop in the birth rate and then a post-war 'baby boom'.

Economic factors can also have a significant influence. During the Depression in the 1930s many couples postponed marriage and having children until the economic conditions improved.

Mortality rates

In the study of demography, mortality is measured most simply by the 'crude death rate', that is, the number of deaths in a given period for each 1000 persons in the population.

As with the birth rate, the figure by itself could be misleading if it is not put into the proper context of the social, cultural and economic factors that affect the society to which the figure refers. Of course, death cannot be avoided. The variables that impinge on this biological fact include the following:

◆ the degree of willingness to risk death, for example, by going to war;

◆ infanticide (which is still practised in some societies);

◆ euthanasia (which is legally available in the Netherlands, for example);

◆ natural disasters such as floods, earthquakes, typhoons, crop failure and famine. (Famines still occur in the modern world, for example, in North Korea);

◆ the current age composition of the society: if the proportion of older people is high, as in Japan, the crude death rate will be higher than that for a country where the proportion of young people is high.

The above factors, and possibly others, need to be considered and taken into account before comparing the mortality rates of different countries. The figures by themselves do not enable much meaningful comparison.

Demographers therefore calculate mortality rates for specific age groups and attempt to standardise the figures, eliminating the distortions that are caused by the differing age composition of different countries. Mortality in different countries can then be compared more fairly.

Migration

Since immigration adds to the population and emigration subtracts from it, migration must be taken into account when analysing other demographic data. An immigrant is a person who comes to reside permanently in a country, other than his or her native land. An emigrant is a person who leaves his or her native country to settle in another.

In the UK, the 'net migration', that is, the difference between the numbers immigrating and emigrating, is small. So the net effect of migration on the size of the population is not great. Marriage, as a source of immigration, continues to be important as the right of entry is given to a fiancée or spouse to join a partner already settled in the UK, even though the immigration rules are being applied more strictly than in the past.

Migration as a demographic variable is easy to understand. What is not so easy is to forecast the movements of people from one country to another. In fact, such movement is very difficult to predict. If we look back to what happened in the past, we see that sometimes huge migrations took place. For example, about 60 million people emigrated from Europe to America and other countries in the nineteenth century. In more recent times there was a sudden influx of immigrants to the UK from the New Commonwealth, to beat a change in the UK's immigration laws. Perhaps such an influx was predictable, but 11 years later there were a large number of immigrants from Uganda, Asians escaping from political persecution from Idi Amin. In 1997, there was concern that there might be another rush of immigrants from Hong Kong so the British government revised the laws to restrict the right of residence in the UK to only a tiny percentage of the Hong Kong population.

Post-war immigration to the UK has altered the national sociodemographic patterns quite significantly. Sizeable communities of non-white and non-Christian people, many of whom did not have English as their first language, have been created, adding new and interesting dimensions to British society and the study of demography.

Further resources

Demography

General

United Nations Population Fund (UNFPA), 220 East 42nd Street, New Street, NY 10017.

The Economist and quality daily and Sunday newspapers. Current affairs programmes on television and radio.

Further reading

Chaliand, G. and Rageau, J-P. (1995) *The Penguin Atlas of Diasporas*. New York: Viking Penguin.

Coleman, D. (1996) *Europe's Population in the 1990s*. Oxford: Oxford University Press.

Dorling, D. (1997) *Death in Britain*. London: Joseph Rowntree Foundation.

Ehrlich, P. (1971) *The Population Bomb*. London: Pan Books.

Maddox, J. (1972) *The Doomsday Syndrome*. London: Macmillan.

Office for National Statistics (1997a) *Annual Abstract of Statistics*. London: The Stationery Office.

Office for National Statistics (1997b) *Social Trends 27*. London: The Stationery Office. (For the first time, this annual volume contains a valuable section entitled, 'Projections: a look into the future').

Purdie, Elizabeth (ed.) (1996) *Guide to Official Statistics*. London: HMSO.

Schoon, N. 'The world won't be overcrowded after all', *The Independent*, 12 January 1998.

Internet addresses

United Nations Population Fund (UNFPA): http://www.unfpa.org

The Sierra Club: http://www.sieraclub.org

Dr Paul Ehrlich: http://www.pbs.org/kqed/population_bomb/bio.html

KZPG: What does KZPG mean?

http://www.iti.com/iti/kzpg/current/kzpg/kzpg.html#stop

World population trends

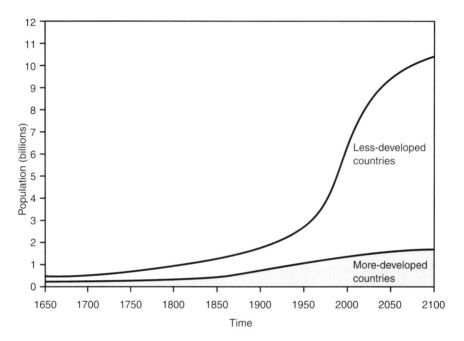

Fig. 8.2 World population growth

Source: Author's projection based on various sources.

Figure 8.2 illustrates the increase in the world's population over the past 200 years or so, and its projected expansion to the year 2100. From the graph, several important points can be noted:

1 The population has doubled, roughly, over the past 35 years.

2 The world population is now around six billion.

3 Most of the expansion is attributable to the much higher rates of population growth in less-developed countries.

4 In advanced countries, population growth is levelling off and may be declining.

Is the world over-populated?

Numerous pessimistic 'environmentalist' forecasters believe that even today's world population of nearly six billion is unsustainable, let alone any further expansion. Some say that the optimal human population of our planet is about two billion and argue that nature will take its course to reduce the current 'over-population'. They point to the dozens of new diseases and epidemics that suddenly appear and sometimes spread rapidly, such as Human Immunodeficiency Virus (HIV) which can lead to Acquired Immunodeficiency Syndrome (AIDS), and Bovine Spongiform Encephalopathy (BSE) (the so-called Mad Cow Disease) which is now linked to the (to date) incurable brain disease Creutzfeldt–Jakob Disease (CJD). These viruses were identified in the 1980s. The unpredictability of whether such viruses will grow to become major epidemics is worrying. For example, whereas another deadly virus, the Ebola, from Zaire, was identified in the late 1970s and appears to have been since contained – reported deaths numbering 'only' several hundred – AIDS has become a major worldwide epidemic, now infecting tens of millions of people, most of them in Africa. The nature and likely effects of BSE/CJD and other new infectious diseases are yet to be fully evaluated.

Other deadly bacteria such as *enterococci*, *pneumococci* and *streptococci* have recently developed resistance to conventional antibiotic treatments. There are others that are also proving to be resistant. One of major concern among microbiologists is Methicillin-Resistant *Staphylococcus Aureus* (MRSA), a bacterium that exists in three completely different strains, is resistant to most antibiotics and strikes in the intensive care and surgical wards of hospitals. It has occurred in at least 190 hospitals in Britain, France and the USA in the 1990s and has been termed 'the silent epidemic' as MRSA is not usually given as the cause of death on death certificates. Instead, a side-effect of the infection is specified as the cause of death.

In view of the problems mentioned above, which necessarily must be taken into account in some way by demographic forecasters, it is possible to feel some understanding for those who are arguing that 'nature will take its course' to reduce the world population.

The influential environmentalist group 'The Sierra Club,' California, and the leading campaigner Dr Paul Ehrlich of Stanford University and author of *The Population Bomb*, first published in the USA in 1968 (*see* Further resources) also argue that the world's population of nearly six billion people and/or its further expansion is unsustainable because of the consequent damage to the ecology – by means of pollution, soil erosion, the depletion of natural resources and the extinction of species of wildlife.

However, one can always find equally credible reports and forecasts to support the opposite view, e.g. John Maddox, then editor of *Nature*, in 1972 through his book *The Doomsday Syndrome* and more recently, the United Nations Organisation (UN) has suggested that in the Third World alone a population of 32 billion would be sustainable if high-yield farming techniques similar to those used in North America were employed. This view is based on the actual increases in yields achieved in some developing countries where three-, four-, or five-fold increases have occurred in as many recent decades (e.g. India). In contrast, other parts of the world (e.g. most countries in Africa) have vast tracts of under-used, low-yielding land. This suggests, in short, that the world's problem is not over-population but backward farming techniques. This author advises against use of the term 'Third World', preferring the more precise 'advanced' or 'developed', 'newly industrialised' and 'less developed'.

Other factors to consider when looking at the 'over-population' question are the following:

1 Countries that have high population density are more prosperous.

2 A country's economic growth seems to be sustainable only when there is a continuing increase in its population: children appear to be one critical resource for a country's economic development, growth and prosperity.

3 Fertility rates are much higher in the less developed countries. However, as more children are surviving (through improved medical and health facilities), parents are having fewer children, that is, the fertility rates are declining. This factor is especially significant as it is the main reason for an expected stabilisation of population in the developing world in the twenty-first century.

The above discussion of world population trends provides an outline of the views and arguments put forward by the pessimistic 'environmentalists' and by one organisation, the UN, which takes a different view. Other bodies such as the World Bank, the Asian Development Bank and OECD also have evidence, forecasts and policies on population growth or on curbing population growth.

The article reproduced in Exhibit 8.5 provides statistics and further details that are relevant to the preceding discussion. Note that the United Nations Fund for Population Activities (UNFPA) forecasts a total number of people in 2050 of 10 billion, but it points out that, by applying other assumptions (a difficulty confronting every demographic forecaster), the total in 2050 could be anything between 7.8 billion and 12.5 billion.

Exhibit 8.5

A host of future problems – Population

Alarm and hope: those are governments' twin reactions to the latest batch of projections from the United Nations on how many people will be occupying the planet in the next century. One message behind the figures is that high population growth in developing countries remains a threat to their prosperity, and through migration, to that of developed countries as well. But other messages are that growing populations need not represent the apocalypse which has been predicted by many, and that there is much governments can do to slow down the increase.

This month's UN conference on population and development in Cairo, the first to tackle the contentious subject for a decade, stirred up controversy on many fronts. The Vatican formally registered its reservations to nearly half the chapters in the final text, on the grounds that it condoned abortion as a form of contraception. The UN Population Fund (UNFPA), which organised the conference, denied that the text had that interpretation, but several Catholic countries in Latin America also lodged reservations to sections.

However, despite an informal alliance between the Vatican and Moslem governments in the run-up to Cairo, governments achieved a much greater degree of agreement at Cairo on responses to the threat

Exhibit 8.5 continued

of population growth than seemed possible at the previous UN conferences in 1984 or 1974. The final document set a target for annual spending on family planning of $17bn a year by 2000, from national programmes and international aid, which marks a threefold increase on present levels.

Most governments acknowledged at Cairo that it is in their own interest to take steps to help people limit the sizes of their families, given the formidable projections of the world's population. According to the UNFPA's annual report, published in August, the total is set to reach a sobering 10bn by the middle of the next century, up from 5.7bn at present.

The UNFPA's projection assumes that the average number of children born to each woman will continue to fall, as it has done for several decades; other assumptions, only slightly different, produce estimates of the total number of people in 2050 between 7.8bn and 12.5bn.

These increases will put increasing strains on natural resources of all kinds, both global resources, such as the atmosphere and seas, and regional. Water, in particular, may prove 'an increasing cause of friction' between countries and regions, the UNFPA suggests.

The implications of these projections for the distribution of wealth between countries and continents are also considerable. The World Bank estimates, in a report released ahead of Cairo, that 61 per cent of the world's population will live in countries with per capita incomes of below $350 a year (in 1990 money values). That compares with 57 per cent in 1985. Over the same period, the proportion of people living in countries with per capita incomes over $19,590 will

fall from 16 per cent to 11 per cent.

Moreover, the bank warns that by 2100, 10 out of 11 people will live in the developing world, compared to four out of five at present, and two out of three in 1950. Much of the increase will come in Africa: the present annual growth in the continent's population of 2.9 per cent a year is the highest in the world. That rate outstrips by some way the annual Asian and Latin American growth of less than 2 per cent, according to the UNFPA.

Within developing countries, people will drift to the cities in search of jobs, prompted by competition for land and water in rural areas. The World Bank estimates that in 2025, 57 per cent of the population in developing countries will live in cities, compared to less than half now.

As a result of those pictures, developed countries should prepare to face growing pressures for immigration, the bank warns. As their populations are growing slowly, they should expect their share of the world's population to shrink. While North America's population is edging up at 1 per cent a year, the rate is only 0.5 per cent a year in the former Soviet Union and 0.3 per cent a year in western Europe.

Meanwhile, their populations are ageing: the UNFPA expects the proportion of people aged 65 and over in indusrialised countries to rise from the present 12.7 per cent to 18.4 per cent by 2025.

To set against those threats, UN figures provide some ammunition to counter fears of a global food shortage, of the kind voiced by the 'Club of Rome' school of forecasters some 20 years ago. The UNFPA observes that 'during the past 10 years, the world's food production has increased by 24 per cent, outpacing

the rate of population growth'.

But the improvement in food production has been unevenly distributed, the UNFPA also points out. In Africa, food production fell by 5 per cent while population rose by a third. While the UN maintains that food supplies 'should be sufficient to meet all needs for the foreseeable future', the poorer regions and countries will face severe shortages.

Reason to worry, then; but the past two decades also provide grounds for hope that governments can help bring down population growth rates. Most developing countries – even, in the past few years, those in sub-Saharan Africa – have seen fertility rates fall.

According to UNFPA officials, a decade ago many African countries saw growing populations as a useful tool to increase prosperity. Now, seeing the growth jeopardise the fruits of investment in health, education, infrastructure and agriculture, they are showing a greater readiness to promote family planning.

The UNFPA says that governments now appreciate that making contraception more widely available helps bring down fertility rates, even if economic development has been slow. Demographers' new message is that if people are given the means to control the number of children they have, even in the poorest countries they frequently choose to have fewer.

The past decade has shown governments the threat which uncurbed population growth can pose to prosperity. But it has also helped generate confidence among governments that growth rates can be tackled, and broad agreement on ways to do that.

Source: Bronwen Maddox, *Financial Times*, 30 September 1994.

Whereas the general consensus of opinion among demographers is that the world's population will level off, in the next century, at around 11 billion (*see* Figure 8.2) the population may stabilise at a lower figure of about 10 billion. At the time of going to press in 1998, the UN is about to publish new long-range forecasts that give a figure of 9.4 billion (medium variant) by 2050, and 10.4 billion by 2100.

Exhibit 8.6

Can Europe compete?
Ageing Europe

20 points about ageing in Europe

1 Two out of three over-65s who have ever lived are alive today.

2 There are around 330m people aged 65 or over alive today. By 2050 there will be 1.4bn.

3 The world's oldest country is Sweden: 18 per cent of Swedes are 65 or over.

4 The average European woman of child-bearing age produces 1.7 children. Around 2.1 children are required to replace the population.

5 If Germany's fertility rate remains at its current level (1.3) its native population will be extinct within 300 years.

6 Ireland and Iceland are the only western European countries with fertility rates high enough to sustain their populations.

7 The country with the lowest fertility rate in western Europe is Italy.

8 Europeans currently account for almost a tenth of the world's population. In 2050 they will be less than a fifth.

9 The number of over-65s in Europe will outstrip the number of children aged 14 and under around 2020.

10 More than 50m western Europeans are aged 65 or over – almost 15 per cent of the population.

11 Of these, almost a quarter are aged 80 or over and 1⅛m are 90-plus.

12 By 2050 there will be 70m western European aged 65-plus – over 20 per cent of the population.

13 A man living in the European Union aged 60 can expect to live until 78; a woman until 82½.

14 Almost half the over-80s in the EU live alone.

15 There are roughly equal numbers of men and women aged 60 in western Europe. But women outnumber men two-to-one between 80 and 84 and three-to-one between 90 and 94.

16 Less than 5 per cent of EU people in their sixties are severely incapacitated. Almost one in three in their eighties is incapacitated.

17 Over-60s in the EU would prefer to be called 'senior citizens' or 'older people', according to a Eurobarmeter survey. They do not like to be called 'elderly', 'pensioners' or 'golden oldies'.

18 Real economic growth rates of up to 1.5 per cent a year are needed to pay the increasing bill for pensions over the next 15 years – more if pensions are to rise with earnings.

19 Public health spending for people aged 65 and over is more than four times higher per capita than for the under 65s.

20 Almost 80 per cent of EU citizens believe that those in employment have a duty to ensure, through contributions or taxes, that older people have a decent standard of living.

Sources: OECD, UN, 3rd Age Marketing
Source: *Financial Times*, 8 March 1994.

Chapter summary

This chapter has explained how demography and sociodemography evolved, and their main elements. It also looked at why the study of sociodemographic trends is so important for governments and businesses to enable them to forecast and plan for the future.

Particular attention has been paid to the major issues currently causing concern, including the ageing of the population in Europe and the looming crisis of funding pensions and healthcare for the elderly.

The chapter also discussed world population trends and illustrates some of the difficulties of forecasting.

Assignment

Undertake one of the following assignments.

1 With reference to Exhibits 8.1 and 9.1 and through your own additional library research on Britain's ageing population, write a report that will lead to, and include, recommendations on what decisions the government should take to overcome the coming pensions crisis. You may wish to comment on the adequacy or inadequacy of any recent government decisions in this area.

2 With reference to Exhibits 8.1 and 9.1 and through your own additional library research on Britain's ageing population, write a report that identifies the growth areas and new opportunities for businesses in the financial services.

9

Social trends

Chapter objectives

By the time you have read this chapter you should:

◆ be able to describe the most significant recent changes and trends in UK society, in other words, in our lifestyles;

◆ understand the main implications of those changes and trends in terms of
  - the looming problems in the next century;
  - the need for both business and government organisations to plan for them;

◆ know how to obtain further detailed information on social trends.

Introduction

Social trends concern how living in the UK has been changing. From analysis of these trends, projections and forecasts about aspects of life in the future can be made. Much of the evidence comes from the sociodemographic research and analyses as described in Chapter 8.

The range of topics and details available seems almost infinite so a somewhat pragmatic approach has been taken, leading to the selection of just seven main areas and the highlighting of some of the notable trends in each area. The seven areas are:

a population;
b households and families;
c housing;
d labour force and employment;
e income and wealth;
f expenditure and leisure;
g crime.

For more details on the topics in this chapter, or on other related topics, you are recommended to refer to the publications listed in 'Further resources:

Social trends' later in this chapter. Among the publications listed, *Social Trends*, now in its 27th edition (1997) is probably the best source of official statistics on the changes in British life, but always bear in mind that these, being *official* statistics, may tend to accentuate the positive, such as annual increases in average disposable incomes, whereas figures concerning, say, poverty and inequality are given less prominence. Official statistics, therefore, ought to be read in conjunction with results of other surveys conducted by non-governmental organisations such as, for example, the Institute for Community Studies, the Joseph Rowntree Foundation, and marketing research organisations – Gallup, MORI, NOP, etc. Other independent organisations, including charities and pressure groups, are also sources of interesting statistics. However, always read survey results with a questioning mind, asking yourself, for example: Does the organisation have an axe to grind? What was the size of the sample in the survey? Is the sample representative of the population quoted in the survey? How was the survey conducted? Were the questions biased?

Very often, statistics have been used to mislead and so Disraeli's statement, 'There are lies, damned lies and statistics' has become famous and is often quoted.

Population

The UK has demographic trends quite similar to those of other western countries, characterised in the twentieth century by low birth rates (apart from the post-war baby boom) and low death rates and, overall, a low growth rate in the total population. Table 9.1 shows figures for the UK, other European countries and the rest of the world.

The most significant trend is longer life expectancy. In the UK, average life expectancy has increased from 47.6 years in 1900 to 73 years in 1989. As shown in Table 9.1, it increased further to reach 74 for males and 79 for females in 1996. That represents, roughly, an increase of one year of life expectancy for every three years that has passed, this century, and this trend is continuing. (Can you now work out your own life expectancy?) But these figures are averages so, of course, many people are living longer than the average and more are reaching their one-hundredth birthday. In 1959, the Queen sent telegrams to about 400 people when they reached the age of 100. By 1996, the number of telegrams had increased to around 3000!

The decline in the UK mortality rate is due to a range of factors including better diet and housing, improvements in medical treatments, higher levels of education and increases in real income levels and in social welfare support.

Low mortality rates, coupled with low birth rates, results in an ageing population for the UK, as touched upon in Chapter 8. This consequence has serious implications for government expenditure on health care and pensions in the future.

However, the problems should not be exaggerated. Exhibit 9.1 explains the issues objectively and suggests that the problems are less than daunting, with the exception of those concerning the issue of how to care for the very elderly – those over 85.

Table 9.1 World population

	Population (millions)		1995–2000				Life expectancy	
	1996	2025	Growth rate (percentages)	Population per hectare of arable land	Infant mortality[1]	Total period fertility rate[2]	Males	Females
Europe	727.7	718.2	0.1	–	12	1.6	69	77
European Union								
Austria	8.0	8.3	0.4	10	6	1.6	74	80
Belgium	10.1	10.4	0.3	–	6	1.7	74	81
Denmark	5.2	5.1	0.1	8	7	1.7	73	79
Finland	5.1	5.4	0.4	14	5	1.9	73	80
France	58.2	61.2	0.4	8	7	1.7	74	81
Germany	81.8	76.4	–	14	6	1.3	74	80
Greece	10.5	9.9	0.2	23	9	1.4	76	81
Irish Republic	3.6	3.9	0.3	8	7	2.1	73	79
Italy	57.2	52.3	–	19	7	1.3	75	81
Luxembourg	0.4	0.4	1.4	–	6	1.7	73	80
Netherlands	15.6	16.3	0.6	26	6	1.6	75	81
Portugal	9.8	9.7	–	39	9	1.6	72	79
Spain	39.7	37.6	0.1	12	7	1.2	75	81
Sweden	8.8	9.8	0.4	10	5	2.1	76	82
United Kingdom	58.4	61.5	0.3	6	6	1.8	74	79
Northern & Southern Europe								
Albania	3.5	4.7	1.0	142	26	2.7	70	76
Bosnia & Herzegovina	3.5	4.5	4.5	–	13	1.6	70	76
Croatia	4.5	4.2	–0.3	–	9	1.6	68	76
Estonia	1.5	1.4	–0.5	–	16	1.6	64	75
Latvia	2.5	2.3	–0.7	–	14	1.6	63	75
Lithuania	3.7	3.8	–	–	13	1.8	65	76
Macedonia	2.2	2.6	0.8	–	24	2.0	70	76
Norway	4.4	4.7	0.4	22	7	2.0	74	81
Slovenia	1.9	1.8	–	–	7	1.5	69	78
Switzerland	7.3	7.8	0.8	11	6	1.7	75	8.2
Yugoslavia (former)	10.9	11.5	–0.3	31	18	2.0	70	75
Eastern Europe	308.2	299.4	–0.1	–	17	1.6	64	74
North America	295.7	369.6	0.9	–	7	2.1	74	80
Canada	29.8	38.3	1.0	1	6	1.9	75	81
United States	265.8	331.2	0.9	1	7	2.1	73	80
Africa	748.1	1,495.8	2.7	–	85	5.3	53	56
Asia	3,513.2	4,960.0	1.5	–	57	2.9	65	68
Of which: China	1,234.3	1,526.1	1.0	155	38	2.0	68	72
Latin America and Caribbean	490.4	709.8	1.7	–	41	2.8	67	72
Oceania	29.0	41.0	1.4	–	24	2.5	71	76
Of which: Australia	18.3	24.7	1.2	–	6	1.9	75	81
New Zealand	3.6	4.4	1.0	2	8	2.1	73	79
World	5,804.1	8,294.3	1.5	–	57	3.0	64	68
More developed[3]	1,170.7	1,238.4	0.3	–	9	1.7	71	79
Less developed[3]	4,633.4	7,055.9	1.8	–	63	3.3	62	65

1 Per thousand live births.

2 The average number of children who would be born per woman if women experienced the age-specific fertility rates of the reference years throughout their child-bearing span.

3 More developed: Europe, North America, Australia, New Zealand and Japan. Less developed: Africa, Latin America, Asia (excluding Japan) and Melanesia, Micronesia and Polynesia.

Source: United Nations.

Source: Office of National Statistics (1997).

Social Trends 27. London: The Stationery Office. © Crown Copyright.

Exhibit 9.1

Survey – Third Age: A time bomb ticking gently

Demography is scarcely the stuff of dramatic headlines. Yet the fact that the proportion of elderly people in the UK population is reliably projected to increase over the next 40 years is a matter of great importance. Such long-run trends can have a powerful impact, inter alia, on house prices, patterns of saving and consumption, and the public finances. Reduced rates of fertility and mortality have led to suggestions that Britain confronts a demographic time bomb.

The fears are exaggerated, although the underlying picture is indeed one of pensioners accounting for a growing proportion of the population. In the year 2000 there will be around 3.4 people of working age for every one of pensionable age. That ratio is projected by the government actuary to decline only marginally by 2020. It then falls significantly, as the post-war baby boom generation reaches retirement, to around 2.4 by 2040. The ability to support this increase in the elderly population will depend partly on trends in employment and labour force participation; also on productivity growth in the economy. It will be easier for the young to look after the growing army of old people if most of the younger generation is in employment and the economy is growing.

That said, Britain has gone through the ageing process much earlier than the other leading industrialised countries. A higher proportion of its adult population was over 65 at the start of the present decade. But the trend is about to change. By 2040 Britain is projected to have more people of working age relative to those in retirement than any other OECD country apart from Ireland.

The immediate policy implication arises from the fact that UK pensioners depend on the state for a majority of their incomes. An older population also requires more expenditure on healthcare. So there is inevitable upward pressure on public spending. But how much?

Mr John Hills of the London School of Economics has taken the projected age structure of the British population in 2041 and calculated what would happen to average spending per head at the government's 1991–92 spending levels. The answer is a 17 per cent rise, equivalent to 3.8 per cent of gross domestic product.

In practice, that is less than daunting. Assuming that key determinants of welfare spending such as benefit levels and health workers' pay were maintained in relation to incomes in general, ageing by itself would imply growth in public spending of a mere 0.32 per cent per annum.

The explanation for this apparently low figure lies partly in the erosion of state pension benefits under the Tories. In continental Europe the problem of ageing is all about how to finance continuing high levels of benefit when budgets are already heavily stretched. In the UK, the financial problem is less pressing. To the extent that ageing poses a problem, it relates to the growing inequality of pensioner incomes and a looming crisis of need. The challenge for the new Labour government will be to find ways of extending private pension provision at an acceptable cost to the lower paid. There is, however, one area where demographic pressure really is severe in the UK. The government actuary has estimated that the proportion of over-85s in the population will rise progressively from 1.9 per cent in 1995, to 2.4 per cent in 2011, to more than 5 per cent in 2056. Between a quarter and a third of people over 85 are in institutional care. It follows that the bills for looking after the very elderly will rise substantially. That, too, presents a challenge to the government, since private insurance has signally failed to provide a solution in other countries such as the United States. The implications of demography for personal savings and investment are related to behaviour over the life cycle. The young and the old tend to spend more than they save. The middle aged save more, as they approach retirement.

In today's global capital markets this no longer has a huge impact on the level of real interest rates in the UK, or on equity prices. In housing, however, where supply and demand are largely domestic, demography will exert a powerful downward pull on the market in the early 21st century. This is because ageing post-war baby-boomers will have ceased to bid up prices. But demography is not just about financial trouble. The existence of an enlarged elderly population creates the scope for more service jobs in the economy. And the elderly will be looking not just for care, but for life-enhancing leisure opportunities, too.

Source: John Plender, *Financial Times*, 31 May 1997.

There will be large increases in the numbers of very elderly people, and there are numerous problems, as yet unresolved, about caring for them.

As can be seen from Table 9.1, low or even negative population growth rates are found in most developed countries, whereas high growth rates are common in the less developed countries – *see*, for example, the figures for Africa, Latin America and the Caribbean. We can now see that in the developed parts of the world the population is more or less stable whereas the population in the other parts of the world is growing fast. This is a cause for concern.

Households and families

Notable changes in households and families in recent decades are increases in cohabitation and in the number of people divorced. Whereas cohabitation is not expected to increase much in the future, the number of divorced could double from around 7 per cent of the adult population in 1990 to 14 per cent in 2020 if present trends continue.

The most notable trends, however, concern the number and average size of house-holds, as the number is projected to increase at a significantly faster rate than the population in the next 20 years while the average household size is expected to continue to fall. A household is defined as one person living alone or a group of people who share common housekeeping, that is, sharing at least one meal a day or a living room. Note, therefore, the difference between a household and dwelling. A dwelling can house more than one household.

Housing

The trend towards smaller households (the average size of 2.91 in 1971 shrank to 2.4 in 1995 and is continuing to shrink), plus the large stock of older houses that will need replacing in due course, is creating a strong demand for new houses. Government forecasts show that 4.4 million new homes will be needed by the year 2016. (*See* Exhibit 9.2.)

The issue of major concern is 'Where will the houses be built?' Even though the (previous) government set a target of 50 per cent of new housing development to be on 'brown-field' sites (that is, previously developed land) there remains the other 50 per cent, to be built on 'green-field' sites, and sadly, it seems these must include Green Belt land, for example, that around Stevenage in Hertfordshire and around Milton Keynes – which is currently proposing to double its size.

Regular reading of quality newspapers will enable you to follow the housing debate. Note the conflicting interests of government and town planners, residents near proposed development sites, landowners, house-building firms (represented by the House Builders Federation) and pressure groups such as the Council for the Protection of Rural England, and Friends of the Earth.

Exhibit 9.2

Gummer lays foundations for national housing debate

The government says 4.4m new homes will soon be needed, and it wants the environmental issues to be considered

The government yesterday launched what it hopes will be a 'great national debate' on where to put the 4.4m new households it says are needed for England during the next 20 years.

'We who live on a small island have nowhere to hide,' Mr John Gummer, the environment secretary, told the annual conference of the Royal Town Planning Institute. 'So let's accept the need for a real debate on the central issues of household formation and the impact on demand for new homes.'

Mr Gummer's call reflects concern in the Department of the Environment about fraught planning conflicts ahead if local authorities try to resist government projections on the need for new homes.

One such battle has already been fought in Berkshire, with Mr Gummer forcing the county council to make provision for more housing than it was proposing in its structure plan. At least four other counties are drawing up plans, and some may again seek to challenge Mr Gummer's figures.

The projections involve about a 20 per cent increase in the number of households by the year 2016. However, percentages disguise the sheer volume of new homes needed, particularly in the south-east where most counties are projected to gain at least 120,000 new households, as are Greater Manchester and West Yorkshire in the north.

Mr Gummer wants local planning authorities to accept as given his department's projections for new homes, and concentrate instead on where to put them. He pointed to the fact that virtually all previous projections have proved too low, not too high. 'We have to face up to the fact that very large numbers of new homes will be needed soon, and deliberate sensibly on the consequences,' he said.

In historic terms the figures mark a continuation of the sharp increase in household numbers over and above population growth which started in the 1920s and has seen the number of households double during the past 60 years.

The growth of one-person households is the driving force. In 1991 there were 5.1m of them; by 2016 there are projected to be 8.6m, two-fifths of them of people who have never married. Mr Gummer, a firm proponent of traditional 'family values', nevertheless regards these demographic projections as the essential basis for policy planning.

Mr Gummer's initiative comes at a time of growing consensus about many elements in planning policy. From local councillors to national strategists, most engaged in planning future development agree that the future lies in more efficient recycling of built land, eschewing big new rural settlements on the lines of the post-war 'new towns'.

The government has set a target of 50 per cent of new housing development to be on previously developed land. Last month it claimed to have achieved 49 per cent, years ahead of target. But that still leaves another 50 per cent, and environmental groups want to see a far higher 'recycling' target. Mr Tony Burton, the head of planning at the Council for the Protection of Rural England, the pressure group, said the existing target 'undervalues the environment gain from urban renewal'.

Mr Burton is adamant that even modest-scale new settlements could cause serious environmental harm. 'The self-sufficient new settlement is a chimera in a densely populated country like England where car travel is so cheap and people are travelling further to work and shop.'

Other issues set to feature in Mr Gummer's debate include urban amenities, out-of-town developments, and the role and provision of new social housing.

Many of the protagonists, however, continue to question the government's household projections. Mr Gummer's immediate challenge is to persuade local planners and environmentalists to accept his ground rules.

Source: Andrew Adonis, *Financial Times*, 6 June 1996.

Social trends

Further reading

Huff, D. (1991) *How to Lie with Statistics*. London: Penguin Books.

Office of National Statistics (1997) *Annual Abstract of Statistics* (ed.: Daniel Wisniewski).
London: The Stationery Office.

Office of National Statistics (1997) *Social Trends 27*. London: The Stationery Office.
(For the first time, this edition contains a valuable section entitled 'Projections: a look into
the future'.)

Purdie, Elizabeth (ed.) (1996) *Guide to Official Statistics*. London: HMSO.

Newspapers

The Economist

Financial Times

Guardian

Labour force and employment

Changes in the labour force can result from the changing size of the population,
changes in the age structure, and/or from changes in economic activity rates.
(Economic activity rates measure the percentage of the population in the labour
force, either working or looking for work.)

In the UK, the workforce is growing and over the ten-year period from 1996 to 2006
it is forecast to increase from 25.8 million to nearly 27 million.

Changes in the age structure, that is, the ageing of the population, is causing
another trend, a rise in the proportion of older people in the workforce together
with a decrease in the proportion of younger people in the workforce. In the ten-
year period 1996–2006, the forecast is that the workforce will comprise 1.8 million
more people aged 35 to 54, 0.8 million more aged 55 and over, whereas there will be
1.2 million fewer people aged under 35.

Employment trends, current and projected to 2006, show marked declines in
employment in the manufacturing, primary and utilities sectors, and increases in
the services industries (for example, education, health, financial and business services, hotels and catering, retailing, etc.). Other significant trends are a decrease in
the number of full-time jobs and an increase in the number of part-time jobs and in
self-employment; it is also forecast that more people will be employed in smaller
firms. Unskilled jobs are in decline whereas there is, and will be, an increased
demand for people with skills and higher qualifications for managerial, professional and technical jobs. According to the British Chambers of Commerce, there is
a growing shortage of skilled workers, and small firms are bemoaning a lack of
skilled managers and sales people.

Unemployment

There is a problem in comparing one year's figures with those of another year, as successive British governments have made so many changes to the methods of measuring unemployment. About 14 such changes were made by the previous (Conservative) government in the years 1979–1997. At the time of writing, unemployment is measured by the number of people actually claiming benefit, and in December 1997 this figure was just over 1.4 million, or approximately 5 per cent of the workforce (the lowest level since 1980), down from around 8 per cent in 1995. Bearing in mind the difficulties of comparing one year's unemployment rate with that of another year, we can summarise the trend over the last 50 years by saying that unemployment in the UK drifted up from around 3 per cent in the 1950s to 5 per cent in the 1970s when it soared to 10 per cent or more in the 1980s, declining as a general trend through the 1990s.

Income and wealth

Official statistics show that the British are becoming wealthier. Average household incomes (after deducting tax, national insurance and pension scheme contributions) have increased by 75 per cent or more over the past two decades. Example figures presented in Table 9.2 reveal dramatic increases.

Table 9.2 Weekly pay for non-manual male workers and for factory workers

	Average 1938	Average 1971	Average 1990
Non-manual male workers	–	£38.50	£354.90
Factory workers	£3.55[a]	–	£229.87[b]

[a] Average hours worked: 47.8 hours per week.
[b] Average hours worked: 43.4 hours per week.

The increase in pay for non-manual male workers, after inflation, represents a real increase of about 80 per cent. Incidentally, in relation to the average hours worked per week by factory workers, generally the British work longer hours than our counterparts in the rest of Europe.

To put the real increases in pay into context, it is useful to examine how much work time is needed to earn enough to buy food and other selected items. Table 9.3 presents some examples.

Table 9.3 Minutes of work time needed (married man working) to buy selected items

	1971	1990	2000 (estimated by author)
Pint of milk	5	3	2
One dozen eggs	22	12	9
Pint of beer	14	11	9
Loaf of bread	9	5	3

Technological advances in production, leading to lower unit costs, and other economies of scale, have effectively made most consumer goods cheaper too. Consider, for example, the trend in prices in real terms of motor cars, colour television sets and white goods.

In material terms, the former Conservative Prime Minister Harold Macmillan's famous saying in the late 1950s, 'You've never had it so good', would seem to apply equally well in the 1990s.

Wealth

Gradually, as indicated in Exhibit 9.3, there is emerging a trend towards growing equality of earnings, but there are still startling inequalities in British society, especially in terms of personal wealth. Various statistics suggest that about 18 per cent of the nation's wealth is held by the richest 1 per cent of the population, and about 50 per cent of the nation's wealth is in the hands of the richest 10 per cent. Poverty and inequality still exist.

On average, British households have about one-third of their personal wealth held in life assurance and pension funds, and another one-third of their personal wealth is tied up in housing.

Leisure

The most popular leisure activity in the UK, outside home, is going to a pub. Roughly two-thirds of the UK population engage in this activity. Eating out is also nearly as popular.

Other leisure activities outside home are, in order of popularity: going for a drive; visiting a library; going to the cinema; taking a short-break holiday; going to a disco or nightclub; visiting historic buildings; attending sports events as a spectator; and going to the theatre.

Significant changes can be seen in travel, over the past 30 years or so, especially the increase in taking holidays abroad which has gone up by over 300 per cent, the most popular destination being Spain.

Exhibit 9.3

Poor catch up on the rich again

After 15 years during which the gap between the rich and poor widened more dramatically than in almost any other industrialised country, the UK has become a marginally more equal society since 1990.

The latest figures from the Households Below Average Income series show that in 1979 the bottom 10 per cent of the income distribution enjoyed just 4.4 per cent of total income, after allowing for household size and make-up. By 1990, that share had fallen by more than a quarter to 3.2 per cent. Over the same period, the share taken by the top 10 per cent had risen from 20 to 25 per cent.

Since 1990, however, the gap has narrowed marginally, the poorest tenth of society seeing their share of total income rise from 3.2 to 3.5 per cent by the spring of last year, while the share taken by the richest tenth declined marginally from, 25 to 24. A similar pattern holds for the top and bottom 30 per cents of the population.

The change still leaves the bottom 30 per cent worse off in relative terms than they were in 1979 and the top 30 per cent markedly better off. Nonetheless, the trend to ever widening inequality has reversed.

Department of Social Security statisticians said yesterday that it was impossible to predict whether that would continue. But a range of factors which had contributed to the rapidly widening gap between rich and poor in the 1980s had been mitigated in the 1990s.

Real earnings growth, and the growing dispersion of earnings had been less marked since 1990, officials said. The big tax cuts of the 1980s, which benefited the better

off, have not been matched in the 1990s. Indeed, since 1992 taxes have tended to rise. The number of households with no one in work has continued to increase, but much more slowly, and pensioners as a group have gained as more have retired with occupational and private provision on top of state pensions.

In spite of the slight narrowing of the gap, there had still been a 'fundamental' change in the income distribution since 1979, officials said. As the graph shows, there are

both many more high earners, and many more households living below half average income after allowing for housing costs – well over 20 per cent against fewer than 10 per cent in 1979.

The groups most likely to be stuck at the bottom of the income distribution are the poorest single female pensioners and lone parents. That justified the government's focus on the new deal for lone parents, Harriet Harman, the social security secretary, said.

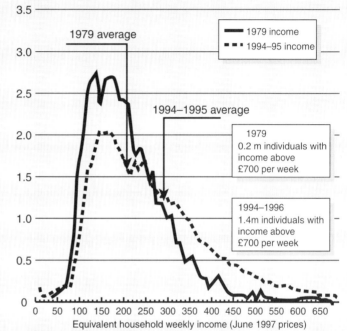

Inequality begins to ebb

Income distribution (ex full-time self-employed)
Millions

1979 average

1994–1995 average

— 1979 income
▪▪▪ 1994–95 income

1979
0.2 m individuals with income above £700 per week

1994–1996
1.4m individuals with income above £700 per week

Equivalent household weekly income (June 1997 prices)

Source: Family Expenditure Survey

Source: Nicholas Timmins, *Financial Times*, 17 October 1997.

At home the most popular ways of spending leisure time are, in order of popularity: watching television (averaging over 25 hours a week); visiting or entertaining friends or relations; listening to the radio (over 16 hours a week); listening to records or tapes; reading books; DIY; gardening; and dressmaking, needlework or knitting. Further study of the statistics in *Social Trends 27* (1997) will, unsurprisingly, reveal sometimes large differences between the percentages participating in the above-listed activities according to gender (for example, about 57 per cent of men engage in DIY activities compared to 30 per cent of women) and according to age (for example, gardening increases with age until about 70 after which it decreases).

Businesses need to identify and monitor these trends in order to adapt to expanding or new markets, and to target their market segments more effectively. For instance, with the increase in ownership of video recorders, a new market for hiring or buying pre-recorded videotapes evolved.

In the 1980s the video rental sector grew dramatically (from £200 million in 1982 to £570 million in 1989) and the retail video market has grown even more spectacularly, to nearly £790 million in 1995. By following the consumer and industry trends, businesses will probably identify a new change in the market as more and more viewers can select their choice of pre-recorded programmes from a cable network.

Television and video no doubt contributed to the post-war decline in popularity of going to the cinema. However, the trend was reversed in the 1980s, stimulated by the introduction of the multiplex cinema where, typically, there are ten screens – thus widening the choice of programmes available. And cinema attendance has continued to increase in the 1990s. Further study of the statistics – *Social Trends 27* (1997) – reveals significant variations in attendance according to social class and age: attendance now being higher among the non-manual social classes and in younger age groups, particularly 7 to 14 year olds.

Car ownership and usage has become an issue of major concern as traffic congestion and pollution from exhaust fumes worsen. At the same time, increasing numbers of families and individuals regard the car as a necessity. Surveys reveal that most trips made are quite short, less than ten miles from home. This is a topic that you will find worthwhile to monitor in the quality newspapers. Note the vested interests of the different groups including: motoring organisations (AA, RAC, etc.); providers of public transport; local governments (consider, for example, the action taken to restrict traffic in Cambridge); and the government, with its commitment to annual fuel price increases, issues of taxation and proposals for road-pricing schemes.

The individual's desire to travel seems insatiable but, gradually, people are realising that there are social limits to the growth of travelling by car. Successive British governments have dithered and delayed in taking necessary radical action, presumably fearing loss of electoral support from car users. Perhaps other technological advances, such as those used in video-conferencing, and having on-line computer workstations in employees' homes, may reduce people's car travel needs. In any event, this whole issue is one of major importance. It will affect us all.

Participation in sports

Recent statistics show that the most popular participation sports, in order of popularity, are: walking; snooker, pool or billiards; swimming; cycling; darts; soccer; golf; weightlifting or training; running; keep fit or yoga; tenpin bowls or skittles; and badminton.

Participation varies, sometimes widely, according to gender (for example, for darts – 9 per cent men, 3 per cent women; golf – 9 per cent men, 2 per cent women; keep fit or yoga – 6 per cent men, 17 per cent women). Also, as one would expect, participation varies according to age. In particular, children participate more than adults in cycling, football and swimming. Approximately 72 per cent of men and 57 per cent of women participate in at least one sports activity.

Pets

The keeping of pets has always been popular in Britain. Pet food manufacturers and other pet-related businesses need to be aware of trends and changes that affect their market. Legal changes, such as controlling or banning certain breeds of dog, and exotic animals or endangered species can have a major influence.

Roughly half of UK households own a pet. Nowadays the pet is most likely to be a cat (there are over seven million cats), whereas dogs have become slightly less popular (around 6.5 million dogs). Other common household pets are budgerigars, rabbits, guinea pigs and fish.

Gambling

About three-quarters of UK households participate in the National Lottery, spending, on average, just over £2 a week. This compares to an average expenditure of around £1.50 a week (a decrease since the launch of the National Lottery in November 1994) on other forms of gambling.

Crime

The statistics on crime in the UK are alarming. Crime rates have soared from 741 per 100 000 of the population in 1938 to over 8000 per 100 000 in the 1990s. Reported offences (in England and Wales) have gone up from 1.67 million in 1971 to 3.7 million in 1990. The size of the police force has increased significantly over the same period (approximately 1.7 times the size of the force in 1961) yet detection rates have fallen from about one in every two crimes committed to one in every three. The prison population has also soared. What is going on?

The true picture may not be as bad as is indicated by the figures above. As with many other statistics, the statistics on crime are fraught with problems. Consider, for example, the distortions caused by the convictions for motoring offences (numbering 171 000 in 1930, 765 000 in 1960 and over two million in 1980) and for shoplifting – arguably encouraged by more shops using self-service displays. There is also always a so-called dark figure, which refers to the percentage of unreported crimes, and which will vary from one type of crime to another. Many reasons are given for not reporting a crime: people may regard it as too trivial, or too embarrassing (e.g. sexual offences), a dislike of the police; a belief that the police 'can do nothing about it'; a wish not to involve the offender in a prosecution; fear of some sort of reprisal, and so on.

An understanding of crime rates and clear-up rates is hampered by the many complexities surrounding the statistics, and there are innumerable problems of interpretation of the statistics on crime. Only a few of those complexities and problems are touched upon above, but they highlight the importance of not accepting figures at face value and of finding out all the factors influencing increases or decreases in the figures.

The importance of looking carefully at what lies behind the figures (and sometimes the emphasis is on the word 'lies') and at how the presentation of the figures can alter the impression, and therefore the message conveyed, cannot be over-emphasised. Try to be aware of the wide range of factors that can affect the statistical trends, and consider whether any significant factors have been omitted.

Chapter summary

This chapter highlights the more important social trends which, together, present a picture of lifestyles in Britain. Most statistics on social trends in Britain reflect significant long-term advances in living standards, education, health and longevity, whereas relatively few areas (e.g. crime) show adverse trends.

Whether in business or in government, to manage effectively we must be able to anticipate the changes in society and in our markets. Arguably, the best starting point for doing so is to monitor and evaluate the statistical information on social trends.

Assignment

Investigate and describe the statistical trends in car ownership and usage in Britain, and outline the social problems caused by the motor car today. Suggest ways in which the problems could be alleviated.

10

The social responsibility of business

Chapter objectives

When you have read this chapter you should be able to:

◆ define, in your own words, business ethics;

◆ explain who are directly affected by ethical and unethical business practices;

◆ understand the stakeholder concept;

◆ provide a meaningful answer to the question, 'Why be ethical in business?'

Introduction

This chapter covers what is often referred to as 'business ethics' or 'corporate social responsibility'.

Business ethics are attracting a great deal of attention these days and, generally, people are taking a more active role to try to persuade businesses to act in a socially responsible way. For example, pressure groups campaign to stop businesses from damaging the environment. A notable example is Greenpeace's actions against oil companies. Another means of exerting pressure is for consumers to boycott a company's products. For example, some consumers boycott Nescafé, because they believe that Nestlé's promotion of powdered milk for babies in less developed countries is harmful. There has also been an instance of students boycotting a bank because they disapprove of its practices.

Companies are facing public scrutiny more than ever before. An example of the extent to which a company's operations can come under public scrutiny, and the high costs of dealing with the various allegations, is given in Exhibit 10.1, about McDonald's, the fast-food chain.

Exhibit 10.1

A historic victory which few companies would relish

McDonald's suffers PR 'disaster' of own making

Mr Paul Preston, the president of McDonald's UK, cut an uncomfortable figure at a press conference after yesterday's High Court judgment. In theory he was acclaiming a legal victory in the company's libel action against two green activists. In practice, he was struggling to defend a public relations disaster of the company's own making.

McDonald's spent two and a half years in court suing Mrs Helen Steel and Mr David Morris over criticisms made in leaflets handed out on street corners. The case, which lasted 313 days, the longest trial in the English courts, tied down McDonald's management and cost it about £10m in legal fees.

Although largely vindicated by the judgment, the exercise is widely viewed as having backfired spectacularly. The case attracted worldwide adverse publicity, presented as a 'David and Goliath' struggle with McDonald's using the big stick of litigation against two people who, denied legal aid, had to defend themselves in court.

The original allegations have received far wider exposure – notably through a web site on the internet but also through international press coverage, television, and a book.

Among public relations professionals, there is a view that McDonald's has comprehensively shot itself in the foot. Mr Simon Brocklebank-Fowler, managing director of Citygate Corporate, said: 'McDonald's has scored one of the most extended own goals in the recent history of public relations.'

'The vast majority of consumers would not have heard about the range of criticisms to which McDonald's has been exposed had they shut up and not said anything.'

Mr Preston denied that the trial had been a public relations disaster or that the 'David and Goliath' image would damage the company.

'The sympathy of the public will lie with the truth. That is more important than big or small,' he said.

He restated the position McDonald's has adopted throughout – that the allegations were a serious threat to the brand and action had to be taken. 'We brought

this case to protect a reputation trusted by millions of customers every day. Very serious allegations were made about our company. They were proved to be false.'

A senior McDonald's executive insisted the brand was under such threat that company no choice but to act. The decision had also been

taken against a background of incidents such as the firebombing of one McDonald's restaurant in the UK which led to fears for staff safety, he said.

He added: 'I won't work for a company that did the things alleged. McDonald's is not perfect.

Judge dismisses bulk of beef but backs

The judgment in the McDonald's libel trial was generally a legal victory for the US fast-food chain and its UK subsidiary with the judge finding that the bulk of the allegations about their business practices were unjustified and untrue, John Mason writes.

However, the companies lost on a number of points, with Mr Justice Bell ruling they were cruel to animals, exploited children in their advertising and their food could cause heart disease if eaten very frequently over a long period. He also ruled the UK company sometimes applied unfair pressure on young staff.

The allegations made in the leaflet accused McDonald's of being respon-

sible for starvation in the Third World, destroying vast areas of Central American rainforest, serving unhealthy food with a very real risk of cancer and heart disease, lying about its use of recycled paper, exploiting children in its advertising, cruelty to animals and treating its employees badly.

On starvation in the third world, the judge ruled there was no evidence to support the allegation that McDonald's had contributed to this by buying large tracts of land and evicting farmers. The allegation that the company had destroyed rainforest, including through the use of lethal poisons, was also untrue. The claims that McDonald's food was 'very unhealthy' were not

Exhibit 10.1 continued

We make mistakes but nobody in the company gets up in the morning thinking how can I be evil? You can't build a successful business like that.'

For Mr Brocklebank-Fowler, the key error made by McDonald's was to mistake the culture in which the UK subsidiary operates and attempt to apply the US solution of litigation.

'McDonald's have mistaken the consumer and cultural context in the UK. Litigation is seen in the US as part of the every day corporate armoury. In Europe we have not got there yet. Litigation is used less

The strength of the McDonald's brand is such that the company will recover, he said. However, the case, like that of Shell over the Brent Spar episode when it reversed its decision to dump the oil installation in the North Sea, shows that large companies can make misjudgments about public perceptions of them.

'Big companies often think that being right is a defence in the public eye. Being right is not always a defence – as Shell found out, he said.

Libel lawyers tend to the same view, arguing that the decision to resort to litigation to defend a per-

on the grounds that the criticisms were insignificant. Even if they were completely successful, in these circumstances there will always be residual sympathy for the little guys. It is very unusual for a company to sue individuals. It is a risky strategy.'

She accepted that a Court of Appeal ruling allowing the two defendants great latitude in questioning witnesses posed problems for McDonald's in court and lengthened the trial. However the company should still have realised how the trial would develop and leave its record exposed.

One of the company's biggest errors was to underestimate the tenacity of its opponents, she said. 'They thought these defendants would give up the ghost. They did not think they would meet two people so committed to the cause.'

animal cruelty and advert claims

justified except when adverts 'pretended to a positive nutritional benefit which McDonald's food, high in fat and saturated fat and animal products and sodium, and at one time low in fibre, did not match', he said.

A small number of customers who ate McDonald's several times a week throughout their lives, encouraged by the companies' advertising, were at risk of heart disease, he said. The untrue claims over third world starvation, the rain forests and the health risks of the food were 'particularly damaging', he said.

McDonald's claims over its use of recycled paper were not untrue, he said. The judge ruled against

McDonald's over its advertising to children.

McDonald's also lost over its rearing and slaughter of some animals, notably chickens. The judge said the allegation that McDonald's knowingly sells food which exposes customers to the risk of food poisoning was unjustified.

On employment practices, the judge broadly ruled in favour of McDonald's, that the claim that McDonald's UK paid low wages and so helped depress wages in the catering trade was justified but the claims it sought to exploit disadvantaged groups, women and black people and provided bad working conditions were not.

Mr Tim Hardy of law firm Cameron McKenna said that in spite of the legal victory the trial has been a 'disaster' for McDonald's.

The decision to bring libel proceedings had spawned a huge campaign against the company with the creation of the 'McSpotlight' internet site. The site, which included the original leaflet and transcripts of the court proceedings, was particularly damaging, he said. This has left the company with a problem since any attempt to sue over an internet publication would be fraught with immense legal hurdles.

McDonald's has a history of robust litigation but getting involved in this kind of litigation was a bad mistake. He said: 'Faced with a similar dilemma, I advise my clients to spend their money on a Porsche as they will get far more satisfaction from it than they ever will out of a libel action.'

often than in the US, particularly against people. It is a last resort.'

The result has been for McDonald's to appear a 'monolith' acting in an inappropriate fashion, he said.

ceived threat to the integrity of the McDonald's brand was misconceived. Ms Sarah Webb, a libel specialist with law firm Russell Jones and Walker, said: 'McDonald's could have put this case on one side

Source: John Mason, 'A historic victory which few companies would relish', *Financial Times*, 20 June 1997.

Exhibit 10.2 Encouraging consumers to take action against McDonald's

What's Wrong with McDonald's?

McDonald's spend over $1.8 billion every year worldwide on advertising and promotions, trying to cultivate an image of being a 'caring' and 'green' company that is also a fun place to eat. Children are lured in (dragging their parents behind them) with the promise of toys and other gimmicks. But behind the smiling face of Ronald McDonald lies the reality – McDonald's only interest is *money*, making profits from whoever and whatever they can, just like all multinational companies. McDonald's Annual Reports talk of 'Global Domination' – they aim to open more and more stores across the globe – but their continual worldwide expansion means more uniformity, less choice and the undermining of local communities.

PROMOTING UNHEALTHY FOOD

McDonald's promote their food as 'nutritious', but the reality is that it is junk food – high in fat, sugar and salt, and low in fibre and vitamins. A diet of this type is linked with a greater risk of heart disease, cancer, diabetes and other diseases. Their food also contains many chemical additives, some of which may cause ill-health, and hyperactivity in children. Don't forget too that meat is the cause of the majority of food poisoning incidents. In 1991 McDonald's were responsible for an outbreak of food poisoning in the UK, in which people suffered serious kidney failure. With modern intensive farming methods, other diseases – linked to chemical residues or unnatural practices – have become a danger to people too (such as BSE).

EXPLOITING WORKERS

Workers in the fast food industry are paid low wages. McDonald's do not pay overtime rates even when employees work very long hours. Pressure to keep profits high and wage costs low results in understaffing, so staff have to work harder and faster. As a consequence, accidents (particularly burns) are common. The majority of employees are people who have few job options and so are forced to accept this exploitation, and they're compelled to 'smile' too! Not surprisingly staff turnover at McDonald's is high, making it virtually impossible to unionise and fight for a better deal, which suits McDonald's who have always been opposed to Unions.

ROBBING THE POOR

Vast areas of land in poor countries are used for cash crops or for cattle ranching, or to grow grain to feed animals to be eaten in the West. This is at the expense of local food needs. McDonald's continually promote meat products, encouraging people to eat meat more often, which wastes more and more food resources. 7 million tons of grain fed to livestock produces only 1 million tons of meat and by-products. On a plant-based diet and with land shared fairly, almost every region could be self-sufficient in food.

DAMAGING THE ENVIRONMENT

Forests throughout the world – vital for all life – are being destroyed at an appalling rate by multinational companies. McDonald's have at last been forced to admit to using beef reared on ex-rainforest land, preventing its regeneration. Also, the use of farmland by multinationals and their suppliers forces local people to move on to other areas and cut down further trees.

McDonald's are the world's largest user of beef. Methane emitted by cattle reared for the beef industry is a major contributor to the 'global warming' crisis. Modern intensive agriculture is based on the heavy use of chemicals which are damaging to the environment.

Every year McDonald's use thousands of tons of unnecessary packaging, most of which ends up littering our streets or polluting the land buried in landfill sites.

MURDERING ANIMALS

The menus of the burger chains are based on the torture and murder of millions of animals. Most are intensively farmed, with no access to fresh air and sunshine, and no freedom of movement. Their deaths are barbaric – 'humane slaughter' is a myth. We have the choice to eat meat or not, but the billions of animals massacred for food each year have no choice at all.

CENSORSHIP and McLIBEL

Criticism of McDonald's has come from a huge number of people and organisations over a wide range of issues. In the mid-1980's, London Greenpeace drew together many of those strands of criticism and called for an **annual World Day of Action against McDonald's**. This takes place every year on **16th October**, with pickets and demonstrations all over the world. McDonald's, who spend a fortune every year on advertising, are trying to silence worldwide criticism by threatening legal action against those who speak out. Many have been forced to back down because they lacked the money to fight a case. But Helen Steel and David Morris, two supporters of London Greenpeace, defended themselves in a major UK High Court libel trial. No legal aid is available so they represented themselves. McDonald's engaged in a huge cover up, refusing to disclose masses of relevant documents. Also, the defendants were denied their right to a jury. Despite all the cards being stacked against them, Helen and Dave turned the tables and exposed the truth by putting McDonald's business practices on trial. Protests against the $30 billion a year fast-food giant continue to grow. It's vital to stand up to intimidation and to defend free speech.

WHAT YOU CAN DO – Together we can fight back against the institutions and the people in power who dominate our lives and our planet, and we can create a better society without exploitation. Workers can and do organise together to fight for their rights and dignity. People are increasingly aware of the need to think seriously about the food we and our children eat. People in poor countries are organising themselves to stand up to multinationals and banks which dominate the world's economy. Environmental and animal rights protests and campaigners are growing everywhere. Why not join in the struggle for a better world. Talk to friends and family, neighbours and workmates about these issues. Please copy and circulate this leaflet as widely as you can.

Source: Greenpeace (London). Reprinted with permission.

As can be seen from the article reproduced in Exhibit 10.1, the allegations against McDonald's concern no fewer than seven serious ethical issues, some of which were upheld by the High Court. McDonald's is still left with the problem that the Court judgment will not stop further campaigning, justified or unjustified, including the annual 'World Day of Action against McDonald's' in October (*see* Exhibit 10.2).

Growing public concern about business ethics is also reflected in the steady rise of ethical investments. Managers of ethical investment funds will not knowingly invest in any company, project or regime which is involved in controversial business such as arms, alcohol, tobacco and gambling; or in activities that abuse human or animal rights; or that are damaging to the ecological environment.

According to a report by the Ethical Investment Research Service, investment in ethical unit and investment trusts is booming, with cash under management more than doubling in the three years to July 1997 to £1465 million, up from £672 million in 1994. This compares with an increase of only 55 per cent for investment in all UK unit and investment funds in the same period. These figures are all the more significant when one considers that ethical funds generally perform badly against the stock market and other unit trusts. Clearly, people are prepared to accept the lower rates of return on their investments in order to avoid investing in companies that engage in controversial business. Ethical investment funds started in 1984 and there are now about 40 in the UK.

International ethical issues

Another example of consumer demand for ethical products, and how it has been stimulated, is given in Exhibit 10.3. This also illustrates how the public has become actively concerned about companies 'doing right' to others when conducting business overseas, particularly in less developed countries; in this case, by helping farmers out of poverty.

Other international ethical issues of public concern include:

◆ the depletion of natural resources, such as tropical rain forests;

◆ exporting products known to be unsafe, such as pesticides that may have been banned in the home country;

◆ the disposal of toxic wastes by exporting them to less developed countries where ignorance and financial inducements enable the waste products to be imported;

◆ disregarding the health and safety of foreign workers so as to save production costs in already low-labour cost countries.

More people are becoming aware and concerned about what they regard as 'exploitation' by international companies operating in the poorer countries. Increased flows of information, reports in the media, active pressure groups, and a

Exhibit 10.3

Clipper Teas: Assam with a difference

Assam is the birthplace of Indian tea and the British tea trade.

At Clipper, we are very pleased to trade with an outstanding organic tea estate in this area.

The tea estate started organic cultivation in response to consumer interest in organic foods and beverages and a growing concern for an ecologically sound environment.

As well as practising organic agricultural methods, the company is also committed to extensive welfare policies for the tea workers and their families. This includes housing, healthcare, fair pay and education for the children. About 50 families consisting of 3 to 5 members in each family depend on this organic tea estate.

There is a local school for the estate children and for higher studies, children are sent to the nearby town by estate transport. The younger children are looked after by qualified staff in a well organised and equipped creche whilst their parents work on the tea estate.

The workers have their recreation club provided by the company, where they have indoor games, reading materials and regular cultural programmes. The expectant mothers receive ante-natal and post-natal care.

The workers are also provided with space for a kitchen garden. Protective weather clothes and equipment such as woollen rugs, umbrellas and footwear are given free to all workers and their families.

Extract reprinted with permission from Clipper Tea Club newsletter, *The Teapot Times*, Issue 5, Spring 1998. (*See also* Further resources for Clipper Teas Website.)

Why Fairtrade?

Whilst only 5% of Third World income comes from aid, a significant 80% comes from trade. Millions of people nonetheless, are kept in poverty by the low prices paid for their products. Globalisation of Industry has made it very easy for manufacturers to pursue low labour costs, and ultimately, we the consumers, must take responsibility as we continually demand low cost commodity products.

The Fairtrade Foundation
Supported by Third World agencies such as Christian Aid, CAFOD, Oxfam and the World Development Movement, the Fairtrade Foundation was set up in the UK in July 1992 to tackle the exploitation of workers in the Third World by offering British consumers the

opportunity to buy products that **guarantee** a better deal for producers.

The Foundation is based on a shared belief that:

'Many of the third world producers of raw materials, commodities and manufactured goods purchased by the developing world are living in conditions of poverty and that poverty is due, at least in part, to the manner in which the developed world trades with them'.

The aim of the Fairtrade Foundation is to recognise and endorse fairly traded products, independent of trading interests and to encourage companies to trade in a way that ensures a fairer deal for Third World producers. They then award the **Fairtrade Mark** to be displayed on products.

Extract reprinted with permission from Clipper Tea Club newsletter, *The Teapot Times*, Issue 4, Winter 1997/1998.
Note: The company Clipper Teas has the endorsement (renewable annually) of the Fairtrade Foundation.

better educated population mean that no company can engage in bad practices and keep them hidden from public scrutiny for long, nationally or internationally. The trends would seem to suggest that we really are living in a more caring society – 'the caring nineties' as opposed to the abrasive profit-grabbing 'yuppie' culture of the 1980s.

This is an appropriate point at which to consider from where and how we acquire our ethical values, as individuals and as a society. We need a clear understanding of what it means to be ethical and why 'being ethical' is important, especially in business.

What does 'being ethical' mean?

Johnson and Scholes (1997) suggest that business ethics exist at three levels, namely, the macro, corporate and individual levels.

Macroethical issues

Macroethical issues concern the role of business in society at the national and international levels. Consider, for example, the different sets of values that underpin society in different countries. A few countries are still dominated by a communist system, others by a military regime or a capitalist system, or are under the dominant influence of religious leaders – as, for instance, in some Islamic states in the Middle East. By comparing the relationship that has developed between the state and commerce in countries where different regimes exist, and thinking about the degree of freedom or the constraints a business has in each country, we can realise how very different the sets of values or 'business ethics' can be. An interesting study of these issues in which, basically, two sets of values have been identified, namely, those of the merchant and those of the guardian, was made by Cullum and Jacobs (1993). These two basic sets of values are described in greater detail later in this chapter.

On the macroeconomic level, there is public debate on the issue of whether the rich nations, and their banks, should waive some or all of their loans to the very poor countries in which the national debt has become so crippling as to prevent normal economic development and growth. In one instance, the UK's National Union of Students has, for the past six years, been advising its members not to use the Midland Bank, on the grounds that it has a poor record in helping to reduce debt in less developed countries.

Corporate ethical issues

Corporate ethical issues concern, or should concern, each company or organisation and how it conducts its business and develops it relationships with its stakeholders. (The concept of stakeholders is discussed later in this chapter.) Many companies today incorporate a code of ethics in their mission statements, or lay down elsewhere in writing the ethical rules and practices which they require their staff to follow. Inevitably, dilemmas and conflicts arise, depending on how tightly the codes are enforced and whether a company's code concurs with the employee's own set of values and expectations. This leads us to consider how we acquire our own ethical beliefs.

Individual ethical beliefs

Individual ethical beliefs concern the set of values or moral outlook we each have. These derive from our family upbringing, school experiences, friends and religious beliefs and from influences from the community we live in and from society at large. As a result, we all grow up to share certain common values such as, 'It's wrong to tell lies, or to steal', etc. We are also taught certain personal responsibilities and virtues such as being concerned for the well-being of others, being reliable, punctual, etc. So, as adults, as well as sharing a common set of values, we also develop our own unique individual set of personal values too.

Understanding these concepts, where our set of moral values comes from and what they are, enables us to see what is meant by being ethical; and why 'being ethical' can be interpreted in so many ways by different people because of their different cultural backgrounds and unique personal experiences. Thus, we can also understand how problems arise when we try to be precise about the extent to which we should obey the rules and carry out our responsibilities in society, for example, in regarding a financial inducement as a gift, or as a bribe; in being charitable; in caring for the environment, and so on.

The 'merchant or guardian' approach

It should now be easy to understand how and why there are such different approaches to running a business. The 'merchant or guardian' approach, mentioned earlier in the chapter, is another way of contrasting the different schools of thought. This approach notes that at one end of the spectrum there are businesses and business leaders ('merchants') that have as their main aim maximising profits whereas at the other (the guardianship approach) there are those whose main aim is to work in harmony with society, for the greater good, while also making some profit. You should be able to categorise some well-known British companies in terms of whether they tend towards one or other of these approaches. There are many companies, however, which it is difficult to categorise as either 'ethical' or 'unethical'.

Companies may engage in particular activities or have an approach to business that some people will admire while others will disapprove of them. Consider, for example, the way in which the Enlightened Tobacco Company (Exhibit 10.4) conducts its business. What are your views on the company and its honest approach to selling cigarettes?

Exhibit 10.4 An ethical approach to the marketing of cigarettes?

In 1991, Mr B. J. Cunningham, with a budget of £20 000, launched the new brand 'Death Cigarettes' from his bedroom in Lewisham. By 1994, annual sales were reported to have risen to £200 000. Building on this success, Mr Cunningham raised £1.5 million in the City to relaunch and reposition the product, and expand market share.

By using a skull and crossbones logo on the pack, Mr Cunningham claims he is breaking the taboo about death and smoking, and that this is the unique selling point. He claims his brand follows 'the principle of honesty' and 'that ethos will run through the company' (named the Enlightened Tobacco Company). The company is committed to donate 10 per cent of pre-tax profits to non-vivisection cancer research and related charities.

'We are being ethical, we are being honest,' Mr Cunningham is also quoted as saying. 'Our business is selling cigarettes, and if somebody in Asia or Africa wanted to buy then we'd sell. We want to make money, make profits and make our shareholders very rich.'

Adapted from: Hague, 'Breathing New Life Into Death', *Independent on Sunday*, 24 April 1994.

Affirmative action

Growing public awareness and concern over ethical issues have encouraged companies to show that they are socially responsible by engaging in high-visibility activities to benefit charities or the local community. Many of these company activities are prompted by the marketing department and some call it 'societal marketing'. This has been defined as making marketing decisions so as to meet:

◆ the company's requirements;

◆ the customers' needs and wants;

while also

◆ benefiting society.

The concept is widely known in marketing and is illustrated in Figure 10.1.

Note that in the societal marketing concept, as illustrated in Figure 10.1, the three considerations are balanced whereas previously the concepts of marketing tended to overlook the interests of society.

Social cause marketing

Social cause marketing refers to the situation where a company links itself to a popular social issue, thereby gaining more business from customers who are sympathetic to the same social issue. The Body Shop is one example of a company that deliberately identifies itself with popular causes such as animal rights, justice

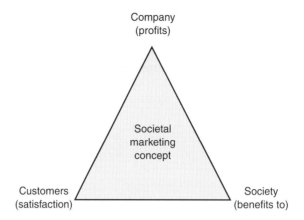

Fig. 10.1 The societal marketing concept

(Amnesty International) and Trade-Not-Aid. Regardless of whether the Body Shop set out to gain more customers and increased business through its campaigns for selected social causes, there can be no doubt that the media coverage has been a powerful, and probably very cost-effective, alternative to conventional advertising.

Cause-related marketing

Cause-related marketing (CRM) has been described as 'the involvement of a company in a charity for commercial as well as purely philanthropic reasons'.

An example of CRM is Tesco's voucher scheme for providing computers to schools. This has enhanced Tesco's image in the community while also increasing customer loyalty, especially from parents and children.

CRM is an alternative means by which companies can support good causes other than by simply making a donation to charity. Instead, companies become actively involved in the community, demonstrating their caring approach. Invariably, the companies then benefit from the media coverage and better public relations.

'There's no such thing as a completely clean company'

The statement quoted in the above heading was made by Anne Simpson, joint managing director of Pirc, a London-based pressure group established in 1986 that aims to promote socially responsible management. Pirc tries to persuade large companies to improve their policies and practices concerning the environment, employment and human rights. Pirc's directors raise issues at a company's annual general meeting, gaining shareholders' support. Many very well-known companies have come under criticism from Pirc, creating publicity and discussion.

Pirc's hope, in taking such action, is that the company directors will be spurred into acting in a more socially responsible way, with the understanding and support of the shareholders. It is, after all, the shareholders who may have to accept a short-term loss of profits if the company institutes tougher environmental standards and better employment practices, or even loses business by withdrawing from operations in countries with oppressive regimes (for example, currently, Nigeria).

The stakeholder concept

Wheeler and Sillanpää (1997) define stakeholders as 'individuals and entities who may be affected by business, and who may, in turn, bring influence to bear upon it.' Stakeholders can be categorised as *primary* or *secondary*. Also, they can be categorised as *internal* or *external*. Internal stakeholders include individuals and groups of employees and managers, whereas external stakeholders include customers and suppliers. A further category of *connected* stakeholders may also be used, as shown in Figure 10.2.

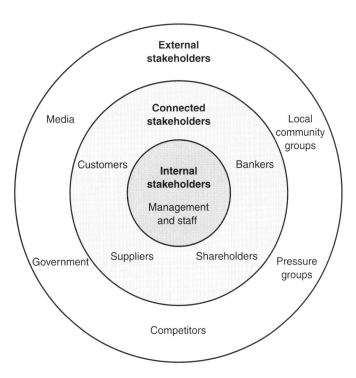

Fig. 10.2 Three categories of stakeholder

Primary stakeholders

Primary stakeholders are the business owners, shareholders and other investors, employees, customers and suppliers of a company. Each of these groups has a direct interest in the performance and well-being of the company.

Secondary stakeholders

Secondary stakeholders have less direct links to the company but still (in the words of the definition quoted above) may be affected by it and may, in turn, influence the way the company operates. Secondary stakeholders include local community groups (who, some publications suggest, could be primary stakeholders), pressure groups, regulatory bodies, trade unions, trade associations, the media and competitors.

Expectations of stakeholder groups

Each stakeholder group will have its own expectations and objectives. The investors will be seeking a good financial return whereas the employees will be expecting safe and pleasant working conditions, fair pay and job security. Clearly, other stakeholder groups will have different expectations and objectives, some that will be in harmony with those of, say, the investors and employees, but others that may cause conflict.

Generally, both the primary and secondary stakeholders will agree that they would like to create a socially responsible enterprise that not only complies with the laws and regulations but also improves the environment and creates benefits to society. However, when the wants of all the different stakeholder groups are considered, it will be realised how varied and far-reaching they can be. The question arises, 'Is it possible for a company to satisfy all the varied expectations of its stakeholders?' If we look at well-run, forward-thinking, socially responsible companies, such as The Body Shop, the answer is that it is probable that no company can be regarded as 'perfect' by all of its stakeholder groups. There will always be trade-offs and compromises. However, by communicating constantly with its stakeholders (communication being a two-way process) and by continuously striving to 'do the right thing', a company can gain their respect and even admiration which, in turn, can lead to greater financial rewards.

The company's approach to stakeholders, therefore, requires the balancing of their various, and sometimes conflicting, demands and expectations. Sensitivity and diplomacy are required. On the other hand, when a company antagonises, avoids or ignores one or more of its stakeholder groups, there are often serious negative consequences. Consider, for example, the case of Shell which suffered from adverse publicity concerning the disposal of its oil rig Brent Spar and again, within a short time, concerning its investment in its Nigerian Liquefied Natural Gas Project.

Shell felt compelled to take full-page newspaper advertisements to explain its actions (*see* Exhibit 10.5); however, this could be regarded as a 'damage limitation' exercise following an earlier lack of communication with some of its stakeholder groups.

Exhibit 10.5

IF WE'RE INVESTING IN NIGERIA YOU HAVE THE RIGHT TO KNOW WHY

Shell plans to invest in the Nigerian Liquefied Natural Gas Project. Some say we should pull out. And we understand why. But if we do so now, the project will collapse. Maybe for ever.

So let's be clear about who we'd be hurting. Not the present Nigerian government, if that's the intention. The plant will take four years to build. The revenues won't start flowing until early next century. Of course the government of that time would suffer, but why should anyone want that?

The people of the Niger Delta would certainly suffer – the thousands who will work on the project, and thousands more who will benefit in the local economy.

And the environment would be hurt, because this plant will bring real benefits, with a great reduction in the need for gas flaring by the oil industry.

Whatever you think of the Nigerian situation today, we know you wouldn't want us to hurt the Nigerian people. Or jeopardise their future.

After Brent Spar, Greenpeace apologised for feeding the public false facts. This time, we thought you deserved to hear the truth.

Source: Shell newspaper advertisement, 17 November 1995. Reprinted with permission from Shell International Ltd, London.

New options for the disposal or alternative use of Brent Spar are still under consideration: clearly it is a sensitive issue under public scrutiny (*see* Exhibit 10.6).

Another example of the power of pressure groups and therefore of the importance to a company of recognising such groups as their stakeholders and of communicating with them, is provided by the reactive decision of the German pharmaceutical company Hoechst which was producing, through its French

Exhibit 10.6

Shell to consider 11 disposal options for Brent Spar

Shell, the Anglo Dutch oil group, has short-listed six contractors to study schemes for disposing of the obsolete Brent Spar oil storage installation anchored in a Norwegian fjord.

Shell said it was considering 11 different proposals for re-using Brent Spar's component parts or scrapping it onshore. Deep sea dumping – an operation abandoned in 1995 after protests across Europe – remained a further option.

However, executives said they were optimistic some of the solutions outlined would prove to be 'as good as, or better than, deep sea disposal'.

Mr Heinz Rothermund, a senior executive with Shell UK, said the final detailed alternative schemes would be weighed against environmental, safety and cost criteria set by the deep sea option. 'At the moment, it is the only one that is technically feasible,' he said.

Greenpeace, the environmental pressure group that organised the original protests against the dumping, welcomed yesterday's announcement as 'a further nail in the coffin of sea dumping. Of the shortlisted options, not one involves dumping the 14,500 tonne structure in the ocean.'

Three of the 11 schemes to be investigated in a further Shell-sponsored study involve scrapping the Brent Spar onshore. Two will focus on re-using the top part of the giant buoy as a land-based training facility.

Three proposals involve cutting it into horizontal sections which could then be used for quay construction or harbour development, and another will study its use in coastal protection schemes off England's east coast.

Shell will pay the contractors £1m–£1.5m to undertake the detailed studies which should lead to firm bids being submitted by the end of April.

UK-based contractors on the shortlist include Brown & Root and Amec, McAlpine Doris, an Anglo-French consortium, and Wood-GMC, an Anglo-Norwegian partnership, were also selected.

A number of alternative uses for the Brent Spar were rejected. These included a plan to turn it into an offshore electricity generating station using wind and wave power or converting it to an offshore desalinisation plant.

Mr Rothermund said the company would have spent about £9m by the time it was ready to award a final disposal contract.

Shell is to ask the Norwegian government to extend by one year its permission for the Brent Spar to remain in the Erfjord, one of the few inshore locations in Europe with the water depths to handle it.

Source: Robert Corzine, *Financial Times,* 14 January 1997.

subsidiary Roussel Uclaf, a pill called RU 486 to induce the abortion of an embryo in the first two months of pregnancy. Although the drug had been approved as safe and effective by regulators, anti-abortion activists in the USA campaigned for US consumers to boycott Hoechst's products including a potentially very profitable new anti-hayfever treatment called Allegra. Consequently, Hoechst was forced to end its involvement with RU 486. (Clark, Corrigan and Green (1997) and Jack, Clark and Green (1997).)

The social responsibility of business

General

Quality daily and Sunday newspapers. *The Economist*.

Further reading

Clark, B., Corrigan, T. and Green, D. (1997) 'Anti-abortion call to boycott Hoechst drug'. London: *Financial Times,* 3 April.

Cullum, L. and Jacobs, J. (1993) 'Where trade began – the renewal and morality of cities (an interview with Jacobs, Jane)', Parabola – The Magazine of Myth and Tradition, Vol. 18, No. 4, pp. 15–20.

Jack, A., Clark, B. and Green, D. (1997) 'Boycott forces Hoechst to drop abortion pill'. London: *Financial Times*, 3 April.

Jacobs, J. (1994) The Death and Life of Great American Cities. Harmondsworth: Penguin.

Johnson, G. and Scholes, K. (1997) Exploring Corporate Strategy (3rd edn). Hemel Hempstead: Prentice Hall.

Mahoney, J. (1992) 'Business ethics', Klein, J. (ed.) *Survive and Thrive – The Path to Prosperity*. Kettering: Duncan Publishing.

Wheeler, D. and Sillanpää, M. (1997) *The Stakeholders Corporation. A Blueprint for Maximising Stakeholder Value*. London: Financial Times Pitman Publishing.

Internet addresses

Ethics Resources: http://ethics.acusd.edu/resources.html

Jane Jacobs: http://www.jacobs97.com

European Institute for Business Ethics: http://www.nijenrode.nl/research/eibe.htl

Clipper Teas: www.clipper-teas.com

Chapter summary

This chapter has explained the increasing importance of paying attention to ethical issues in business today. The reasons are clear. These issues must be taken into account, not only because people should behave altruistically, but also to bring longer-term benefits to the business. These benefits include:

◆ building a positive company image;

◆ attracting investment;

◆ recruiting better calibre staff;

◆ increasing sales; and

◆ creating customer loyalty.

Thus, the competitive position of a business can be sharpened by operating it deliberately in a socially responsible way.

This chapter has explained recognised modern concepts of social responsibility, including:

◆ the societal marketing concept;

◆ social cause marketing; and

◆ cause-related marketing.

Above all, this chapter has explained the relevance of stakeholders and the different expectations and influences of various stakeholder groups. It is vital that a company is very careful in cultivating its relationship with each stakeholder group. When this is done, the result is good for business. When it is not done, as shown by the examples quoted in this chapter, a company can lose the support of those who influence its performance and can even come under attack from the public, with consequent damage to its image.

Assignment

An American entrepreneur, Paul Hawken, is quoted as saying:

> Business is the only mechanism on the Planet today powerful enough to reverse global environmental and social degradation.
>
> (Quoted in Harvey, B., 'Corporate Governance And Non-Executives', *Financial Times*, 3 May 1996.)

Do you agree or disagree with Hawken's statement? Give reasons to justify your answer, and compare the social responsibilities of business with those of not-for-profit organisations, such as: charities, schools, the BBC, the National Health Service, the armed forces.

Part 4

THE TECHNOLOGICAL ENVIRONMENT

Introduction

Technology is not something which was born in the twentieth century. It is both old and new, and the old does not necessarily become obsolete.

The kitchen knife could be termed the old but it is still in use. However, today we also have the electric food processor and the microwave oven. Similarly, in biotechnology, the old is baking bread, the new is cloning (for example Dolly, the sheep).

The most remarkable aspect of technological developments in the late twentieth century must surely be the speed at which they happen. Technological advances occur at an ever-accelerating pace, making forecasting more and more difficult. Looking back, who could have forecast 50 years ago that a man could be landed on the moon? Or that today's 'ordinary' desktop computer would be more powerful than the computer used to guide the craft to the moon in 1969? Conversely, looking forward 50 years or even five years, forecasting the further technological advances and their impact on society has become almost a guessing game.

The power of computers still increases dramatically, along with miniaturisation and lower costs. For nearly ten years now, it has been possible to store the entire contents of the *Encyclopaedia Britannica* on a chip the size of a pinhead. Society has begun to take many of these remarkable developments and changes as normal. When the Space Shuttle blasts off or returns to earth, it is barely given a mention in the news; it is regarded as a matter of routine. However, while some such technological advances are taken for granted, others are happening so fast that society cannot always cope. Reactions and ethical issues have to be worked out later, and many individuals are quite bewildered by the impact of new technology.

One particular area of technology worth watching is robotics (created by combining automation with computing), as the usefulness of robots spreads from factories to offices, hospitals to homes, and so on.

The impact of technology on business and individuals

Chapter objectives

By the time you have read this chapter you should be able to:

◆ define what is meant by the word technology;

◆ assess the impact of technolgy on:
  – factories;
  – offices;
  – shops;
  – financial services;
  – education;
  – communication;

◆ appreciate the impact of technology on employment and work practices;

◆ appreciate the impact of the Internet.

Introduction

The Penguin Dictionary of Economics defines technology as '*the sum of knowledge of the means and methods of producing goods and services*'. Further, J. K. Galbraith (1974) defines technology as 'the systematic application of scientific or other organised knowledge to practical tasks'. In short, therefore, technology is 'the use of knowledge'.

In the early part of the nineteenth century, a group of textile workers in northern England smashed up newly introduced manufacturing machinery, as they considered it to be a threat to their jobs. Even today, newspaper headlines such as: 'New Technology could put five million out of work' (*Guardian*) and 'Electronic revolution may lead to the dole' (*The Times*) appear.

So what exactly is this new technology and has it actually resulted in such frightening consequences as far as employment is concerned? In this chapter we will examine the impact of technology in the workplace – in factories, offices and shops, on financial services and on employment and work practices. In addition we will assess its impact on communication and appreciate a recent innovation – the Internet.

The impact of technology in the workplace

In the factory

In the factory, computer-aided design (CAD), computer-aided manufacturing (CAM), and integrated manufacturing systems (IMS) have all, it would appear, resulted in the need for less labour. CAD occurs where products are designed on a computer screen. CAM refers to the situation where production processes are controlled by computers. For example, we have all probably seen pictures of robotic arms in use in the manufacture of cars. IMS is the integration of CAM sub-systems. Further, just in time (JIT) is a production technique whereby finished and partly finished goods and components are produced and delivered when needed by customers. They are therefore delivered 'just in time', thus avoiding the costs of holding large amounts of stock.

In the office

In the office, word processors have replaced typewriters and databases have replaced vast rows of filing cabinets. Word processors create and correct documents. Now, e-mail is replacing the telephone and the fax for increasing numbers of communications. Spreadsheets formulate and analyse information. Databases enable information to be collected and analysed. Electronic data interchange (EDI) enables data to be directly transmitted between one organisation's computer system and those of another. Voice messaging makes it much easier for people to get in touch with one another.

The use of new technology has meant that many companies that might once have had to relocate to larger premises in order to expand their business are either staying put or actually reducing the amount of office space they need, while increasing their numbers of staff. How is this possible? Some of the means used are desk sharing, flexible working hours, telecommunications and computer work-stations at home. The intelligent use of existing technology, combined with flexible working practices, also improves productivity. The term 'virtual office' has come into being, meaning one which is simulated by various communications links between employees who may be located in widely dispersed places.

Exhibit 11.1

Check out tags

Sainsbury, the UK supermarket group, is set to begin a pioneering trial of technology this month that could, it hopes, ultimately transform the running of its supply chain.

The three-month trial will experiment with RFID (radio frequency identification) tags on crates of ready-prepared food and fresh produce. The purpose of the tags, which were designed by Singlechip Systems of the US, is to allow information about the goods stored in its warehouses to be collected automatically – rather than by manually checking the barcodes on crates.

The tags contain chips and antennae: when a reader directs a radio signal at the tags, the chips respond by transmitting information. Using a sophisticated 'anti-collision algorithm' that distinguishes between the messages from different tags, the reader can read 250 tags in under one minute.

The benefits of the system are those of cost, speed and the accessibility of the information. A company like Sainsbury spends large sums in confirming the exact position of goods as they make the journey from the supplier to the depot to the store. RFID technology would be a quick and cheap alternative to manual checks.

The technology could also improve the freshness of products that arrive in the supermarket, because it will become easier to identify goods with particular expiry dates. 'We could check the life of products all along the chain,' says John Rowe, a director of Sainsbury. 'It would allow us to make sure we could give fresher products to the customers.'

Mr Rowe says that he has been amazed by the rapid progress of the technology. 'Six months ago, if you had asked me about case tags, I would have said that they were five years away,' he says. Although the cost needs to come down still further. It is 'definitely in the right ball park', he says.

Sainsbury is part of a consortium of 24 companies in businesses including wines and spirits, pharmaceuticals, clothing and logistics which are pooling their experiences with various RFID trials. The goal of the projects is to demonstrate whether the technology works and get a sense of the potential return on investment.

One issue which will be carefully scrutinised by the participants concerns standards. 'The standards issue could be one of the main constraints,' says Mr Rowe. For example, it would clearly be problematic if data could only be read by a certain type of reader. In many cases, suppliers would find they had to provide different tags for different retailers.

Martin Swerdlow, chief executive of Integrated Product Intelligence which is co-ordinating the trials, is confident that attempts under way to sort out international standards will be successful. He is also confident that prices of tags will drop drastically. He predicts that the price of tags that, until recently, cost $2–4 (£1.20–£2.40) each could be as low as 20 cents by next year.

Currently, the cost of the tags means that it is not feasible to use RFID for anything less durable than a crate – or 'talking box', as it is sometimes called.

But what if individual items, such as bags of sugar or cans of beans could be labelled with tags? The notion of the 'talking can' would make it possible to push a trolley full of goods through a supermarket checkout, which could automatically tot up the bill.

This vision has been technologically feasible for several years. But it seemed that it would be too expensive ever to become a reality. Now people are beginning to think again. In the view of Mr Rowe, the falling cost of intelligent tags could make disposable RFID labels a reality within five to seven years. When that happens, it will open up a huge market, according to Mr Swerdlow. In his view, the RFID market could then be worth $5bn to $10bn a year.

Source: Houlder, V., *Financial Times*, 3 October 1997.

The impact of technology in shops

When we go shopping in our local large supermarket, the impact of technology is evident. The items of stock on the shelves are not individually priced, instead there are bar codes. These were devised by the Article Number Association (ANA), to allocate a unique number to each product. Each product is laser scanned at the checkout. This results in improved operational efficiency for the supermarket:

◆ time is not spent attaching price tags to individual stock items;

◆ price changes can be implemented more quickly;

◆ it leads to better stock control.

When we take the goods to the checkout, the computerised till reads the bar codes and produces an itemised receipt giving details of all purchases made. We can pay with a debit or credit card which is 'swiped' through a machine and funds are transferred electronically. This is known as Electronic Funds Transfer at the Point Of Sale (EFTPOS). The use of this system means that there is no need for customers to carry around large amounts of cash. For the retailer, there is faster checkout throughput and reduced operator error. Another benefit for the retailer is that payment by card results in faster payment to them and reduced cash handling.

The rapid progress of technology has led also to the creation of RFID (Radio Frequency Identification) tags which can be put on to items, including crates of fresh produce, in a supermarket. The RFID tags would enable the supermarket company to monitor the movement of goods from supplier to depot and to store, automatically instead of by means of the more costly manual system of checking bar codes that is used today. Trials using RFID tags were taking place at the end of 1997.

The next step envisaged is to have some form of tag on individual items so that when the customer pushes a trolley full of goods through a checkout each tag transmits its signal to a reader that automatically calculates the total bill. This may become a reality within five to seven years. For more information *see* Exhibit 11.1.

The impact of technology on financial services

Home banking

Once it was necessary to visit your bank, or at least telephone, in order to conduct your financial business. With modern communications it is possible to plug in to your bank's computer system and use a home computer to effect transactions. Progress has been slowed by concerns about the security of the link between the home and the bank, but encryption techniques appear to have overcome this difficulty. The data are converted into a complicated code which is very difficult to decode.

Automatic teller machines

Automatic teller machines (ATMs) have become a familiar sight in the high street, and recently in motorway service areas, railway stations and airports. Cash can be withdrawn or deposits made on a 24-hour basis. Financial organisations have entered into arrangements which allow their customers to use the ATMs of other companies – for example, the LINK or CIRRUS networks – in the UK as well as overseas.

The impact of technology in education and on communication

In education

With greatly enhanced means of communication comes the feasibility of education no longer having to take place in a school, college or university. It is true that 'education no longer has to be bound by place' (Cornwell 1997).

For many years, children in the Australian outback have been provided with a school education, of a sort, by radio because of the impracticality of long-distance travel to a school. The newer technology has enabled a natural progression to the wider provision of higher-quality, effective education. For example the Open University now has the largest number of students of any university in Europe. In the USA, television and video are complemented by the use of laptop computers in education. (Already some schools in New York provide laptops to each pupil, as an aid to teaching and learning.)

The implications of new technology for education are phenomenal. 'Distance learning', traditionally a rather difficult, solitary activity using documents sent through the post, is now, thanks to new technology, turning into 'learning at a distance' in which participants can log in to an inspiring range of materials and activities, including interactive discussions. One example is the Western Governors' University (WGU), better known as the 'Virtual University', in the USA where students will be able to enrol and learn via the Internet. The WGU was due to start early in 1998. One advantage will be the facility to draw on the expertise of academics in hundreds of colleges and universities across the West, as 13 states from North Dakota to Hawaii are cooperating to deliver personalised courses to students at home or in the work-place in any city or far-flung place.

In the UK, companies are also setting up their own training and development programmes using all the modern technology. British Airways is one such company; Unipart is another. The 'Unipart U' as it is called, (not being allowed to use the term university), could, effectively, offer much the same courses as colleges or universities do in the UK. It would have the added advantage that the courses would be tailor-made to suit the company's precise needs, and the company's employees would have the convenience of being able to study at the time and place to suit themselves.

The convenience and lower costs of the 'Virtual U' style of education will create valuable new business opportunities for the colleges and universities that wish to become providers in this high-tech industry. However, no doubt many other colleges and universities that fail to recognise that 'education no longer has to be bound by place' will be left behind.

The impact of technology on communication

The growth of commerce in the nineteenth century was necessarily accompanied by the development of postal services. Yet even with jet travel it can take days to deliver a piece of mail from one place to another. The advent of e-mail has permitted the exchange of information almost instantaneously and at low cost. Drafts of large documents can be sent for quick amendment and return. The frustration of encountering an engaged telephone or fax machine is avoided. It is not even necessary for the user of e-mail to be at their normal place of work to receive messages.

Video-conferencing allows groups of people to hold a meeting, without the costs and stress of travel. Cameras and microphones enable two or more groups of people to hold simultaneous discussions. The technology has existed for many years, but it is only recently that costs have dropped sufficiently to make it worth while. Lloyds Bank experimented with video-conferencing between its commercial managers based in Bristol and the IT specialists in London who were developing new applications. Within nine months, in addition to the time saved, there was a 20 per cent saving on rail travel. Global operations are making even greater savings, by cutting the need for air travel.

The impact of technology on employment and work practices

It is not so much the new technology in itself which has resulted in changes in work practices, but the new forms of work organisation that go with it. Technology may liberate workers from exhausting physical tasks but can be repetitive and dehumanising in both the factory and office. Research has shown that there has been some loss of jobs caused by new technology. On the other hand, new jobs have also been created in new-technology firms. Further, with both manufacturing and professional jobs alike, there has been little job displacement; the major impact of new technology has been on clerical work.

Research has also shown that there will always be the need for high-skilled and low-skilled employment. The main effect of new technology, it would appear, will be on semi-skilled jobs. There will be more part-time work and work subcontracted. Also there will be more working at home with the advent of portable computers and more sophisticated communication systems, such as, voice mail. Hence, the question, 'Daddy, what was an office block?' (as suggested in *Business Computing*) may become a reality.

It is difficult to find any convincing evidence that, in the long run, new technology either destroys more jobs than it creates or creates more jobs than it destroys. What is clear is that new technology eliminates the need for certain types of jobs. (For example, telephone switchboard operators are replaced by automated systems.) It also creates the need for other new types of jobs (for example, computer programmers and systems analysts). Dirty and dangerous jobs are now performed by robots. Thus, the application of new technology is changing the pattern of employment – fast. Overall, there appear to be compensating effects, suggesting little difference in the total number of jobs available.

A major (continuing) difference will concern output, as the application of new technology facilitates not only a rise in productivity but also better, superior products. Consumers will benefit from faster and higher-quality services too.

Whereas the possible future applications of new technology and innovation are limited only by our imagination, suggesting a rich and exciting future, at least in the developed economies of the world, we must not overlook the misuses to which technology can be put, and the mistakes that technology can cause. Two examples are the nuclear bomb and the forthcoming 'millennium bug' problem when many computers will mistake the year 2000 for the year 1900, causing systems to crash or to put out wildly incorrect information. The cost of trying to avert the problem is currently estimated at well over £150 billion worldwide. Further information, also highlighting the problem of ensuring that data from external sources are date compliant, is given in Exhibit 11.2.

Exhibit 11.2

Year 2000 Date Switch

Companies face threat from their external business links

Companies face threat from their external business links. Businesses may feel confident that their computer systems will be ready for the year 2000 date switch. But with the rapid growth of electronic commerce, how can they ensure data from external sources is also date-compliant? Those organisations in the throes of preparing computer systems for the year 2000 may be forgiven for feeling smug that at least they are on the road to compliance, given the indications that many businesses have yet to recognise the threat, let alone act on it.

But in a networked world, ensuring internal systems are adapted to handle the date change will not fireproof a company against 'the Millennium bomb'. To avoid problems, all data from external sources must be compliant, as must all systems to which data is transmitted.

'The irony is that companies are focusing on changes to internal systems that are not the most important element in avoiding Year 2000 problems,' says Mr Martin Caddick, practice manager for Year 2000 business at the consultancy, DMR.

'Traditionally, IT has had an internal focus. IT departments concentrate on things in their own domain – 'We own this application: we'll fix it.' Many are taking the same approach with the date change.'

But in the race to be compliant, this is a misuse of resources. 'Rather than dealing with the Year 2000 problem, an application at a time, companies need to assess what has to be done in terms of business processes. They should track data through from one end of the process to the other, and consider whether it can move through all the interfaces between systems,' he adds.

Exhibit 11.2 continued

Broad impact

The Year 2000 problem arises because most older computer systems use only two digits to designate the year. Unless they are changed, systems are likely to respond to the start of a year ending with the digits 00 by assuming there is an error and stop working, or interpret the year as 1900. This will invalidate all kinds of date-related calculations, sort routines and indexing procedures.

The Edifact standard for electronic data interchange uses only two figures in the date field, making it inevitable that many computer-based trading links will be affected.

So it is not sufficient to ensure internal systems are compliant. Companies must collaborate with all partners who have interfaces with their systems to agree how to handle the date change. BACS (Bankers Automated Clearing System), which handles all transfers of money between banks, has, for example told all its data partners that it intends to take a windowing, or logic approach to handling the date change. It will expect data in the existing format, that is, with two figures in the date field, and will be responsible for inferring the correct date.

The alternative to the logic approach is to expand the date field to four digits to make the year unambiguous. 'The changes that are required are not difficult, but you need to agree a common strategy for each interface,' says Mr Caddick. 'And you need a strategy for external interfaces before you go making changes to internal computer code.'

Putting the focus on external interfaces will make it easier to get directors to take the Year 2000 problem seriously. Senior managers can appreciate the impact that the

failure of external business links will have on the company, and will be more worried by this than the issue of whether an internal application is date-compliant.

Mr John Secker, director of the UK Millennium Practice at the outsourcing company, Origin, agrees that the impact of Year 2000 on trading links 'will be very serious'.

He adds: 'There is less risk from "bad" (non-compliant) data getting into your system and causing a problem than that good data you send out is not dealt with because the receiving system is non-compliant.'

For example, a car company which operates a just-in-time manufacturing system may find orders are not fulfilled. 'A day later, you have no windscreens – and the production line stops.'

Since just-in-time systems often work on very fine tolerances, with components delivered half an hour before they are needed, a delay of only half a day could have a serious impact on a business. Companies have to do more than simply ask electronic trading partners if they are Year 2000-compliant, says Mr Secker. 'As it was put in the BBC television comedy, Blackadder – "Just asking a chap if he is a spy, isn't really good enough."'

Companies should extend their testing programmes to all external links, he suggests. 'When it comes to testing for Year 2000 compliance, companies should regard suppliers as part of their internal organisation.'

Although the modifications required to ensure that interfaces continue to work are straightforward, it is very hard to test the changes unless they are tested in a live environment. Setting up a full environment to test interfaces will cost a large company tens of millions of pounds.

Difficult issue

Nor is it enough to ensure that suppliers are Year-2000-compliant. If customers are affected it could have an equally serious effect on your business. 'It may be more difficult to approach customers than suppliers on this issue, but you need your customers to stay in business, too,' says Mr Secker.

'If you are a big corporation – or a government – you can dictate how you make the changes,' says Mr James Johnson, director of Global Renovation Centres for the Year 2000 at EDS. 'But if a system you are sending data to is unmodified, you have no choice but to continue to provide the data in the format expected. This is one of the key reasons why EDS believes it will be one of the leading players in the "Year 2000 industry". We're one of the few companies that can work with a customer and its vendors, if appropriate, in a beginning-to-end solution.'

There are indications that companies are beginning to realise they should not view Year 2000 compliance as an internal issue. In the UK, BT has taken the strong-arm approach to ensuring all suppliers are compliant and will involve them in its testing programme which begins later this year. Lloyds TSB has set up teams of senior managers to handle the delicate business of ensuring anyone with whom the bank has electronic links is taking an agreed approach.

Meanwhile, Railtrack is trying to persuade UK rail companies to co-operate in dealing with the Year 2000 problem. It wants an industry-wide agreement on the format for date-compliance, and will require key suppliers to demonstrate compliance.

Source: Nuala Moran, *Financial Times*, 4 June 1997.

The impact of the Internet

The Internet has been the success story of the 1990s. At the start of the decade few had heard of it, by 1997 many private homes were linked to the fast expanding World Wide Web of interconnected computers. President Clinton and the Prime Minister, Mr Blair, have encouraged schools in their countries to link up.

The Internet came into being because of the demands of the Cold War. The US Department of Defense sought to avoid having its computer network disabled by a single 'point of failure'. The answer was to build a decentralised network that could continue in operation even if parts of it were destroyed. That first network was known as ARPANet (after the Advanced Research Projects Agency). It became operational in 1969. Between 1969 and 1983 many advances in the lower-level internetworking protocols led to the transmission control protocols (TCP) and image processing (IP) protocols we use on the Internet today.

In the late 1980s these protocols were used in other networks. Soon these networks were open to universities and then later to the public. The mid-1990s saw an explosion in public interest, and business recognised the Internet's potential. Many firms use the Internet to advertise their services, and in some cases it is possible to shop using your home computer.

The speed of data transfer has greatly increased. The top-of-the-range modems in early 1995 permitted speeds of 14 400 bits per second. By 1997 modems of 56 kilobits were available in the high street. Other technology is now available to allow data transfer at a speed of up to 10 megabits a second. Eventually it is hoped that full-motion videos will be available as an alternative to the television.

The current approach of the American government may be seen in a recent set of proposals from the Clinton Administration called 'A Framework for Global Electronic Commerce'. The basic principles are that the private sector should provide the leadership in the development of standards. Government should avoid the imposition of regulations, restrictions or Internet-specific taxation.

**Further
resources**

The impact of technology

General

Quality daily newspapers have regular supplements on the latest developments in information technology, for example, the *Financial Times Review* on Wednesdays.

Specialist engineering, medical and particularly computing journals all contain examples of technological advances.

Further reading

Cornwell, T. (1997) 'Logging is out as West logs into learning at a distance', *The Times Higher Education Supplement*, 11 July.

Galbraith, J.K. (1974) *The New Industrial State*, London: Pelican.

Chapter summary

This chapter has explained that technology affects business in many different ways: in the workplace – whether it be a factory or an office; and also affects the life of the individual, for example, in shopping and at work; but perhaps one of the most significant results of technological advance in the 1990s has been the impact of the Internet on both business and individuals alike.

As the speed of technological advance appears to be increasing, it becomes difficult to predict the impact that technology will have in the future.

In this book we have examined aspects of the politico-legal environment, considered elements of both the UK micro- and macroeconomic environments and looked at major developments in the European and wider international economic environment. We have also considered the impact of demographic and social trends on business. Of all the environmental factors considered in this book, the impact of rapid technological advance appears to be the most dynamic.

Exhibit 11.3

Self-service rings change at supermarkets

Supermarket chains could greatly reduce their labour costs while improving customer service by adopting new checkout technology.

NCR, the US-based computer group which is a leader in the fields of bank automated teller machines and retail point-of-sale systems, is planning to launch a 'self-checkout terminal' at the Retail Solutions exhibition in Birmingham next week.

The new terminal, which combines the look-and-feel of a bank ATM with retail scanning technology, is designed to let customers scan, bag and pay for groceries in express checkout lanes without cashiers.

NCR claims the terminal provides benefits for both the retailer and the customer. 'Shoppers are looking for ways to avoid checkout lines, and grocers are focusing on enhancing customer service while reducing front-end labour costs,' says Ms Joanne Walter, NCR's vice president of future retailing systems.

Research in the US has suggested that a supermarket checkout lane costs more than $100,000 (£62,000) a year to operate, of which 90 per cent is wage costs.

Although some store owners might be concerned about potential theft, NCR's studies suggest that far from encouraging theft, self scanning is more likely to lead shoppers to double scan the same item.

'Retailers face the challenge of providing better quality services while also facing pressure on margins,' notes Mr John Owen, who is in charge of NCR's retail operations in Europe.

He says self-scanning will allow stores to cut wage costs and redeploy staff to other areas to improve customer service.

Customers will enjoy faster checkouts and more flexibility

NCR's research suggests that shoppers are tending to make more shopping trips, but buy fewer items each time in order to use the express lanes. It also says more men are doing the shopping, and that men 'love self-checkout'.

Source: Paul Taylor, *Financial Times*, 12 May 1997.

Assignment

With reference to Exhibits 11.1 and 11.3, briefly explain how developments in technology have affected supermarkets, and from your additional research outline further changes we can expect from the use of new technology in supermarket retailing.

Index

Index